Redeeming Time

Redeeming Time

Atonement through Education

TIMOTHY GORRINGE

Foreword by Lesslie Newbigin

Nondum considerasti quanti ponderis sit historia
(You have not yet considered what a weighty thing history is)

Darton, Longman and Todd
London

First published in 1986 by
Darton, Longman and Todd Ltd
89 Lillie Road, London SW6 1UD

ISBN 0 232 51701 0

British Library Cataloguing in Publication Data

Gorringe, Timothy
Redeeming time: atonement through education.
1. Redemption
I. Title
234′.3 BT775

ISBN 0–232–51701–0

Phototypeset by Input Typesetting Ltd, London SW19 8DR
Printed and bound in Great Britain by
Anchor Brendon Ltd, Tiptree, Essex

To my parents

Contents

Foreword

Timothy Gorringe has written the work which follows in the midst of his ministry as a theological teacher at the Tamil Nadu Theological Seminary in Madurai, South India. This institution is already widely known throughout the world as a centre of adventurous innovation in relating theological training to the realities of the Church's mission. The present work will confirm and advance that reputation.

In seeking to clarify the nature of the mission for which ordinands are being trained, Gorringe invites us to look in a fresh way at the atonement. Acknowledging both the strengths and the limitations of classical theories of the atonement as sacrifice, as ransom, as victory over evil powers, Gorringe invites us to consider the atonement as part of the divine education – but not merely (in the Gnostic manner) as the dispelling of ignorance; rather as the bringing of human beings to the fullness of what God intends them to be. Such an approach involves giving a much larger place to the ongoing work of the Holy Spirit, and a much more serious consideration of the meaning of human history as a whole, than is normally found in discussions of the atonement.

This approach enables Gorringe to set a great many old questions in a new and penetrating light. The relation of salvation in Christ to world history, the relation of the gospel to the world religions, the nature of inter-faith dialogue, the relation between evangelism and political action, and the nature and purpose of the Church's mission are all (at least for this reader) freshly illuminated by being placed within the concept of the divine pedagogy.

Here is a theology which grapples with the real issues which confront serious Christians everywhere and not only young pastors in South India – the issues of justice and liberation, the issues of religious pluralism and the central issues concerning the nature of Christian discipleship. These pages will provoke the reader to fresh thinking, sometimes to dissent, always – I think – to gratitude for fresh insight. I hope the readers will be many.

Selly Oak
Pentecost 1986

LESSLIE NEWBIGIN

Preface

This essay is an attempt to think through from a fresh vantage point, and thus to re-state, one of the most ancient strands in theology of atonement, the theory that God redeems us through the practice of a divine education. As such it works on a fairly abstract level. At a meeting of Asian theologians in Japan a prominent Asian theologian is supposed to have remarked that whilst Barth taught that the Bible should be kept in one hand and the newspaper in the other there was precious little evidence of the newspaper in his *Church Dogmatics*. Many, especially those taught by Marquardt, would wish to contest this judgement. In case the abstraction of the present essay should lead to similar misunderstandings, something may be said about its origin. It arose in the first place from engagement in the practical training of theological students at the Tamil Nadu Theological Seminary, Madurai, South India. Required to spend one full semester in practical work, students were sent as far as possible to so-called 'action groups' engaged in consciousness-raising education amongst rural and urban poor on the lines suggested by Paulo Freire's *Pedagogy of the Oppressed*. Contact with these groups started the train of thought which led to the book and, as will be obvious, suggested the line of much of the discussion. In this educational work students found poverty and all its attendant evils combated not by aid or charity but by the establishment of solidarity amongst the poor themselves, and they were often able to see small but measurable gains for the people concerned.

Many of the activists the students encountered had no religious faith. For some students the contrast between the commitment of these 'unbelieving' activists and the platitudes they were accustomed to hear in church was so sharp that their faith suffered a change in form. Henceforward what they really believed in was the human project: revolutionary struggle for a new human future. Critique of earth led to a devastating critique of heaven. Faith in God seemed a moralising irrelevance, worship a frivolous waste of time. Taught by Cardenal and others they could still read the Bible as the book of people's liberation, but church traditions appeared to have nothing to say to the concerns they now saw to be vital.

After this period of active engagement there followed attempts both to understand the Indian situation through social and political analysis and, at the same time, to reflect theologically on this engagement, an attempt which took the form of reflection on the Third Article of the creed, on God the Holy Spirit, on the Church, on grace and the sacraments. In this area, and in terms of these doctrines, the tradition has attempted to grasp the reality of God's engagement with human history, or, to put it less abstractly, what the reality of God means for the day-to-day lives of men and women. Contexts change, philosophical presuppositions change, the social position of the theologian changes greatly from one age and one culture to another, but this question remains urgent and inescapable for those whom the question of God will not let go. Across every divide of culture and time the attempt to answer this question with integrity evokes an answering response. In seeking to articulate what the reality of God means in a situation of great social inequality and injustice, and at the same time in the midst of a religious tradition vastly different from the Jewish–Christian tradition, previous attempts to do the same – the attempts of an Irenaeus or an Athanasius for example – are indispensable, 'strong landmarks in the uncertain out-of-doors'.

Western readers brought up on the myth that there is a 'mystic' East and a 'materialist' West may be disappointed that there is so little in the book which relates to the former. There are two reasons for this, which may be briefly indicated.

The impression that Hinduism is a 'mystical' religion rests partly on experience of its ascetic and yogic traditions, and partly on the identification of Hinduism with Vedantic spirituality fostered by the movement which began with Ramakrishna. It describes a genuine element of Hinduism, but one which always related more to the tiny literate and Brahmin minority than to the masses. Long ago the Abbé Dubois recognised that Hinduism is not so much an ascetic religion as a sacramental religion of village square and street, of hearth and home, of pilgrimage, of folk song and story – and of caste. Seventy per cent of India's population still live in villages, and theirs is not a literate religion grounded in the reading of the Upanishads and the Gita but a peasant religion rooted in response to the harsh facts of agricultural practice. It is very doubtful if peasant religion is ever properly described as 'mystical'.

In the second place the reality of India is not appropriately described in terms of a non-material sprituality. The reality of India includes the fact that 300 million people live on or just above the poverty line defined in terms of 'the minimum diet required for a moderate activity', and another 300 million live below this. Of this latter group, four out of ten of their children go blind from vitamin-A deficiency due to malnutrition.[1] It is fine to covet spiritual values on a comfortable salary; less fine when your children cannot eat, have no medical facilities, and cannot go to school.

It follows that to do theology in India is not to 'do theology at 120°F', as it has been romantically described, but to take part in a struggle between death and life (Deut. 30:19). This struggle cannot be waged primarily by Christians, who constitute only 2 per cent of the population, but they too, along with everyone else, are called to take sides on the fundamental issues which confront the country: poverty and justice. The dialogue with Hinduism, cherishing those elements which are beautiful within it, and those elements which make for human fullness, takes place within this other and far more urgent imperative.

Besides this social and political context one other, more church-related context needs to be mentioned. The Church of South India is born of the evangelical mission, and to this day evangelism remains a high priority. During the seventies some Christian groups passed through the slow process of education undergone by so many groups in Third World countries, from trying to 'help' the poor through lavish development projects to a commitment to solidarity with people's struggle. This raised afresh and with new urgency the question which always attends church involvement, as to motivation: was the motivation for involvement with the poor a better future for them, whatever their creed, or was it conversion? It was the former, of course. But traditional evangelical work continued and this raised in many people's minds the question whether involvement in people's struggle was not simply a new tactic adopted by the churches, and some Hindu organisations were not slow to make this charge. Nor were they altogether wrong, for here and there the voice of Christian triumphalism was heard behind the talk of people's liberation. An energetic debate about the nature of evangelism and the content of the good news naturally followed and this debate too is presupposed.

The book makes rather free use of the language of liberation and humanisation. Writing of the beauty of Wales, R. S. Thomas remarks that there you can 'grow rich with looking'. But he goes on

> Have a care;
> This wealth is for the few
> And chosen. Those who crowd
> A small window dirty it
> With their breathing, though sublime
> And inexhaustible the view.[2]

The word 'liberation' is such a small window. It has been taken up by theologians to translate the Hebrew *'yosh'av'* (salvation) or the Greek '*katallasso*' (redeem), because long centuries of use have privatised and spiritualised these. To translate by 'liberate' is to point out that these words have an historical material connection, that they imply a critique of earth. 'Salvation' is not only for the soul because human beings are a body-soul unity; 'redemption' may be from sin, but sin is an historical as well as a moral category. But the word and the slogans connected with it are speedily found in the mouths of ecclesiastical statesmen, of 'Bible-based' Christians with no critique of existing structures, and even of reactionary politicians trying to please a Christian constituency. 'Since when has the Church been interested in liberation?' asked a sceptical Marxist worker when asked to take a theological student for six months' training, and the question is just. In order not to dirty the small window which looks out on the long road to human freedom the distance of engagement and action is required and not pious or theological heavy-breathing. At the same time, as Freire has taught us, action needs the critical distance of reflection, and it is with such an apology that these reflections are offered.

Returning from a meeting for feminist theologians and activists a colleague remarked that the meeting did not happen at the sudden inspiration of the Holy Spirit, but as the result of a long historical process. The question which this book puts is simple: should we not discern in those long historical processes which make for mutuality and real humanity the slow and patient pedagogy of God's Spirit?

> For we know that the whole creation with one consent groans and travails up to this moment. And not the creation only: we ourselves also, who have the first fruits of the Spirit, we ourselves also groan inwardly, while we still look forward to our adoption as God's children, the redemption of our body. For we were saved in this hope. And hope really means hope; for a hope you can see is no hope at all – for why does anyone endure patiently for what he can see? (Rom. 8:19–25)[3]

Any book which arises primarily out of teaching always owes a large debt to the students who were partners in the process: to these, and to colleagues with whom the ideas of some of the chapters were discussed, warm thanks. Above all a special debt of gratitude is owed to Bas Wielenga and Gabrielle Dietrich, a debt only very imperfectly indicated by the references to their books and articles, and which, beyond criticism and discussion, relates principally to a vision of the messianic lifestyle, in which may be discerned (though they will not thank me for saying so) something of the Spirit's pedagogy.

In conclusion, I am aware that at certain points in the book, in the effort to understand how God makes history through men and women, and how the great purpose of redemption is advanced through that history, I may seem to be speaking of God by 'speaking of man in a loud voice', as Barth accused Schleiermacher of doing. But so far as that goes I can only say that on this matter at least I am in complete agreement with Augustine: *Soli Deo gloria.*

Madurai 1986 TIMOTHY GORRINGE

Acknowledgements

Thanks are due to the following for permission to quote copyright material: Faber and Faber Ltd, from 'The Incarnate One' in *The Collected Poems of Edwin Muir*; Grafton Books, from 'The Small Window', in *Selected Poems 1946–68* by R. S. Thomas; Helicon Ltd, from 'The Fool', in *Plays. Stories. Poems* by Padraic Pearse; Macmillan, London and Basingstoke, from 'The Presence', *Between Here and Now* by R. S. Thomas.

1

The Divine Pedagogy

DIVINE EDUCATION IN THE CLASSICAL TRADITION

In 1780 in Germany the Enlightenment playwright and theological controversialist Gotthold Ephraim Lessing published the full version of a series of theses entitled 'The Education of the Human Race'.[1] The opening thesis averred that, 'What education is to the individual man, revelation is to the whole human race.' Education and revelation are equated: 'Education is revelation coming to the individual man; and revelation is education which has come, and is still coming, to the human race.' The sting in the tail of this proposition was revealed in the fourth thesis: just as education gives a person nothing which they could not get from their own resources, so 'revelation gives nothing to the human race which human reason could not arrive at on its own; only it has given, and still gives to it, the most important of these things sooner'. Even this concession is ironical, for Lessing remarks that whilst Israel was guided by revelation, amongst the remaining nations, guided only by the light of reason, 'Only a few had got in front of them' (thesis 20), and when, during the exile, Israel found itself in foreign lands it found others who knew more than it did and who lived more becomingly. Persian worship of a supreme God challenged their own theological understanding and, whereas 'revelation had guided their reason . . . now, all at once, reason gave clearness to their revelation' (thesis 36).

The fact that this caustic irony did not provoke outrage when it first appeared in 1777 is doubtless due to the fact that the first fifty-three theses relativised only the revelation in the Old Testament. 'Every primer is only for a certain age' – and the coming of Christ, the better instructor, to tear the exhausted primer from the child's hands conformed exactly to the Lutheran understanding of the relation of Law and Gospel. According to a certain reading of Galatians Christ was indeed the replacement for an outmoded primer (Gal. 3:24). Those who could accept the argument thus far were, however, thoroughly discomfited at the appearance of the whole essay, for there the New Testament was accorded the dignity only of a second primer. Lessing speaks for those who find themselves fretting and impatient on the last page of that second primer. The thesis is deeply reminiscent of Kant's proposal, made only four years later, that 'the Enlightenment is the emergence of man from immaturity', which Kant understands as 'the incapacity to use one's own intelligence without the guidance of another person'.[2] The aim of education, for Lessing, is that a person should do his duty, should do right simply because it *is* right. That aim, he senses, is now almost realised. He feels poised on the verge of a 'third age of the world', of the realisation of the 'new eternal gospel' about which Origen had speculated, and in this age the second primer could also be dispensed with. Truths taught by revelation, amongst which he singles out the immortality of the soul, the doctrine of the Trinity, of original sin or of the Son's satisfaction, all become truths of reason and in that process human education is completed.

Whilst paying lip-service to revelation, Lessing asserted the primacy of reason in the contention that the biblical primers were in fact illuminating only 'through the light which human reason itself put into them' (thesis 65). In so far as it remains possible to speak of revelation it is therefore identical with the immanent development of reason, a proposal which strikingly anticipates Hegel. To this extent it is history itself, the growth of humankind to the very verge of being able to dispense with primers, which is revelation. Lessing's 'education' is simply the flowering of an immanent potential. Behind history Lessing did not discern a personal God, the Lord of history, but an inscrutable Eternal Providence in which the great slow wheel is turned by innumerable smaller and faster wheels, 'each of which contributes its own individual part to the whole' (thesis 92). It is not a surprise to learn that not long before his death Lessing is supposed to have confessed that he believed only in the monism of Spinoza, the doctrine that all reality is one, and that therefore history is simply a form of God's self-expression. Rather than the education of the human race Lessing is thinking of its evolution or development, a process in which there need be neither educator nor educated.

In speaking of revelation as education Lessing is undoubtedly stimulated by his study of the Christian Platonists of the second and third centuries, especially Origen. From the time of the Apostolic Fathers onwards a favoured, though never an exclusive model of redemption, had been that of illumination and education. Origen above all is 'the Christian philosopher of "educative providence" '.[3] The presupposition of his understanding of divine education is the fundamental kinship between God and the human mind. He speaks of 'a certain affinity between the mind and God, of whom mind is an intellectual image' (*De Principiis* 1.1.7) and even of 'a kind of blood-relationship with God' (4.4.10).[4] History may be regarded as the story of how souls fell away from God and how they are slowly won back to him through the educative work of the Logos, a process which Origen considers may involve rebirth and education in the different spheres. Christ, the Logos, is at the heart of this process. He is the Word who 'interprets and presents to the rational creation the secrets of wisdom and the mysteries of knowledge', but he is also a mediating light which leads us to the ineffable brightness of the Father. In a beautiful passage Origen speaks of the brightness of Christ which

> falls softly and gently on the tender and weak eyes of mortal man and little by little trains and accustoms them, as it were, to bear the light of its clearness; and when it has removed from them all that darkens and obstructs their vision . . . it renders them capable of enduring the glory of the light, becoming in this respect even a kind of mediator between men and the light. (*De Prin.* 1.2.7)

Human beings are capable of varying degrees of participation in God, 'in proportion to the earnestness of the soul and the capacity of the mind' (4.4.9). Because Origen thinks in terms of genuine education, there is no compulsion or force used but souls are made obedient 'by word, by reason, by teaching, by the exhortation to better things, by the best methods of education' – and then he adds, rather like someone cautioning another to give up smoking, 'and also by such merited and appropriate threatenings as are justly held over the heads of those who contemptuously neglect to care for their own salvation and advantage and their spiritual health' (3.5.8). Origen even pictures heaven as a school where pupils will first learn all about the stars (which he considered spiritual beings) and then come to 'the things which are not seen'.

> And so the rational being, growing at each successive stage, not as it grew when in this life in the flesh or body and in the soul, but increasing in mind and intelligence, advances as a mind already perfect to perfect knowledge, no longer hindered by its former carnal senses, but developing in intellectual power, ever approaching the pure and gazing 'face to face' . . . on the causes of things. And it attains perfection . . . while it has for the food on which it feeds the problems of the meanings of things and the nature of their causes. (2.11.7)

The essence of this spiritual food is the contemplation of God.

Naturally any theology which concentrates on the educative work of the Logos must have an important place for Scripture, as the witness to the Word's self-revelation and as the text around which the reflecting community gathers itself and in which it finds its identity. For Origen Scripture is not a primer, as it was for Lessing, but a living thing, the creation and vehicle of the Spirit. This Spirit leads us through and beyond the literal and moral senses of Scripture to the spiritual sense where the unspeakable mysteries of God are revealed, so that we become partakers 'of all the doctrines of the Spirit's counsel' (4.2.7). Through this instruction people are drawn into fellowship with the Logos and thus *redeemed*, restored to their original state of communion with God.

It is clear that, in contrast to Lessing, Origen speaks of a real process of divine education, a history in which there is dialogue and relationship. The incarnation of the Logos, the life, death and resurrection of Jesus have in this connection the significance of an accommodation to the weak – almost a kind of remedial teaching. Souls which have fallen are punished by their bondage to mortality and decay, and it is from this state that the education of the Logos frees them and restores them to their proper state in the heavenly sphere. Origen's Platonic world-view means that the value, not to mention the centrality, of this worldly experience is hedged with questions and the educational process continues even more decisively in heaven than here. Nevertheless, Origen offers us a bold and typically full-blooded attempt to conceive of what God is redemptively up to in terms of education. In the next three sections of this chapter we shall attempt to explore this analogy for the divine work, to see where it leads and whether it can be rescued from the pitfalls usually associated with it. We begin with the question of the mutual relationship of the concepts of education and salvation.

EDUCATION AND SALVATION

In the New Testament, but above all in Paul, there is an attempt to grasp and fathom what God has done for us in Christ through a whole series of metaphors. The most important metaphors are drawn from the slave market (redemption), the law court (justification), diplomacy (reconciliation) and the cultus (sacrifice). All these metaphors presuppose that there is something seriously out of true in the human situation from which human beings need to be 'saved' or 'delivered'. Each metaphor focuses attention on one particular aspect of this problem and one aspect of God's way of meeting it. The metaphor of 'redemption', for instance, focuses on all the dimensions of human bondage, on sin as a structure, and thinks of Christ as the price paid to free human beings from that bondage. The metaphor of justification focuses on the human tendency to arrogate the role of judge, and it speaks of the divine subversion of that arrogance. The metaphor of reconciliation focuses on the breach between the holy God and sinners, and on the costliness to God of making peace, whilst the cultic metaphor concentrates more on the crippling effects of guilt which has to be shriven and seen to be shriven.

Description of God's redemptive work in terms of education has often seemed to focus attention on three things: on ignorance as the state from which we need to be saved, on knowledge or 'gnosis' as the means of salvation, and on the image of Christ as teacher. All three dimensions are rightly felt to be inadequate as a description of what is involved in salvation. In the first place 'ignorance' is not a satisfactory description of the human malaise. Not only does it pay no attention to the dimension of pain and suffering, but it is notoriously short-sighted in respect to the existence of deliberate wickedness. Ignorance may be part of the human problem but it is not, by a long way, identical with what the Jewish–Christian tradition has spoken of as 'sin'.

Again, coming to see things in a new light or in a new perspective is an essential part of that conversion which is involved in all redemption. But undoubtedly for Origen there is the implication that we are actually saved by knowledge, and that the possession of saving knowledge constitutes an intellectual elite. 'Happy are they', says Origen, 'who no longer need the Son of God as a physician who heals the sick, nor as a shepherd, nor as redemption, but as wisdom, and as Word, and as righteousness' (*In Johannis* 1.20.124). This seems a far cry from Jesus' exultation that the gospel is 'hidden from the wise and understanding and revealed to babes' (Matt. 11:25). Moreover, in his teaching Jesus never emphasises right knowledge or right belief as such but only what it is necessary to *do*. Salvation for Jesus is a matter of doing his Father's will.

Thirdly, Christ is of course rabbi and teacher, and a large part of his ministry seems to have consisted in teaching. From the beginning the Church felt the need to pass on and to reflect on these teachings. But in describing Jesus as Lord and Saviour, as Son of God and Son of Man, and in the whole galaxy of titles applied to him, the New Testament writers are trying to express the fact that Jesus was something more than an inspired teacher and that we are saved not by attending to his teachings but through following him as the way, the truth and the life.

It is these weaknesses that the great missionary theologian Hendrik Kraemer had in view when he said that to think of God primarily as the Pedagogue amounted to 'a complete disavowal of revelation, which means God's sovereign Will creating an entirely new situation'.[5] For him education meant assisting in developing innate forces, a view which we have seen could be legitimately derived from Lessing, for example, and to think of God's work in these terms was a fundamental misunderstanding of the human situation 'under sin'. But does conceiving of God's redemptive work as education necessitate this kind of jejune and intellectualistic picture? This depends on how we conceive of education.

Implicit in the very idea of education is the notion of process, whether from the latent to the explicit (Socrates), or from the less to the more complete. 'In contrast to other animals who are unfinished, but not historical, men know themselves to be unfinished; they are aware of their incompleteness. In this incompleteness and this awareness lie the very roots of education as an exclusively human manifestation.'[6] Where conceptions of education vary is, in the first instance, in their understanding of what constitutes completeness. Education obviously involves the acquisition of knowledge about the world, and completeness might then be thought of in terms of an ever more comprehensive and penetrating grasp of reality, or at least one segment of reality. Put in another perspective, education in an art or craft – including 'the art of loving' – involves a progressively deeper grasp of mystery and nuance, understanding the other, understanding the medium of a particular form of art. Again, there is an important connection between education and 'the pursuit of excellence', which may be understood as a way of speaking of the possibilities of human self-transcendence. Kant chose to define completeness in terms of the ability to think for oneself, without tutelage. Lessing seems to have thought in terms of a spontaneous willing of the good, and perhaps that is not so far from Origen's understanding also, when 'the good' is understood as God himself. Behind all these ideas of what completeness in education might mean lies a judgement of value, and this is that the human project is worthwhile. Underlying all notions of completeness (and utilitarian and purely technical courses of education are not a counter-instance to this) is the notion of *human* fullness, the realisation of personhood, of authentic subjectivity, of the human capacity for freedom and for love. Education is not computer-programming: no human education is concerned to produce robots. The only purpose of any education is that human beings should have life and have it more abundantly, that through the educational process persons may be more fulfilled, and therefore more creative, more free and therefore more loving, more loving and therefore more free. The ultimate aim of education is the becoming of human being.

At the same time, if 'salvation' is defined from a centre which is Jesus of Nazareth, then it must be understood in terms of what is necessary to make and to keep human life human.[7] 'It does not yet appear what we shall be,' says the author of the first letter of John, 'but we know that when he appears we shall be like him' (1 John

3:2). Salvation means 'becoming like Christ', and it is in virtue of this insight that it has been identified with humanisation. Christ is what Luther called 'the proper man', the true and normal human being. To become like him means therefore to become fully and truly human. But if this is the case the goal of education and the goal of salvation are the same: both are concerned with the realisation of human fullness, with becoming human, the liberation of the whole wealth of human potential.

How is this completeness and fullness to be realised? Of course all education, 'awareness education' not excepted, involves the imparting of knowledge, but if a fully dimensioned human completeness is the goal this is but the beginning of education. 'Man becomes an I through a Thou' (Martin Buber). All education, even technical education, proceeds only through relationship. This is true even when the teachers involved are long dead (this is the core of the hermeneutics of Dilthey). Persons are shaped, formed, educated, freed, helped to completion, by persons and through relationship and through no other means. 'Relation is reciprocity,' said Buber: 'My you acts on me as I act on it . . . How are we educated by children, by animals! Inscrutably involved, we live in the currents of universal reciprocity.'[8] This 'universal reciprocity', relationship, is education. To say this is not to minimise the importance of the sharing of knowledge, nor of the pursuit of excellence (if that phrase is rescued from its elitist connotations). It is simply to recognise that relationship is their inescapable presupposition, that without which true education, progress towards human fullness, does not occur. And this is at the same time to recognise that education cannot be exhaustively defined in terms of the development of innate forces, for there is always, in education, the question of the other.

Origen speaks of a 'blood relationship' between human beings and God. The language is strange, heretical – but we can also see what might be called its necessity, at least if we begin our reflection with Jesus Christ. We do not have to postulate any essential kinship between human and divine mind, nor any theory of an immortal soul in a mortal prison house, to recognise this. There is between human beings and God an I and a Thou, a relationship, and this relationship, both according to the redactor of Genesis who introduces the covenant with Abraham as the clue to the meaning of the creation history and according to the doctrine of the incarnation, is the clue to the whole of reality. God becomes human in Christ because the fulfilment of the whole of creation is most decisively forwarded in that way. If for no other reason, the fact of Jesus Christ forces us to talk of a divine–human relationship. The relationship expressed most concretely there is the heart of the divine education.

In identifying education with what happens in relationship we have rephrased Lessing's opening theses, replacing 'revelation' by 'relationship'. Yet at its deepest level relationship always involves revelation, and there is no revelation without relationship. Implicit in the doctrine of the incarnation is the recognition that human beings are the most profound mystery we encounter, and it is a matter of common experience that the more we know a person the more mysterious they become (cf. Eph. 5:32). 'God' is the name of that reality which grounds this 'prosaically' encountered mystery. If we speak of the Trinity as 'a holy mystery' this is not because our finite intellects cannot 'grasp' the truth of God, for no true mystery can ever be 'grasped', and that includes the mystery of my neighbour. God is a mystery because he is the ultimate depth of personhood, perfect and mutual relationship in himself, not three persons but One, not one but three persons. 'In the beginning, God' means, as Buber said, 'In the beginning is the relation.' This is why God is an eternal mystery, a mystery which can never be fathomed but only explored. Exploration of this infinite because personal dimension is the meaning of education. Understood like this, as the realisation of the human potential to love, God's work of salvation is, as Justin, Clement and Origen described it, a pedagogy, the education of the human race.

If this is the case, if the making and keeping of human life human is what is meant by salvation, and if this is achieved by the divine education, then this image functions differently to the other great metaphors for God's redemptive activity, closer, in fact, to the way the word 'salvation' functions. 'Salvation' and its cognates is used to describe historical situations of deliverance from enemies or from sickness or death which are ascribed directly to God. It is not an image to help us understand how and from what God has delivered us. If God's educative work were simply the removal of human ignorance, then education or pedagogy would be a metaphor on a par with the other metaphors for salvation, and to the extent that ignorance is a poor description of the fundamental human problem, it would be a very partial and imperfect metaphor. But if education is concerned not primarily with the removal of ignorance but with the realisation of the human potential for freedom, love and goodness, then the divine education is a category under which the other metaphors must be subsumed. Subverting the structures of sin in which human beings are trapped, and freeing them from guilt and the compulsion to judge others, is part of the realisation of human fullness, of the divine pedagogy. To speak of the education of the human race does not make God the Supreme Lawgiver of Enlightenment imagination, for education is infinitely varied in its methods and the heart of the divine education, it will be argued, is an act of solidarity, God's taking the form of a slave.

PEDAGOGY AS REDEMPTION

To define education thus in personalist terms, in terms of 'relationships' abstractly conceived, is not yet to have become concrete, and thus far can rightly be accused of romanticism. If the goal of education is human fullness then this involves overcoming what Marx called 'alienation'. According to him human beings seek to realise themselves in their labour, but this labour becomes alienated when it is bought and sold. In this situation we do not express our creativity in our labour but instead expend this labour for the profit of another. For human fullness to be achieved therefore this alienation has to be overcome and people must become the masters of their own labour. Long before Marx, Christian theology had spoken of a fundamental human alienation from God as the root of a whole series of other alienations, including that of a person from their labour (Gen. 3:17). This means that in all true education there is included, as well as the positive element of the drawing forth and enabling of a person's potential, the need for redemption and this has both a critical and a constructive aspect.

Prominent in Origen's soteriology, as it is not in Lessing's, is conflict with the demons. At first sight this might seem to have no connection with the theme of redemption as education, and might perhaps be taken as part of Origen's accommodation to the weaker brethren. In fact the exorcism of demons is part and parcel of education, a fact J. M. Robinson recognised in his work on Mark. According to Robinson, Jesus' debates with the Pharisees and his casting out of demons are two parts of the same struggle: 'Mark not only presents the debates in a form similar to that of the exorcisms but also envisages the meaning of the debates in a way similar to the exorcisms'.[9] Especially in the disputes with the Pharisees, Jesus is concerned to attack and expose all forms of dehumanising behaviour – the fetishising of the Sabbath, for example (Mark 3:22ff.), or the use of Mosaic law to evade clear obligations to one's parents (Mark 7:10ff.), or to legitimate male abuse of women through non-mutual divorce (Mark 10:2ff.). In Jesus' ministry both debate and exorcism have the same goal, which is the freeing of human beings from all that enslaves and dehumanises them. In his reflection on the significance of Jesus, Paul is also led to view Jesus' death as an exposure of the evil powers which threaten human life with ruin. On the cross, says Paul, God 'disarmed the principalities and powers and made a public spectacle of them' (Col. 2:15). This public exposure of the 'powers' of religion and state which destroyed Jesus is not a gratuitous triumph. The exposure is part of the *means* of victory, part and parcel of God's assault on evil. The cross shows up once and for all the falsehood of absolutised systems of religion or culture or state because what is done there is done to truth itself. John too speaks of the Spirit 'convicting' (he uses the word *elenchein*, to convict or expose) the world of sin, righteousness and judgement in the light of the cross (John 16:7ff.). The light shines in the darkness, through that exposure of the real nature of evil which the rejection of Jesus brings about.

In contemporary educational theory it is above all Paulo Freire who has drawn attention to this aspect of education. The situation from which he starts is that of an educator in what Nehru called 'the Third World' where the vast majority of people, constituting two-thirds of the world's population, live a precarious existence on or below the poverty line, unable to enjoy basic human rights of adequate shelter, food, medical care or education. Freire realised that the deep pathos in their situation was not just its objective condition but the fact that most people had internalised their oppression, had come to see it as an unchallengeable fate, as part of the necessary way of things. As Rabbi Hanokh put it, 'The real exile of Israel in Egypt was that they had learned to endure it.'

Freire therefore sought to initiate what he called a 'pedagogy of the oppressed', an 'education for critical consciousness', the purpose of which was to awaken people to the fact that they were not under the sway of necessity, but that they were oppressed and that something could be done about this. The purpose of such education is to see that people no longer endure what is unendurable if the humanity of both oppressed and oppressor is to be restored. This process involves the naming of dehumanising forces – their exposure and exorcism. This exposure is the beginning of death for the demons, whose power rests principally in the lie (cf. John. 8:44), but commonly it exacts the same price for the educator also, as it did for Jesus. The martyrology of the recent Church consists to a large extent of those who have named, and so threatened and exposed, the demons of race, nation and capital.

It is often remarked that the Enlightenment period had a very inadequate understanding of sin, and an over-optimistic account of human nature. It is this which accounts for the fact that Lessing had no place for conflict or exorcism in his understanding of education. From Lessing we can learn that redemption takes the form of education, but the converse must also be stated, that the divine pedagogy has the form of redemption, a rescue of the human race from powers which are beyond the capacity of the individual to counter. The gospel 'conquers' in the sign of the cross which exposes every false claim to ultimacy. Whilst it is true that the Church has repeatedly betrayed its Lord by making itself an ultimate, at the same time it has over and over again taken issue with dehumanising forces. This is the significance of the patristic polemic against the demons of the Roman world; it is the point of the monastic and Franciscan protest against the medieval concordat between Church and State; of the radical critiques of Anabaptists, Diggers and Levellers against self-righteous Puritan theocracies; of the protest against slavery and child labour in the factories of a complacent 'Christian' Europe. The 'liberation theology' of the past fifteen years looks to this tradition in its opposition to the idols of death, and its naming of the powers, and ultimately it looks beyond this to the ultimate exposure of the powers on Calvary. It is extremely naive therefore to dismiss it as a Marxist product simply because it uses Marxist tools of analysis: rather, it is rooted in the most central facts of the Christian gospel.

This unmasking of the demons, this work of exorcism, may be considered the critical or negative moment in the work of redemption. Alongside this is the great movement by which, in the face of human solidarity in sin, God effects and makes real a solidarity in redemption (the theme of chapter 3), and this too is the work of the divine education.

PEDAGOGY AND PRESENCE

In returning to the patristic and Enlightenment theme of redemption as education we have sought to conceive of education in terms of relationship. Not only is there no education without relationship (which is simply to state the obvious), but relationship is the very heart of education. In relation to the divine mystery this involves a theology of presence. Whilst we shall have to return to this when considering the reality of 'grace', an outline of the connections between the divine education and the divine presence needs to be attempted here. God's presence as pedagogy has four related aspects: it is, as Samuel Terrien has styled it, elusive; it is known in an ellipse between intra human encounter and prayer; and it is oriented towards the future.

(a) An Elusive Presence

There is no pedagogy without presence – relationship – and though presence is neither the sum nor the goal of the divine education (as it was in the theory of the Beatific Vision for example) the mode of the divine presence is crucial to this education. As if to underscore this fact the Bible at this point presents us with a paradox: God is not a 'hidden God' (as in the apophatic tradition of theology) but he is a God who 'hides himself' – the verb is active (Isa. 45:15). Although both prophet and psalmist cried out for God's presence and protested this self-hiding, the tradition had a twofold answer to why it could not be otherwise. It explained first that God was not at human disposal, and could not be manipulated through ritual or cult (Exod. 33:19). It was thus not possible to 'bargain or huxter' with God. At the same time Israel saw the contrast between God and humankind not so much in metaphysical terms, as between mortal and immortal, but more in moral terms as between holy and sinful. Because human beings were sinful it was believed that God's naked and holy presence would destroy them. It was therefore necessary for God to veil himself even in the moment of unveiling (Exod. 33:20). As Irenaeus put it, 'He might easily have come to us in his immortal glory, but in that case we would never have endured the greatness of his glory; and therefore it was that He, who was the perfect bread of the Father, offered himself to us as milk, because we were as infants' (*Adversus Haereses* 4.38.1). Humankind is created for relationship with God and this demands a freedom of response which would be eliminated by anything but an 'elusive presence'.[10]

In the New Testament this elusiveness is witnessed to especially by the resurrection stories. Jesus would most certainly be lost to the obscurity of other first-century messianic claimants had his death not been followed by a renewed experience of presence. The stories which relate this presence are more broken and difficult to give systematic content to than is usual, even for theological discourse, but it is a rationalist error to mistake such brokenness for unreality – quite the contrary. Whatever happened here, it is difficult to set it down just as fantasy or illusion, and certainly not to retrospective interpretation. All the circumstances pointed to yet another unredeemed defeat in Israel's history – and yet there was an experience of presence. Whilst the presence of this event, like the experience of presence of Moses and the prophets, was short-lived, the Church understood this presence as continuing through the fellowship meals which were so important to Jesus. But there too presence was elusive, not to be pinned down and made into a guarantee. When Jesus took, blessed, broke and gave, 'their eyes were opened and they recognised him; *and he vanished out of their sight*' (Luke 24:31). Presence which is creative of human freedom cannot have any other mode of reality.

The existence of mutuality between God and humankind cannot be proved, and the very wish to prove it is a kind of spiritual Philistinism.

> Man desires to have God; he desires to have God continually in space and time. He is loath to be satisfied with the inexpressible confirmation of the meaning; he wants to see it spread out as

> something that one can take out and handle again and again – a continuum in space and time that insures life for him at every point and moment.[11]

And so begins the quest for 'real' presence, the theology of sacred space and time, the theology of the change and the monstrance. But real presence, presence 'face to face' as the Bible calls it, is always elusive. The Welsh poet R. S. Thomas captures this quality in his poem 'The Presence'. When he prays he 'incurs silence', but he does not take the silence as refusal but feels the nudging of an invisible power:

> I know its ways with me;
> how it enters my life,
> is present rather
> before I perceive it, sunlight quivering
> on a bare wall.
> Is it consciousness trying
> to get through?
> Am I under
> regard?
> It takes me seconds
> to focus, by which time
> it has shifted its gaze,
> looking a little to one
> side, as though I were not here.
> It has the universe
> to be abroad in.
> There is nothing I can do
> but fill myself with my own
> silence, hoping it will approach
> like a wild creature to drink
> there, or perhaps like Narcissus
> to linger a moment over its transparent face.[12]

This elusiveness of God's presence contains also a strictly pedagogical point. In what Freire calls the 'banking concept' of education the teacher functions as depositor, prescriber and domesticator, and the method of education is through propaganda, slogans and deposits. The pupils are thought of as empty vessels who need to be filled with a ready made content. Conceiving God as essentially Eternal Mind, much Western orthodoxy has reduced his work to 'revelation' propositionally conceived in terms of 'deposits' of doctrine and moral prescriptions which serve to discipline and school the human race. Hardly surprisingly, a Church with this view of God could establish the Index and require every theological publication to receive the imprimatur, or alternatively could reduce evangelism to propaganda and pious slogans, the Gospel to the level of a tract, and could be co-opted by reactionary governments to keep the masses quiet. Thus one of the most reactionary prime ministers of Britain in the nineteenth century, Lord Liverpool, voted one million pounds for the construction of new churches because the masses were 'exposed to vicious and corrupting influences dangerous to the public security as well as to private morality'.[13] The elusiveness of God's presence, however, does not encourage such a view of the divine education. Education, remarks Freire, is a process of action. 'Even if the people's thinking is superstitious or naive, it is only as they rethink their assumptions in action that they can change. Producing and acting upon their own ideas – not absorbing those of others – must constitute that process.'[14] The fact that both creation and history evolve, and that no finite thing is produced 'ready made', seems to indicate that God operates much more on the lines of this pedagogy which, at enormous cost, allows people to become the subjects of their own history, to make their own world, and to find and relate to God only in that process.

(b) Presence in the neighbour

In the biblical writings the touchstone of the reality of the presence of God is the neighbour, the fellow human being – it is not in the first instance an experience of cultic space or time. The Hebrew word to denote God's presence is *panim*, at the same time the ordinary word for the human face. A forceful comment on the relation of these two meanings is to be found in the story of Jacob's encounter with God at Penuel.

By necessity Jacob is forced to return to the territory of the brother he has cheated of his inheritance. When he hears that Esau is coming to meet him with four hundred men his guilty conscience suggests the worst; he is 'greatly afraid and distressed' and devises a scheme for the survival of at least some of his family and possessions. In the extremity of his distress on this occasion Jacob wrestles in prayer and sees God 'face to face' (Gen. 32:30). The next morning as Esau, like the father of the prodigal, runs to meet his brother and falls weeping on his neck, Jacob cries, 'Truly to see your face is like seeing the face of God, with such favour have you received me' (Gen. 33:10). Jacob encounters God 'face to face' in the meeting with his alienated brother 'face to face'. Conversely, Cain excludes himself from the 'face' of God because his own 'countenance' (*panim*) is distorted by a murderous jealousy (Gen. 4:5, 14).[15] This idea, that God was to be encountered in and through other human beings, was taken up and generalised by the prophets. Thus for Jeremiah to 'judge' the poor and needy (which in Israel is to deliver them) is to know God (Jer. 22:16). Conversely the absence of knowledge of God is proved by the total breakdown of human relations:

> There is no faithfulness or kindness,
>   and no knowledge of God in the land;
> there is swearing, lying, killing,
>   stealing and committing adultery;
> they break all bounds and murder follows murder. (Hos. 4:1–2)

It is this tradition, of what encounter with God means, that Jesus recalls when he speaks of action on behalf of the hungry, the naked and those in prison as being action on behalf of the Son of Man who is also the judge of the historical process (Matt. 25:31ff.). This account of God's presence should not be taken just as a metaphor, part of a vivid exhortation to 'help' the poor. Rather it tells us, much more radically, that God is 'revealed' in and through the poor, that we can learn what he is like there, and what his mode of working is. As Paul was later to express it, it reveals a God whose strength is in weakness and who works through those who are of no account (1 Cor. 1:27ff). It is because God is really *present* in the poor that he is worshipped by behaviour which establishes justice (Isa. 58:6).

The doctrine of the incarnation represents to some extent a

further reflection on this theme of presence. On the one hand it tells us that just as Jacob met God 'face to face' in his brother so God may be encountered in all the brothers and sisters of the Son of Man. But it goes further in affirming the presence of God not simply in 'a man' but in the humiliated and crucified Jew, in the Son of Man who had nowhere to lay his head and who 'took the form of a slave'. It speaks of God's presence being most specific and most concrete not just in 'humanity' but in someone on the margins of society, who died the death of a slave and rebel.[16]

Because God was in Christ human beings are, as Paul described them, the 'temple of the Spirit'. Reverencing them we reverence God, despising them we despise God, rejecting them we reject God, in and through their presence we stand in the presence of God. God 'dwells' in, and his education is conducted in and through, relationships of friendship, kindness, mutual acceptance and forgiveness, and beyond that in those aspects of human work upon the world which are life-enhancing and life-fulfilling.

To recognise God's presence thus and in this manner is, of course, a large part of the elusiveness of that presence. If God is in Christ, then he is present in 'the Rabbi of Nazareth, historically so difficult to get information about, and when it is got one whose activity is so easily a little commonplace alongside more than one other founder of a religion and even alongside many later representatives of his own "religion".'[17] As Barth remarked, 'the veil is thick', and it is thicker still around God's presence in the poor, which cannot be romanticised. Beyond this deeply veiled 'unveiling', however, there is another pedagogical aspect to this presence. If God is really present in Christ and in other human beings, then his presence can only be known in dialogue. The God of Feuerbach and Freud, the divine Headmaster who delivers stern moralising monologues to his pupils, and punishes them if they break the rules, is not the God and Father of Jesus Christ. The God of whom Jesus speaks is engaged in an 'alternative education', the goal of which is the realisation of human creative potential, and thus that education proceeds through a dialogue. 'Dialogue requires an intense faith in man, faith in his power to make and remake, to create and re-create, faith in his vocation to be more fully human (which is not the privilege of an elite, but the birthright of all men)'.[18] Is this faith in dialogue not a poignant way of describing the book of Hosea, for example?

> . . . behold, I will allure her,
> and bring her into the wilderness,
> and speak tenderly to her . . .
> And there she shall answer as in the
> days of her youth . . . (Hos. 2:14–15)

This dialogue, this speaking and answering, is the history of the divine pedagogy. 'Man is inclined by nature to hate both God and his neighbour,' said the Heidelberg Catechism, summing up in this respect the tradition deriving from Augustine. Very often this was taken to imply that there could be no divine faith in the human creature, but only a creation *de novo* from the corrupted mass of humanity. But is not the movement which takes the Son of God to the cross the supreme instance of 'an intense faith in man' which recreates not by fiat but, as Hosea represents it, by wooing, by dialogue, and in patience?

(c) Prayer and presence

The characteristic locus of the divine–human dialogue is intra human encounter, but to say this at once raises the question of prayer. To say that God is present in and through other human beings is not to reduce the divine to the human. Jacob, Moses and Jesus all found the need to be alone, to withdraw to 'a lonely place', and there to wrestle 'until the breaking of the day'. The practice of presence is a practice with two poles, both of which consist in attention. On the one hand, there is presence in the neighbour, and especially in the poor. But to be sensitive to that presence as the presence of *God* requires that wrestling with silence, that listening and waiting, which Jesus underwent in Gethsemane and which is the other side of Jacob's wrestling with his brother. These two poles belong together. There is never a question of presence for its own sake, divorced from the concrete, historical and relational. On the other hand, the language of presence is not just a vivid way of talking of the 'transcendence' of the human project. The concrete and the relational speak 'the vernacular of the purposes of One who is', what Bonhoeffer called 'the beyond in the midst'. This dimension of presence must be considered more fully in the context of the discussion of the historical reality of grace.

(d) Presence and the future

The presence of God which is known in prayer is never, in the biblical witness, an abstract enjoyment of 'mystic sweet communion', but always stands in intimate connection with God's future. In the story of Elijah at Horeb it is pointed out that God is not known in the normal manifestations of theophany but in the commissioning to a specific historical task (1 Kings 19:15). The story of the revelation to Moses at the burning bush both includes the bi-polarity of experience of the divine presence, but also concludes with a promise and an historical summons. The story actually starts when Moses, who has been brought up in the household of an elite and oppressing class, sees someone beaten before him. 'One day, when Moses had grown up he went out to his people, and looked on their burdens; and he *saw* . . .' (Exod. 2:11). The fruit of this first seeing is a wild action which accomplishes nothing but forces him to flee into the 'wilderness'. There, where he has time for reflection rather than just a wild action, he again 'sees': 'And Moses said, "I will turn aside and see this great sight, why the bush is not burnt" ' (Exod. 3:3). The experience of Moses at the Burning Bush should certainly not be reduced to the record of 'the internal brooding of a man over the problems of his people'. We may take it as the record of an encounter with one who is 'Wholly Other'. On the other hand, these two possibilities do not constitute an 'either–or'. The encounter with God and the experience of his presence recorded in Exodus 3 cannot be reduced to, but on the other hand cannot be taken apart from, the encounter with the slaves of the earlier chapter.

In this encounter God reveals himself fundamentally in terms of promise: the only 'name' that he gives is 'I will be who I will be', the one who is known through his faithfulness to the promises, and whose presence is promised on the path of historical liberation in the future. Similarly the angel at the tomb promises the disciples the presence of Christ ahead of them in the 'Galilee' of the messianic mission to the nations. 'The God of the exodus and resurrection "Is" not eternal presence, but he promises his presence and nearness to him who follows the path on which he is sent into the future.'[19] God is therefore 'present' 'where we wait on his promises in hope and transformation'.

This aspect of God's presence likewise has its pedagogical reflection. Freire speaks of education as happening in the bi-polarity of action and reflection. In an echo of the idea of the prophetic Word, which changes reality, and of Jesus' critique of the idle word, which accomplishes nothing, he speaks of the 'true word' by which reality is changed. 'To exist humanly is to *name* the world, to change it. Once named, the world in its turn reappears to the namers as a problem and requires of them a new *naming*. Men are not built in silence, but in word, in work, in action-reflection'.[20] The divine education is not conducted 'directly' through revelations which have no bearing on the historical situation, neither is it to be reduced to an intra-human social activism, as though theology were anthropology, but is conducted in a constant interaction between the two.

The awareness of presence, in relation to situations, bearing on the situation and to some extent springing from it, but going beyond it in the dimension of a definite encounter, is the beginning of the *circulus fiduciae*, the circle of faith, which is also a pedagogical circle. Presence is fleeting, but it calls into being faith in the present and hope for the future. It calls into being a tradition of faith: history read in the light of the presence of the Other who discloses himself. This tradition in turn gives content to the cult, to the celebration of the Passover and of the supper of the Lord. People recite the traditions in the cult and they know God present in the mode of story, or Word. They repeat significant actions recalling past events in which God was understood to be present, sharing unleavened bread or a cup of wine, or eating bitter herbs, and they know God present 'sacramentally', in the mode of sign. They understand their corporate existence as bound up with the self-revelation of God, and they know God present in and through the community as the 'people of God' or 'the body of Christ'. This traditional, liturgical and community experience provides in turn a context for the more fundamental experience of God in the neighbour, and for the biblical tradition very specifically in the poor. From presence *remembered and anticipated* the community receives its interpretation of historical existence, a framework for making sense of reality.[21] The circle of action and reflection therefore produces action in a particular direction, towards the realisation of what Jesus called 'the kingdom'.

The heart of education is relationship, but in respect to the divine human encounter relationship means presence. Experienced in an ellipse between intra-human encounter and prayer, always elusive and never a quantity we can bank on and count our own, always directed to the realisation of the completely new, the presence which is the reality of what Lessing called 'the education of the human race' guides, woos, directs and elicits – or, as Origen said, uses 'the best methods of education' – towards the fulfilment of the divine purpose, that human beings should be conformed to the image of God's Son. It is this 'grammar' of God's presence, this account of its fundamental structure, which will guide us as we seek to understand the divine education.

CONCLUSION

The object of the essay which follows is to explore some of the dimensions of this pedagogy through presence as a way of trying to understand how God acts redemptively in history. Whilst history itself is not identified with God's redeeming action, as by Hegel and his followers, it is argued that redemption is an historical process, and that history is therefore not simply the backdrop or stage-set for redemption, as it was for Augustine, but the medium of redemption. Accordingly, chapters 2 and 3 attempt, first, to establish that the 'kingdom' of which Jesus spoke had an historical dimension and that 'progress' may be meaningfully affirmed of human history and, secondly, to explore the significance of the incarnation as part of God's redemptive pedagogy. To do this the patristic word *homoousion* is taken up, understood in terms of solidarity, and this is in turn illuminated by means of the root analogy of the book, the practice of 'education for critical consciousness'.

To speak of God's engagement with his creature we need, according to the tradition, to speak of both incarnation and the Spirit. Since what is meant by 'Spirit' is far from obvious, two further chapters trace the significance of language about Spirit in the biblical writings and attempt to establish that this is centrally concerned with the 'coming' of God's kingdom, that situation where

God's will for his creation is realised. Its concern, in other words, is to give content to such assertions as 'God works in history' or 'God makes history'. 'Grace' language also shares this concern but speaks more of the quality of God's presence to history and the nature of his engagement. A further chapter explores this qualitative dimension. The argument with Augustine developed in the third chapter is here taken further in a challenge to his understanding of grace. The extent to which grace may be considered as an historical category, which appears to have been the concern of Aquinas's language about 'created grace', is also pursued.

The remaining chapters all deal with the 'economy' of the Spirit, the concrete ways in which this work of God is known, in each case reflecting on its role in the divine education. Within the community which derives from Jesus God's presence is known in sign and story, and chapters 7 and 8 consider the role of the sacraments in general, and the eucharist in particular, in the divine education. Chapters 6 to 8 all contain brief reviews of the development of doctrine in the tradition. For those for whom to mention Aquinas and Calvin is to induce a yawn, these sections can be omitted without harm to the argument. They are included partly to put the present argument in its context, but more fundamentally as part of a concern to understand how what was said then relates to me now, a concern which runs throughout the essay.

Chapter 9, dealing with religion, represents, it must be admitted, something of a bracket between the treatment of Word and sacraments and that of the Church. It is, nevertheless, an essential prelude to the discussion of the role of the Church in human history, whilst on the other hand it presupposes to some extent the account of the role of human stories in chapter 8. From a very early period Israel believed that God worked not only in their history but in the histories of the nations. How are we to understand that work? A common and influential answer is that his work is to be seen in the great religions of the world. In evaluating this answer the pedagogical tradition of Israel, Wisdom, is drawn upon. From this discussion we turn naturally, and at last, to the question of the role of the Church in the divine economy of redemption, which is the question of its mission. Its relation both to political structures and to the wider sphere of human culture is considered.

The book may then be seen as an essay in theology of the atonement. It was one of the merits of the great book on this theme published at the very beginning of the present century, R. C. Moberly's *Atonement and Personality*, to perceive that it was not possible to speak of the atonement without speaking of Spirit, Church and sacraments. 'An exposition of atonement which leaves out Pentecost, leaves the atonement unintelligible', he remarked. 'Calvary without Pentecost would not be an atonement *to us*'.[22] In its own way Moberly's book was an exposition of the theme of atonement through education, though he did not spell out the connection. The reasons for that have perhaps been indicated in the present chapter, as deep and well founded suspicions attend this model for God's redeeming work. With a different understanding of education, however, the theme can perhaps be rescued. In this attempt another classic book on the atonement plays its role, Gustav Aulén's *Christus Victor*, published thirty years after Moberly. As already hinted in the present chapter, and developed further in chapter 3, the theme of the battle with the powers and the theme of divine education are inextricably linked, for the powers are defeated, according to both John and Paul, by their *exposure*. No lack of contemporary illustrations of this truth will occur to the reader. In attempting to understand God's redeeming work, both in Christ and through the Spirit, we have taken up an analogy from the present political situation – the attempt to create more human conditions through 'the education for critical consciousness' – and lest this be thought to indicate too heavy a debt to so-called 'Liberation theology' we note that in doing this we are but following Anselm, who also used a political analogy for this purpose.

As a final point, entitling chapters 4 and 5 'The Spirit and the Kingdom – I' and ' – II' follows not just from the fact that the biblical material cannot be handled in one chapter but is designed to make a fundamental hermeneutical point which underlies all the exegesis of the essay. The present order of our Christian Bibles derives from the Septuagint. It begins with the Pentateuch and progresses through historical, poetical and prophetical books. The 'New Testament' is tacked on as the last of the series, and this easily suggests that the earlier books no longer have anything but archaeological significance. Numbers and Judges might be interesting as containing illustrations of how society was organised in the ancient Near East but they are not 'prophecy', a word of the divine education spoken to the present. However Ton Veerkamp has recently pointed out (and it is the implication also of 'canonical criticism') that the order of the Hebrew Bible, the Tenakh, is more synchronic, and avoids this regressive scheme. There the historical books are included under prophecy, and together Torah and Nebiim (Prophets) constitute the heart of God's revelation, the disclosure of his will for human life and society. Around these writings are placed the Khetubim, the Wisdom writings and 'poetical books', to be heard as a commentary on law and prophets. Veerkamp's suggestion is then that the New Testament as 'the Messianic writings', the writings which speak of the coming of the Messiah promised to Israel, should be placed around these as in the diagram, as a further commentary on Khetubim, Torah and prophets, and the whole

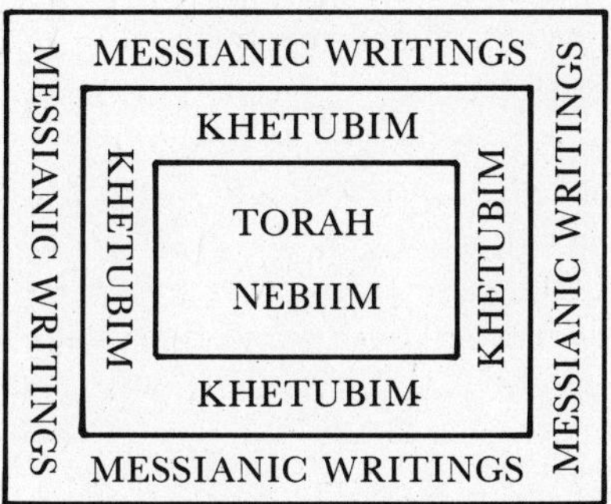

witnessing to God's will for his creation. This model emphasises that the Messianic writings do not supersede Torah but presuppose it and together with it form a whole. The argument is fundamental not only to chapters 4 and 5 but also to chapter 2, the elaboration of Jesus' understanding of the kingdom.[23]

Possibly a still more appropriate image for understanding Scripture is to picture a sheet of music scored for three or four parts. Torah is the ground theme, and Prophets, Wisdom and the Messianic writings are all themes introduced above this, not in dissonance but as constituting the full harmony of the revelation of God's will. Though any theme may be taken and examined on its own, as in musical analysis, the music is not properly heard until all the themes are heard together.

The opening up of the whole person which can be achieved by

music – the liberation of body, mind and emotions as the Renaissance masters understood dance – is doubtless a more appropriate model for the divine education than that more political model which is pursued here. On the other hand, the fact that not only Karl Barth but also Hermann Hesse might welcome this musical analogy should warn us once again that history as a whole is not to be identified with the divine pedagogy, which would all too easily suggest that human suffering and wickedness were but the necessary counterpoint to the main theme of God's elicitation of love from the creature. The divine music is shaped from the raw materials of human history, but history itself is not that music. The music that will form the final vindication of God's purpose is *redeemed*, rescued, corrected, set aright. The choice between death and life which we are called upon to make, the struggle for life in which we are caught up, is part of that redeeming composition.

2

The Kingdom of God and Historical Process

Pedagogy involves process: there is no instant education. If God's redemption of the human race is through education, then this entails that history is the scene of that education, even if the whole of history cannot be identified, as it was by Hegel, with 'the self-realisation of Absolute Spirit'. History itself is not revelation, but revelation (education) happens only in and through historical process. In the synoptic gospels the phrase which is used to describe God's interaction with this process is '*Hē Basileia tou Theou*' (God's kingly rule, or 'the kingdom of God'), but what precisely is meant by this phrase has been the subject of intense debate for more than one hundred years.

Fixing on the proclamation of the kingdom of God as the heart of Jesus' message, the liberal theology of the nineteenth century understood this kingdom as 'an immanent force in history, culminating in a universal society of brotherhood and justice'.[1] For Ritschl, the doyen of liberal theology in the mid-nineteenth century, 'kingdom' was an active word, 'the organisation of humanity through action inspired by love', in the course of which activity human beings, inspired by grace, 'built' the kingdom which is the goal of the purpose of God's love. Ironically, it is precisely this gospel of the kingdom which has been used to deny that there is any inner meaning to history. Thus the philosopher of history Karl Löwith maintains that 'since the kingdom of God is not to be realised in a continuous process of historical developments, the eschatological history of salvation also cannot impart a new and progressive meaning to the history of the world, which is fulfilled by having reached its term'.[2] For Löwith, 'Historical processes as such do not bear the least evidence of a comprehensive and ultimate meaning. History as such has no outcome'.[3] It is the presumed 'radical eschatology' of Jesus' teaching about the kingdom which is used to justify this scepticism. The church historian Edward Norman, on the other hand, likes to read into Jesus' call to 'a Kingdom not of this world' a relativisation of all human values and strivings, a need to 'turn away from the preoccupations of human society'.[4] Clearly, the attempt to discern in human history a redemptive pedagogy must try to clarify what Jesus meant in his proclamation that 'the kingdom of heaven is at hand' (Mark 1:15), and this is the concern of the present chapter. The central contention will be that Jesus' proclamation of the kingdom is only properly understood in the light of the fact that at all points Jesus presupposed 'Moses and the prophets'. Once this is grasped, radically discontinuous and radically other-worldly readings of the kingdom become impossible. We begin however with a brief review of the 'kingdom debate' of the past century, develop an alternative contention that 'kingdom' is to be understood in terms of the doing of God's will, and then turn to the question of whether Jesus envisaged any period of time, whether short or long, for the realisation of this kingdom. Finally we turn to the content of the gospel of the kingdom.

THE KINGDOM AS THE END OF HISTORY

Contemporary rejection of the idea that the kingdom of God involves historical process begins with the publication in 1892 of Johannes Weiss's essay *The Preaching of Jesus on the Kingdom of God.* In a thesis later taken up and forcefully elaborated by Albert Schweitzer he argued that Jesus was an apocalyptic prophet who expected the catastrophic end of all things. Weiss wished to oppose as sharply as possible the idea of the immanent kingdom of love and justice of his father-in-law, Ritschl. The kingdom was not the work of men but of God, and Jesus did not expect the continuation of history but 'stands at the end of the world and the end of history'. He considered that the apocalyptic expectation of the later prophets was the background for Jesus' proclamation. For him eschatology means apocalyptic. Agreeing with this, Schweitzer drew the necessary inference that Jesus was mistaken in his expectation of the kingdom. At first, he argued, Jesus thought that the kingdom would come upon his sending out the messengers. When that failed he expected his death to usher it in, an expectation which was tragically mistaken:

> There is silence all around. The Baptist appears, and cries 'Repent, for the kingdom of heaven is at hand'. Soon after that comes Jesus, and in the knowledge that He is the coming Son of Man lays hold of the wheel of the world to set it moving on the last revolution which is to bring all ordinary history to a close. It refuses to turn, and he throws himself on it. Then it does turn; and crushes him.[5]

Despite this failed expectation Jesus still means something to our world because 'a mighty spiritual force streams forth from Him and flows through our time also'.[6] Jesus still rules in history 'through the power of his inmost being'. By a nice irony the conclusion of consistent eschatology, the doctrine that the coming of the kingdom meant the apocalyptic end of the world, is identical with liberalism, and in fact proves the triumph of the christology of Schleiermacher which began the nineteenth century as the 'impulse' which comes from the man Jesus shapes human history. An eschatology which is completely transcendent (the end of the world, the Second Coming) is transformed into one which is completely immanent – insofar as we can talk of kingdom it means the continuation of the spiritual movement which Jesus started. Followers of Ritschl must have been greatly amused and gratified by this outcome.

This combination of the identification of eschatology with apocalyptic on the one hand, and a basically liberal and individualistic interpretation of the significance of Jesus on the other, is determinative for a great deal of suceeding discussion of the meaning of the kingdom. Lecturing in 1899 the liberal theologian Harnack had spoken of the kingdom as 'the rule of the Holy God in the hearts of individuals' which comes 'by coming to the individual, by entering into his soul and laying hold of it'.[7] The result is scarcely different for Bultmann who begins by rejecting this liberal interpretation but then finds the need to demythologise the New Testament concept and reinterpret it in terms of existential decision. Similarly, another scholar who accepts that the kingdom is an apocalyptic concept, Norman Perrin, likewise believes that the language of the kingdom points to 'the sphere of individual human existence as the sphere in which the kingdom of God is manifested', and Jesus' eschatological teaching is 'concerned above all with the experience of the individual'.[8] To the extent that this contains no social reference whatsoever it is not only not an advance on Harnack but a definite step backwards.

Although the identification of eschatology with apocalyptic is still current in many quarters, Adolf Schlatter pointed out as long ago as 1923 five crucial differences between the teaching of Jesus and apocalyptic: Jesus does not offer an elaborate and unified picture of the future, as apocalyptic does; he nowhere refers to apocalyptic writings; he nowhere refers to the favourite themes of apocalyptic, such as the fall of the angels or the figure of Enoch; he nowhere appeals to special experiences like the apocalyptic writers; and he does not build up one total picture of past and future, like apocalyptic. Commenting on these differences Perrin remarks that 'there is still one crucial thing in common between Jesus and the apocalyptic writers: the use of "Kingdom of God" in connection with the future hope'.[9] But Billerbeck could only find five instances of the phrase 'kingdom of God' in the apocalyptic literature, which Perrin expands to seven with two instances from the Dead Sea scrolls, and in any case what is meant by 'kingdom of God' and 'future hope' is precisely what is under discussion!

Thirty years after Schweitzer, C. H. Dodd was able to show that a purely futurist understanding of eschatology did not do justice to the New Testament. In the teaching of Jesus there is a word about the present realisation of God's kingdom, which comes in the ministry of Jesus himself, which is 'the impact upon this world of the "powers of the world to come" '. But Dodd's Platonist framework yielded a result more or less identical to Bultmann's, as for him history is not important as a process but only as the sphere of moral decision: 'The preaching of the Church is directed towards reconstituting in the experience of individuals the hour of decision which Jesus brought'.[10]

There can be no doubt that some of Jesus' sayings about the kingdom think in apocalyptic terms of the coming end of all things: 'The kingdom of heaven is like a net which was thrown into the sea and gathered fish of every kind; when it was full, men drew it ashore and sat down and sorted the good into vessels and threw away the bad. So it will be at the close of the age' (Matt. 13:47–50). At the close of the so-called 'eschatological discourse', in which Jesus speaks of the signs which precede the coming of the Son of Man, Luke amends the Marcan version by concluding, 'So also, when you see these things taking place, you know that the kingdom of God is near' (Luke 21.31). Texts such as this (though we note that the Marcan text refers to a process preceding the consummation), when taken together with those which speak of the 'Day of the Son of Man', clearly indicate that Jesus thought of a divine 'winding up' of the historical process at some time in the future. Equally clearly there are a number of texts which speak of the present realisation of the kingdom: The time is fulfilled (Mark 1:15), the kingdom is at hand (Matt. 10:7), it has come upon you (Luke 11:20), it is in your midst (Luke 17:21). To these texts Dodd appealed for this thesis. On the basis of this clear duality scholars such as Kümmel and Cullmann proposed that the kingdom had both present and future aspects, an 'already' and a 'not yet', or as Cullman felicitously put it, a distinction between 'D-day', the decisive battle, and 'V-day', the final overcoming of the enemy. Whilst for Cullman this duality indicated a salvation history between the two, for the followers of Bultmann 'the intention is always to depict the relationship between the coming kingdom and the present activity of Jesus and thereby to bring about a decision in face of the present offer of salvation'.[11] It remains a question however whether this twofold categorisation is adequate to the evidence.

THE KINGDOM AS THE DOING OF GOD'S WILL

To test the adequacy of the 'present–future' scheme for interpreting the meaning of the kingdom we can take the petition from Matthew's version of the Lord's prayer:

> Your kingdom come
> Your will be done – on earth as in heaven. (Matt. 6:10)

It was Weiss who proposed that this should be understood in the light of the Kaddish prayer: 'May he establish the kingdom in your lifetime and in your days and in the lifetime of all the house of Israel ever speedily and at a near time.' Dalman, who originally drew attention to the prayer, understood it as referring to the individual taking upon himself 'the yoke of Torah', which meant putting oneself under all the obligations of the law – in other words as both a present and a moral reality. Perrin on the other hand regards the petition as 'clearly eschatological' (which means apocalyptic):

> But we must remember that those who are being taught to use this petition are those for whom the kingdom is already a matter of personal experience.[!] They are therefore either being taught to pray that others may share this experience;[!] or, more probably, they are being taught to pray for the consummation of that which has begun within their experience.[!] In this case we have here another example of this highly characteristic tension between present and future; caught up in this tension the disciples are to direct their prayer to the future in which it will be resolved.[12]

Aside from the 'higher Moravianism' of this interpretation (the centrality of the concept of 'personal experience'), which is very characteristic of this kind of liberalism, the interpretation is wholly unconvincing on two grounds. In the first place the similarity with the Kaddish prayer is greatly overstated: what we have here is no parallel. If Jesus is consciously referring to it then precisely the important thing is how he alters it. But in the second place, in looking for an aid to interpretation outside the gospels it ignores the much more obvious evidence in the gospels themselves. Matthew has two instances where Jesus speaks of 'doing God's will'. The first comes in the same teaching section in which the Lord's prayer is included, where Jesus warns that 'Not every one who says to me, "Lord, Lord," shall enter the kingdom of heaven, but he who does the will of my Father in heaven' (Matt. 7:21). Later, when his family come to find him, Jesus says to the crowd, 'Whoever does the will of my Father in heaven is my brother, and sister, and mother' (Matt. 12:50). These two remarks are part and parcel of Jesus' emphasis on 'doing' which is a very characteristic part of his teaching.[13] By this 'doing' he does not mean 'decision' in the face of 'the challenge of the hour', according to Matthew, but 'doing and teaching' the law and the prophets (Matt. 5:17–20). This emphasis of Jesus, in turn, appeals not to the apocalyptic of the later prophets but to the emphasis on 'doing' which is highly characteristic both of Deuteronomy (e.g. Deut. 4:1, 5:1, 19:9) and the prophets (e.g. Isa. 56.1, Jer. 11:6, Ezek. 18:5).

Schlatter has pointed out that Jesus never once refers to apocalyptic literature. By contrast we have very clear citation, and even more frequent allusion, by Jesus of 'Moses and the prophets'. In his reading of the Scriptures of Israel does Jesus pick out those elements which Weiss appealed to for his understanding of the apocalyptic kingdom of God? Strangely, he does not. In the story about eating with unwashed hands (Mark 7:1–13) Jesus cites Isaiah 29:13 and then Exodus 20:12 in order to establish that the commandment should be kept in its proper sense (or as we might say, that God's will might be done) and that the word of God should not be made void. On the question about divorce (Mark 10:2ff.) Jesus cites Genesis 1:27, 5:2 and 2:24 in order to establish that God's will in creation should be respected and that woman should not be treated as an object. In the incident of the Temple cleansing (Mark 11:15ff.) Jesus cites Isaiah 56:7 and Jeremiah 7:11 to establish that a narrowly nationalistic reading of Israel's vocation is a perversion of God's intentions (or, as one could also say, his will). The story of the question about the greatest commandment (Mark 12:28ff.) is particularly important. Jesus responds to the question as to which is the greatest commandment by citing the Shema, Deuteronomy 6:45. The scribe replies with an allusion to a series of texts which put obedience above sacrifice (1 Sam. 15:22; Hos. 6:6; Mic. 6:6–8). According to Matthew Jesus himself cited Hosea 6:6, 'I desire mercy and not sacrifice,' in response to the accusation of breaking the sabbath. In Mark's version of the present story Jesus concludes by saying to the scribe, after his citation of these texts, 'You are not far from the kingdom of God' (Mark 12:34). This means the kingdom neither as future(!) nor as present in Jesus' person and demanding decision, but as doing the will of God in obedience.

MOSES AND THE PROPHETS

In Matthew's account of the story of the great commandment Jesus follows the citation of Deuteronomy with the words, 'On these two commandments hang all the law and the prophets' (Matt. 22:40). The gospel records consistently depict 'the law and the prophets' as forming Jesus' frame of reference, and in turn Luke considers that it is only through 'the law and the prophets' that we rightly understand Jesus.

Both Matthew and Luke record sayings in which Jesus firmly underscores the eternal validity of the Torah. In Luke this affirmation is put together with a saying about the kingdom:

> The law and the prophets were until John; since then the good news of the kingdom of God is preached, and every one enters it violently. But it is easier for heaven and earth to pass away, than for one vowel of Torah to become void. (Luke 16:16–17)

The preaching of the good news of the kingdom does not negate Torah but on the contrary confirms it. Luke emphasises this further with his story of the rich man and Lazarus, where the answer to the rich man's request that a messenger be sent to warn his brothers is, 'They have Moses and the prophets; let them hear them' (Luke 16:29). In what appears to be a post-resurrection saying it is further underlined that the revelation of God's will in Moses and the prophets is no less clear than in the resurrection (16:31). Luke returns to Moses and the prophets in the story of the walk to Emmaus where it is these writings which interpret the significance of Jesus (24:27).

In Matthew we find a variant tradition of Jesus' affirmation of the importance of law and prophets:

> Think not that I have come to abolish the law and the prophets; I have come not to abolish them but to fulfil them. For truly, I say to you, till heaven and earth pass away, not an iota, not a dot, will pass from the law until all is accomplished. (Matt. 5:17–18)

Significantly Jesus then goes on: 'Whoever then relaxes one of the least of these commandments and teaches men so, shall be called least in the kingdom of heaven; but he who does them and teaches them shall be called great in the kingdom of heaven' (Matt. 5:19). 'The kingdom of heaven' is Matthew's reverential periphrasis for Mark's 'kingdom of God'. Greatness 'in' the kingdom is determined by the observance of all that is taught in Moses and the prophets. For Jesus Torah is the heart of God's self-giving to history, and all else is commentary upon that.

Thus whilst Jesus did not presuppose apocalyptic writings, as far as we can tell from the gospel, he did presuppose 'Moses and the prophets' as witnesses to God's will for human beings, what he wanted them to do here and now. When Jesus teaches his disciples to pray, 'Your will be done on earth,' Dalman's suggestion that this might be similar to the rabbinic 'taking on the yoke of Torah' is far more probable than the idea that it is a prayer for an apocalyptic consummation such as we have in the cry 'Come Lord Jesus' (so Perrin). But the petition that God's will be done stands in parallelism with the petition for the coming of the kingdom. In the same way the command to 'seek first his kingdom' is in parallel with the command to seek 'his righteousness' (Matt. 6:33). Is this righteousness something which is known 'in the sphere of individual human existence'? Not according to Moses and the prophets. For them the righteousness of God calls forth an answering righteousness of man which transcends all individualism, and which is known in the establishment of justice and in concrete programmes for a new order in society (Deuteronomy).

Dismissing the possibility of finding meaning in historical process Karl Löwith concludes that for Christianity the history of salvation is 'internationalised because it is individualised'. For Jewish theology, however, he feels that a 'theology of secular history is indeed a possibility and even a necessity'.[14] Löwith is able to arrive at this individualising of salvation only by separating Jesus from Moses and the prophets, and this is the hermeneutical presupposition which underlies the individualism both of liberalism and existentialism: notoriously neither Schleiermacher nor Bultmann could make much sense of the Old Testament.

Behind the rejection of the Old Testament is an evolutionary scheme which begins with 'gross', 'unrefined', 'materialistic' ideas and moves to a peak in 'purely spiritual' ideas, a scheme whose values derive from Plato. For the Old Testament however the spiritual is known only in and through the material. It speaks of the goal of the historical process in terms such as 'salvation', 'blessing', and 'peace', and these are all conceived in a thoroughly materialist way: 'the saving blessings held out to the people are for the most part material – fertility in man and beast, peace from enemies, political greatness. Yahweh's grace produces everything that furthers life (Deut. 28:8–14). This material view of salvation extends even to the kneading-trough of the individual household (Deut. 28:5).'[15] This materialist understanding was not due to a lack of spirituality but on the contrary to the perception that God's love and grace were apprehended *in* creation, and that the purpose of creation was 'life in all its fullness'. The view that, opposed to this materialist understanding, the New Testament offered a pure and 'spiritual' religion was fought in the second century as a deadly error. Confronted with the depreciation of creation in Gnosticism Irenaeus asserted that 'those who say that our created world was made of "decay, ignorance and passion" sin against their Father' (*Adversus Haereses* 4.18.4). For him both incarnation and Eucharist established the 'unity of flesh and spirit', so that the spiritual is understood only in and through the material. Historical materialism, said Marx, is concerned with people 'in their actual empirically perceptible process of development under definite conditions'. Irenaeus agrees: 'Since there are real men, so must there also be a real establishment, that they vanish not away among non-existent things, but progress among those which have an actual existence' (5.36.1). It was on grounds such as these that, in the eighth century, John of Damascus elaborated a theology of matter: 'I do not worship matter. I worship the God of matter; who became matter for my sake, and deigned to inhabit matter; who worked out my salvation through matter . . . Do not vilify matter, for it is not dishonourable. Nothing is dishonourable which God has made. This is the Manichaean notion'.[16] Manichaean too is Edward Norman's view that Christ believed in 'the worthlessness of human values' – as expressed, for instance, in the law and the prophets, which did not fall from the skies, but which are the human response to the revelation known in God's 'elusive presence'. Only as human values are they also divine values.

'Bread for me is a material question; bread for others is a spiritual question' (Berdyaev). This is the correct account of the relation of spiritual and material found in the Scriptures Jesus presupposed. The painful elaboration of the doctrine of the incarnation in the second century is an affirmation by the Church that it understood the 'New' Testament in this way. 'Spiritual' salvation comes only in and through the material, and the attempt to divorce the two – as in the major and recurring heretical tendencies of docetism and ebionitism – is a heresy, an option incompatible with the Church's life. When the Bible is read not as the second-century heretics and as Schleiermacher and Bultmann read it – as a superseded 'Old' Testament and a relevant 'New' Testament (even though the mythology needs working out, both for Valentinus and for Bultmann) – but as one book with two parts neither of which is properly understood without the other, as Irenaeus read it, then it becomes impossible to spiritualise or moralise or radically individualise that salvation which Jesus spoke of in terms of the kingdom of God.

TIME FOR THE KINGDOM?

In announcing the kingdom did Jesus reckon with a period of time before the 'Day of the Son of Man'? In his argument for a salvation history Cullmann adduced a number of texts to show that Jesus expected an interval of time 'even if a short one' between his death and the Parousia.[17] He pointed to Mark 14:62, which distinguishes between the moment when the Son of Man will take his seat at the right hand of God, and when he will come again on the clouds of heaven; to Mark 13:10, which speaks of the necessity of the gospel being preached to all nations; to Mark 9:1 which only says that 'some' will not taste death before the kingdom comes; to the words about fasting in Mark 2:18ff.; and the promise of resurrection: 'But after I am risen, I will go before you into Galilee' (Mark 14:28). Of these quotations the most decisive is Mark 13:10, because it confirms precisely what we learn from Paul.

A whole series of prophetic texts spoke of the ingathering of the Gentiles in the last days to Zion. According to 'Third Isaiah' it was to be a manifestation of the glory of the Lord which summoned the nations (Isa. 60:3). Paul, who together with John and the author of Hebrews believed that this glory was manifested in the crucified and risen Christ, understood his mission to the Gentiles as accomplishing this ingathering. The urgency of his mission to break down the wall of partition, to preach that 'there is no distinction' between Jews and Gentiles, stems from his conviction that in this mission the vocation of Israel to be a blessing to the nations is fulfilled, and that this fulfilment would usher in the consummation: 'For salvation is nearer to us now than when we first believed; the night is far spent, the day is at hand' (Rom. 13:12). Why? Paul has already explained: 'A hardening has come upon part of Israel until the full number of the Gentiles comes in, and so all Israel will be saved' (Rom. 11:25–6). Paul is convinced that his work, traipsing from synagogue to synagogue round the Mediterranean and establishing worshipping communities of Jews and Gentiles, is hastening the realisation of God's purposes. His eschatology is not purely apocalyptic, but includes essentially a task for the messengers (Rom. 10:14ff).. His vision of history begins with the promise to Abraham (Rom. 15:8) continues through Torah, which is the schooling of Israel for her historical destiny, and is realised in the inclusion of all in the messianic promises.

This perspective of Paul gives the clue to understanding the contradiction in Jesus' ministry, pointed out by Jeremias, that Jesus both avoids the Gentiles and yet clearly thinks of their inclusion in God's promises.[18] On the one hand, he warns the disciples not to stray into Gentile territory and rebukes the Canaanite woman with the words: 'I was not sent but to the lost sheep of the house of Israel' (Matt. 15:24). On the other hand, Jesus enters Jerusalem in fulfilment of the prophecy of Zechariah 9:9–10, which promises that the Messiah will 'speak peace to the nations'; he cleanses the Temple to make it a house of prayer 'for all nations' (Mark 11:17); at the supper he speaks of his blood as being shed 'for many', which is probably a deliberate allusion to the Gentiles, for whom there was otherwise no atonement. In his teaching he promised a share in the resurrection to the Gentiles (Matt. 12:41f.) and eliminated the words of vengeance from the messianic promises.[19] This contradiction is explained if Jesus understood his task as the final preparation of *Israel*, which is the essential prerequisite for the ingathering of the Gentiles. That ingathering, he made quite clear, was not his task. The view that he expected it to be accomplished by an apocalyptic miracle, of the kind anticipated in Isaiah, fails to make sense of many aspects of Jesus' ministry: his calling of the twelve, who did not represent the Israel of his day (which consisted only of the remnant left in Judah after the Assyrian destruction of northern Israel) but the 'new' Israel which included the Gentiles; his creative reading of Torah as a way of life; his teaching on prayer, and on discipleship and service. The reaction against liberalism led to the assimilation of all Jesus' teaching to eschatology, but to interpret all this teaching only in terms of 'the challenge of the hour' is as distorting as the liberal reduction of it to moral generalities. The fact is that a great deal of Jesus' teaching looks as if it was intended for an ongoing historical fellowship, for a pilgrim people, exactly as the original Torah was intended.

If this is the case it raises afresh the question of the meaning of the so-called parables of growth (the Sower, the Tares, the Seed growing secretly, and the Mustard Seed.) For both Dodd and Jeremias the point of these parables is not growth and process but the secretness and suddenness of the coming of the kingdom. Dodd refers the words about growth to the period before Jesus, the period of law and prophets which culminated with John the Baptist, on the grounds that the kingdom is 'realised' in Jesus. But if Jesus envisaged the ingathering of the Gentiles, as promised repeatedly in the Scriptures he studied, how can the kingdom be supposed to have 'come' without that event? Refuting the claim that 'the oriental mind' does not think in terms of growth(!), Nils Dahl argued that these parables must be understood 'in the light of the contrast between the eschatological expectations and the actual process of the coming of the kingdom into the present time'.[20] They teach that the kingdom has a 'history', a period of its secret presence preceding its final revelation in the 'Day of the Son of Man'. This history is the history of the messianic mission, of the fulfilment of Israel's destiny to be a 'light to the peoples' so that God's salvation might 'reach the end of the earth' (Isa. 49:6).

THE CONTENT OF THE GOSPEL OF THE KINGDOM

Three essential presuppositions have determined discussion of the kingdom since Weiss: the identification of eschatology with apocalyptic; the idea that Hellenistic ideas and background are more decisive for understanding the New Testament than the Old Testament is (Schweitzer, Bultmann, Dodd); and an individualistic concept of salvation (actually part and parcel of the second presupposition.) One of the more bizarre results of this interpretation has been to empty the proclamation of kingdom of any *content*, reducing it to a demand for 'decision'. But if in fact it is 'Moses and the prophets' who are decisive for Jesus, and that not in the relatively few apocalyptic texts contained in those writings but in the mainstream reference to the revelation and the doing of God's will, then this reduction of Jesus' proclamation is inadmissible. Certainly Jesus looks to a final consummation, perhaps in the near future. Meanwhile the 'present' of the kingdom is not simply a matter of 'decision' (an idea impossible before Romanticism) but of the doing of God's will, of the doing of Torah, and this, according to the parallelism of the petition in the Lord's prayer, is part and parcel of the coming of the kingdom.

According to Weiss and many later followers of his, such a notion is equivalent to saying that the kingdom is a work of man rather than being something which is brought by God. As a reaction to Ritschl, that 'archetypal bourgeois of the age of Bismarck' as Barth called him, with his deistic Kantian division between God and the world, this might be a legitimate criticism. Its mistake, however, is continuing to presuppose this same kind of deistic disjunction. For Moses and the prophets it is not 'either God or man' but the hand and work and will of God through the hand and work and will of man. A text like the 'call' of Jeremiah illustrates this with great clarity:

> See, I have set you this day
> over nations and over kingdoms,
> to pluck up and to break down,
> to destroy and to overthrow,
> to build and to plant. (Jer. 1:10)

What God does, he does through the prophet. Without this presupposition there is not only no prophecy but no court history, no Deuteronomistic history and no Torah, for all presuppose that God's will is done and his purpose furthered through men and women. They presuppose in other words what Martin Buber called 'active history', history which is not pre-planned but is realised in a dialogue between God and the creature. 'God's promise opens up a new possibility for human beings, but the particular realisation of the possibility depends on human decision, on their faith or unbelief. God's kingdom, in other words, does not by-pass human faith, but comes where God is recognised in faith as Lord.'[21] Once this is accepted a great many other of the kingdom sayings of Jesus, which do not fall neatly into either present or future categories, call for reconsideration.

The paucity of references to the 'kingdom of God' both in the apocalyptic writings and in the Old Testament indicates the extent to which Jesus is an innovator. To understand what the word 'kingdom' means in Jesus' usage it is first necessary to understand that neither Jesus nor the writers of the New Testament were concerned with precise philosophical definitions. The great words of the New Testament gospel, words such as 'grace', 'sin', and 'kingdom' all have as it were an atomic structure. Their 'meaning' is constituted by the inter-relationship of significantly variant but not contradictory meanings grouped around a 'core'. The core meaning of 'kingdom' is not 'decision', but that situation where God's will and purpose are perfectly fulfilled, the situation which law and prophets spoke of as the realisation of peace, freedom, justice and life. Thus when Jesus says to the scribe, 'You are not far from the kingdom of God,' he means the realisation of God's will as referred to by the prophets whom the man has just quoted, which is given to be done on earth. Again, entry to the kingdom is said to be almost impossible for the rich because their riches camelise them and get in the way of doing that will. Similarly, the 'word of the kingdom' (Matt. 13:19) rightly understood, involves 'doing' and bearing fruit.

At the heart of Jesus' proclamation, as what Jeremias calls its 'most decisive feature', is good news to the poor. This good news is 'that God will intervene; nor are they [the poor] put off with hopes for an indefinite future; the time of salvation is manifested, realised, actualised for them even now'.[22] But Jeremias' description of this actualisation in terms of forgiveness and the call to table fellowship fails to refer to just those aspects of 'Moses and the prophets' which would make Jesus' announcement really good news. According to Luke, Jesus began his ministry by taking to himself a quotation from Isaiah which announced the realisation of the year of Jubilee (Luke. 4:18–19). The year of Jubilee involved release and liberty for slaves and restitution of rights to the poor (Lev. 25:10) a proclamation which would certainly be 'good news'. And yet Jesus was no Zealot nor was he interested in a rising of slaves, and so it seems that he has no programme which could help the poor attain their freedom. But Jesus' discernment went much further at this point than most programmes for revolutionary action, and took his hearers deep into what Lehmann calls 'the darkness of the Gospel'. The key to the good news to the poor which Jesus announces is solidarity, his own consistent, forthright and joyful 'taking the form of a slave'. The question is how the redemption of both rich and poor may be achieved, how there can be good news for the poor which is at the same time good news for the rich. Freire puts it this way:

> Although the situation of oppression is a dehumanized and dehumanizing totality affecting both the oppressors and those whom they oppress, it is the latter who must, from their stifled humanity, wage for both the struggle for a fuller humanity; the oppressor, who is himself dehumanized because he dehumanizes others, is unable to lead this struggle.[23]

Jesus is amongst his fellows 'as one who serves' because a redemption which consists in humanisation can only be effected from below. Thus when he pronounces the poor or those persecuted for righteousness' sake blessed because 'theirs is the kingdom' (Matt. 5:3, 10), when he says we can only 'receive the kingdom' as children (Mark 10:15), and when he says that the least in the kingdom are greater than John the Baptist (Matt 11:11), he is talking about the 'revaluation of values', the surprising announcement that God's will and purpose is not accomplished through the rich and pious, but through the poor, rejected, marginated, those with no voice – he is discerning a disturbing and scandalous pattern in God's activity. This is 'the secret of the kingdom' which the disciples, who share Jesus' homeless life, should discern (Mark 4:11), and it is in making *this* central (and not in making apocalyptic central as Perrin maintains) that the new thing in the teaching of the kingdom comes. Jesus' proclamation is good news to the poor because it is an annoucement of God at work amongst them, active to 'save' them, to bring them 'life'.

It should be emphasised that this is not to follow a fashionable trend which would like to see in Jesus a social revolutionary. It is quite simply to understand Jesus, as his contemporaries understood him, and perhaps as he partially understood himself (Mark 8:28; Matt. 23:29ff.) as standing in line with the prophets of Israel. Jesus' revolution goes far deeper than zealotry, and consists essentially in a solidarity in hope for a new world 'in the process of realisation' as Jeremias put it. To understand Jesus thus is at once to be freed from the entirely unnecessary embarrassment of the 'interim ethic', of which the reduction of Jesus' ethical teaching to a call to decision is but a rationalisation. Jesus is neither the deluded apocalyptic visionary of Schweitzer, nor the pietist of Bultmann, Dodd and Perrin but, standing clearly on the ground of Moses and the prophets, he announces God's will for men and women, what he expects them to *do*.

For both Jesus and Paul, as for Moses and the prophets, it is not human beings but God who brings the kingdom, but not over the heads of his people and the historical process but through that process. Only thus can we understand Jesus' ethical teaching. And it was for this reason that, when one of Paul's congregations misunderstood his urgency and allowed apocalyptic enthusiasm to preempt the toil of the historical process, Paul reacted so sharply: 'If any one will not work, neither let him eat!' (2 Thess. 3:10). No less than the liberal Jesus who preached about the Fatherhood of God and the brotherhood of man, the apocalyptic prophet concerned only with the sudden termination of history is 'a figure designed by rationalism . . . and clothed by modern theology in an historical garb'.[24] This figure replaces the real scandal of the gospel of the kingdom, which is the overturning of conventional values (of which the cross was for Paul a sign), with a scandal derived from Lessing and the Enlightenment, the difficulty of how to understand 'outmoded' first-century categories. For the Enlightenment, the scandal was first and foremost an intellectual scandal, to be met by demythologising and a new hermeneutic. But Jesus was a scandal for his own day, for Paul's audiences in Asia Minor, for second, third, and fourth-century intellectuals, and was only rendered moderately safe when the books which spoke of him were encased in gilt and no longer read but chanted in the course of a gorgeous imperial liturgy. The scandal of the kingdom was the same kind of scandal that Amos caused at Bethel, and Jeremiah at the court of Jerusalem – not identical, but the same kind – the demand that God's will be done on earth in a way quite foreign to what the guardians of religion (who may include professors of New Testament!) and pietists and men of power find acceptable. The contemporary attempt to render the scandal safe is on the one hand to push it into a remote and unintelligible past, and on the other hand to reinterpret it as essentially the affair of the individual, the nurturing of individual piety which can disturb no one. But of one thing we may be certain: Jesus would not have been crucified for preaching such a gospel.

Jesus proclaimed the kingdom both as present and future. The present consisted in, or at least involved, the doing of God's will, and the realisation of his purposes thereby. The future certainly involved an end to the historical process, a 'day of the Son of Man', but before that event the disciples had a task, the messianic mission to the nations. The good news was not simply that 'God has acted and demands a response to that action' but it had a particular direction and content, en-fleshed in Jesus' life, good news to the poor. In his preaching Jesus emphasised that hearing this news properly implied doing it, and it is this hearing and heeding together which is the future of the kingdom prior to its final consummation.

CONCLUSION

In one sense, what has been attempted in this chapter is a digression from the main theme of the essay – God's relationship to human history understood in terms of education. On the other hand, it must be regarded as the essential presupposition of that theme. Education is a process and, if Jesus thought in terms of an immanent catastrophic ending to history, it would be an extremely dubious enterprise to try and conceive the redemption he brought in terms of education. Whilst the majority of recent scholars have favoured an existentialist or individualist reading of Jesus' gospel of the kingdom, in opposition to the optimistic views of progress with which it was allied in the last century, it seems highly doubtful whether such interpretations can stand once the Bible is read as a whole. According to the Scriptures of Israel, God gives himself to history through Law and in Covenant, and this self-giving evokes a response and imposes a task. It is in terms of this doing of God's will, more specifically of the messianic mission to the nations, that the language of the kingdom must be understood – but in this case the kingdom involves process. But what is the nature of this process? Can there be process without progress? And dare we take up this notion after Auschwitz? These are the themes of the following chapter.

3

Solidarity and Redemption

If the goal of the divine education is to realise the possibility of full humanity, how does God achieve this goal? What is the mode of his education? According to the New Testament we must give a twofold answer, in terms of both Christ and the Spirit. In this chapter we shall seek to understand the significance of the so-called 'Christ event' as a moment within the divine pedagogy, which means also within the historical process.

When Anselm of Canterbury came to reflect on the nature of God's redemptive work he focused his thought in a question: *Cur Deus homo*?, Why did God become man? The same question lies behind the present exposition, and like Anselm we shall attempt to answer it by means of a political analogy. Anselm took an analogy from the feudal society of his day and conceived sin as a shattering of the proper order of the universe, just as an insult to the king would be a shattering of the proper order of society. Beginning from a very profound perception of human solidarity in sin, Anselm saw God himself doing that which was necessary (*satis fecit*) to restore this order.[1] The real problem with Anselm's exposition is perhaps not so much the concept of 'satisfaction', which can probably be rescued from the idea of the vengeful God, as the political model he used. The feudal model inevitably implied an image of God as unquestionable absolute power. Even in terms of Anselm's own framework (where honour rather than power was the point of the analogy) this was an extremely dangerous model, but if we think in terms of divine education it is disastrous. Were the education of the human race conducted by such a being it could only be through the impartation of knowledge, truths of revelation which could not be questioned. By contrast we begin from the perception that, as Freire puts it, 'Authentic education is not carried on by A *for* B, or by A *about* B but rather by A *with* B mediated by the world'.[2] This characteristic of authentic education is the innermost rationale of the incarnation. In Freire's terms this is not only an educational but at the same time a political model, for the goal of education is human freedom, and it is education which motivates people for political struggle. Unlike Anselm's feudal model this analogy begins not from the powerful but with the powerless. Rather than thinking of the restoration of a shattered honour, it conceives of the establishment of the 'radically new'. To effect this, God does not come to people with a message of a ready-made salvation but adopts the 'radical posture' of solidarity so that human beings may themselves participate in the humanising process as subjects of the redemptive transformation. Solidarity is the category which replaces that of satisfaction. Through this category we attempt to grasp the nature of God's act in Christ (*cur Deus homo*), suggesting that this is the necessary precondition for the divine education. As a prelude to this the arguments developed in the last chapter for conceiving history as a redemptive process are taken further and generalised. Solidarity without a continuing process would be an isolated moment, an empty gesture. It is only because history is a genuine process that God's act of solidarity can take root and bear fruit to redemption.

HISTORY: THEATRE OF REDEMPTION OR REDEMPTIVE PROCESS?

C. H. Dodd considered that from the realised eschatology of Jesus' parables 'a Christian view of history emerges' in contradistinction both to liberal ideas of immanent progress and to views which reject any overall design in history at all. In the light of his concept of realised eschatology he believed that Jesus envisaged 'no long historical perspective', and we should not therefore think of a long process of development introduced by his ministry. Rather, the significance of history is that, through the life and death of Jesus, it 'became the field within which God confronted men in a decisive way and placed before them a moral challenge that could not be evaded'. The thought of Jesus 'passed directly from the immediate situation to the eternal order lying beyond all history' declaring the eternal order present in the actual situation. For Dodd,

> The series of events is neither a veil of illusion hiding the eternal from our eyes, nor a process working out its own values from within apart from any reference to a timeless reality beyond it. It is instrumental, or more properly sacramental, to the eternal order. The several events in the series, in which the minds, wills and affections of individual men and women are implicated, are each of them capable of confronting these individuals with the Kingdom of God, that is, with the ultimate good and final power in the universe.[3]

This view of history, which must be considered the fore-understanding of Dodd's reading of the parables, is not original with Dodd but looks to St Augustine. For Augustine the reality of history is the sum of individual histories. There is indeed a beginning and an end of history, but the process *as such*, between the one and the other, does not have meaning. Historical time is but the stage and backdrop for each human actor to play his or her part. The city of God and the earthly city are two communities of persons, the one determined by love of God and the other by love of self, the one destined to salvation, the other to damnation. God is the Lord of history as he controls the minds of persons, by his irresistible grace bringing the two groups to their respective ends. History is thus the tale of the perfecting of a certain number of souls through their testing in this vale of tears. Any notion of progress in history is vehemently rejected on account of the manifest facts of sin. Naturally this view gains cogency in times of catastrophe: how can we talk of moral progress after Auschwitz? Thus it was that Karl Löwith, writing directly after the Second World War, championed Augustine's as the authentically Christian view of history. For Löwith history is 'a divinely appointed pedagogy, operating mainly through suffering'.[4] 'Seen in the light of the faith that God is revealed in the historical man Jesus Christ the profane events before and after Christ are *not a solid chain of meaningful successions but spurious happenings* whose significance or insignificance is to be judged in the perspective of their possible significance of judgement and salvation.' In Christ salvation is radically individualised.

> The message of the New Testament is not an appeal to historical action but to repentance. *Nothing in the New Testament warrants a conception of the new events that constitute early Christianity as the beginning of a new epoch of secular developments within a continuous process.* For early Christians the history of the world had come to an end and Jesus was not a link in a chain of historical happenings but the unique redeemer.[5]

It is significant that Löwith speaks of 'nothing in the New Testament' warranting his view, which indicates the failure to see that the New Testament presupposes the Old at every point. Within the biblical tradition only Ecclesiastes possibly thinks of history as a set of 'spurious happening'.[6] In different ways most of the Old Testament traditions think of history precisely as a 'meaningful chain of successions'. Particularly important in this context is the idea which first comes clearly into view with the Yahwist in the ninth century, that God's purposes are fulfilled through Israel's vocation to be a blessing to the nations. This theme reappears in the Isaianic school as the promise of peace and justice for the nations, established either through Israel or the Messiah of Israel (Isa. 42:6–7). An oracle, which Kaiser dates in the third- or early second-century BC, even thinks of the great traditional enemies of Israel as being 'a blessing in the midst of the earth' on the occasion of the ingathering of the diaspora:

> In that day Israel will be the third with Egypt and Assyria, a blessing in the midst of the earth, whom the Lord of hosts has blessed saying, 'Blessed be Egypt my people and Assyria the work of my hands, and Israel my heritage'. (Isa. 19:24–5)

This theology of Israel and the nations attributes importance to history as the sphere of God's rule and thinks of a 'new epoch' of 'secular developments' – peace and justice established between nations 'on earth'. It thinks of history therefore as a meaningful process. It was this view of history that Paul took up in Galatians, beginning from the promise to Abraham fulfilled in the one man Jesus and now opening up to all human beings (Gal. 3:6–4:7). It was again presupposing this tradition that in the second century, on the basis of the earlier constructive work of the Logos theology,

Irenaeus came to outline a creative theology of history later taken up by Athanasius.

For both Irenaeus and Athanasius, God's act in Christ is part of a *process* of redemption, a process in which the incarnation is the decisive moment, but which is continued *post Christum* by God's work as Spirit. The argument is set out in most detail in the fourth book of Irenaeus' *Adversus Haereses*. Irenaeus there understands history in terms of the process necessary for human beings to enjoy God: 'God directs all things to achieve the ends of man's perfection and man's edification; and to display his own character, so that his goodness may be demonstrated and his righteousness fulfilled, and that the Church may be conformed to the image of his Son, and man may at length reach maturity, becoming ripe through these experiences for the vision and enjoyment of God' (4.37.7). Man was made in God's image, but must grow into his likeness. For this to happen a long historical schooling was necessary: 'Therefore it was necessary that man should in the first instance be created; and having been created, should receive growth; and having received growth, should be strengthened; and having been strengthened should abound; and having abounded, should recover; and having recovered, should be glorified; and being glorified should see his Lord' (4.38.3). This schooling is carried out under the pedagogy of the Spirit: 'Therefore he renews these things in himself, uniting man to the Spirit; and placing the Spirit in man, he himself is made the head of the Spirit, and gives the Spirit to be the head of man, for by him we see and hear and speak' (5.20.2).

The same understanding of redemption as a process may be found in Athanasius, notably in the second discourse against the Arians. There he argues that human beings are not created perfect but with a potential for perfection which it is the task of the 'firstborn' (Christ) to lead us to (*Contra Arianos*, 2.66).

This is a view of history, therefore, which we may call the 'Irenaean' view and which does not see it merely as the locus of the intersection of the eternal with time but as a process which itself is meaningful, the sphere of God's redemptive education.

The strength of the Augustinian view is the comfort it brings, in some respects, to the 'non-person'. It is a gospel for Mr Prufrock. It assumes, as Dodd puts it, 'that history in the individual life is of the same stuff as history at large; that is, it is significant in so far as it serves to bring men face to face with God in His kingdom, power and glory'. Such a meeting with God and his kingdom is not exclusive to 'the makers of history'. The important thing in history is not the process but each individual's meeting with God which is as available to a life 'measured out in coffee spoons' as it is to a life lived in sound and fury. It asserts therefore the eternal significance of each individual's life, and on this ground relegates the process to an entirely secondary importance. If this strength is conceded, it remains a question whether the contrary Irenaean view necessarily involves devaluing individual experience. If the meaning of the whole process is 'humanisation', growing to the stature of Christ, then this is something which can and must be measured both for the individual and for the process as a whole, the one contributing to the other, and both understood within the divine economy.

Apart from the Augustinian concentration on the salvation of the individual soul, another common reason for refusal to speak of the importance of history as such is the idea that salvation is totally concentrated in the life, death and resurrection of Jesus in such a way that all that remains to be done is to reveal the significance of these events at the end of time. Such a view is present in Dodd's concentration of the kingdom in the person of Jesus, in Löwith's reference to the 'unique redeemer', and was stated very forcibly by Karl Barth in a lecture he gave, like Löwith's, at the end of the Second World War. After cross and resurrection, said Barth,

> The war is at an end – even though here and there troops are still shooting, because they have not heard anything yet about the capitulation. The game is won, even though the player can still play a few further moves. Actually he is already mated. The clock has run down, even though the pendulum still swings a few times this way and that. It is in this interim space that we are living . . .[7]

Many questions attend such a complete identification of salvation with the historical 'Christ event'. In the first place it is, as many of Barth's critics have seen, inadequately trinitarian. The work of the Spirit is relegated only to the revelation of what has already passed, whereas Paul understands the Spirit as the Spirit of the new future and the new creation (Rom. 8:23). But it also seems to presuppose an inadequate understanding of sin, and therefore of sin's remedy. Schleiermacher has taught us that sin is 'in each the work of all and in all the work of each', and psychological and sociological studies have only served to deepen this perception. There is a human solidarity in sin which has an inescapably historical dimension, and it is this which Paul calls 'the power of sin' (Rom. 3:9) and the tradition 'original sin'. This power of sin, the principalities and powers which oppress us, may be named in structures such as racism, casteism, patriarchy, class – structures and deeply rooted attitudes into which an individual is born, which form a 'second skin' which it is not possible simply to jump out of.

This solidarity in sin cannot be disowned. It was for this reason that Gandhi rejected an abstract pacifism and opted for ambulance service in the Boer War, as a way of showing that he did not put himself pharisaically outside the guilt of the conflict, but took it upon himself. In the same way Jesus stood in line with his people, going to receive baptism 'for the remission of sins'. There is a solidarity in sin which reaches back to the very 'origin' of human history and which is embedded in the structure of every human society, in its patterns of family life, of relationships, of education, of employment and so on. But this means that if we are to speak meaningfully of redemption we must also speak of a *redemptive solidarity* there which, like human solidarity in sin, is also an historical reality. Because human beings only exist in complex patterns of social relationships they can only be redeemed in those patterns – they cannot be miraculously lifted out of the historical process which would in any case be a reverse of the redemptive movement of the incarnation. If there be such a thing as redemption it too must be, in Schleiermacher's phrase, 'in each the work of all and in all the work of each'. Thus David Jenkins speaks of a future community 'where love fulfils love so that everyone is fully human because everyone is fully human' and this is the 'concrete utopia' of the kingdom.[8]

To achieve this redemption the Word becomes 'flesh', for *sarx* is not simply matter but being which is real only in its history. The assumption of flesh is the assumption of history, and thus Irenaeus in his conflict with the Gnostics, and Athanasius in his conflict with Arius, were contending both for the redemption of history and an historical redemption which naturally led, towards the end of

Athanasius' life, to a recognition of the role of the Spirit in the redemptive process – for 'Spirit' language speaks of God's continuing presence to history. In the quotation from Barth's Bonn lectures, on the other hand, we truly have the Christomonism of which he was accused, and to this attempt to make Christ the very sum rather than the substance of redemption we have to reply (paraphrasing Anselm); *nondum considerasti quanti ponderis sit historia* – you have not yet weighed what a tremendous matter history is if the Son of God dies in the midst of it. On the cross, 'those scales most true', it is human *history* which is weighed and revealed as the object of God's redeeming love. If the Word truly became flesh the force of this cannot be to reduce all succeeding history to an interim, to the slowing down of the pendulum. The New Testament witness does not think like this but looks to the new age of the Spirit of the crucified. The *hapax* of the cross, its 'once for allness', means not the end of all real history but rather that here uniquely the inner redeeming dynamism of history is present and seen to be present. The incarnation is the vindication of history as a process full of meaning and purpose, as a movement which is going somewhere, from image to likeness as Irenaeus puts it.

PROGRESS AND THE TRULY HUMAN

If it is agreed that we have to talk of history in terms of process this is still a long way from granting any real possibility of *progress*, and against this possibility also there are fundamental theological objections. Thus for Emil Brunner, like Weiss and Bultmann in this respect, talk of progress seemed to compromise the sovereignty of God and the fact that it is he, rather than human beings, who 'brings' the kingdom:

> The idea of progress means a movement from here to there, from below to above, reaching more or less steadily to a point in the far future where perfection is conceived as materialised. The Christian message of the coming kingdom however means just the opposite – a movement from above to below, from the transcendent to earth.[9]

The last part of this statement need not be disputed, but the question is, what is meant by 'above' and 'transcendent'? If it is true that God is in Christ, then the transcendent cannot be conceived as something detached and remote from human history, like the early Barth's notorious 'tangent on a circle', but the transcendent is immanent, the power of God's future is in the man Jesus disturbing and breaking open the premature closures and facile syntheses of human history. The process of redemption, begun, continued and ended in Christ is always 'fully human and fully divine' and only in this way a transcendent happening. Thus there is not, as Brunner seems to think, any inherent contradiction between historical progress and God's bringing the kingdom. Such a contradiction would both make the incarnation an arbitrary miracle, a stone heaved into the pool of human history, and also deny the reality and power of God's work as Spirit. But the incarnation is the revelation of the nature of transcendence, of God's *modus operandi* 'in the power of weakness' in and through human history. The coming of the kingdom is not to be equated with human progress, but to be understood in terms of an 'eschatology in the process of realisation'. There is an advancement of God's sovereign rule, accomplished by God's Spirit in and with men and women which goes to meet, makes possible, and makes sense of the final glorification of this entire creation which Jesus spoke of as the Day of the Son of Man.

Brunner made a more formidable point when he challenged talk of progress on the grounds of the ambiguity of historical experience: 'The Christian conception of man', he said, 'includes the belief that the higher differentiation of intellectual powers, as well as the increase of the means of civilisation, is most ambiguous with regard to goodness and the truly human . . . The highly developed human mind and the highly developed human civilization may come to a point where they are capable of destroying all gains and goods in one frantic moment of diabolical madness'.[10] After Auschwitz and Hiroshima, and in the shadow of the neutron bomb, how can we deny this? Such an ambiguity is part of human solidarity in sin. But this sinful solidarity is not the last word, and there are pressing arguments for talking of progress, even when it comes to 'goodness and the truly human'. In the first place the idea of promise and fulfilment is fundamental to the entire biblical record, the thread on which its history is strung, beginning with the promise to Abraham that his family will be a blessing to all the earth (Gen. 12:3) with the promise of descendants (Gen. 15:5), the promise of the land (Gen. 15:7), of the Messiah, and of peace and blessing (esp. Isa. 32:1–2, 15ff.). The fact that in Christ all God's promises are confirmed (2 Cor. 1:20) does not mean that they no longer require fulfilment, for the promise of 'rest' remains (Heb. 4:1) and the excess of promise in the resurrection is not to be fulfilled until God is finally all in all (1 Cor. 15:28). The messianic age is inaugurated in Jesus, but the age of peace and justice remains to be realised. The biblical promises never retreat into an abstract individualism but 'effectually strain towards a real, future event of fulfilment'. As Moltmann puts it,

> Hope, where it holds to the promises, hopes that the coming of God will bring it also 'this and that' – namely, his redeeming and restoring lordship in all things. It does not merely hope personally 'in him', but has also substantial hopes of his lordship, his *peace and his righteousness on earth.* Otherwise hope itself could unobtrusively change into a kind of fulfilment and there would be nothing more in which our hopes could be fulfilled.[11]

If the possibility of progress were denied, for example on the grounds of the total perversion of human nature, there would be no ground for struggling for a more just, more peaceful or more human future. But such a denial would be in itself a denial of the 'truly human'. The problem with the liberal views of progress against which Brunner and Bultmann reacted, and which can be found today in the evolutionary optimism of Teilhard de Chardin and in Process theology, is not simply that they took insufficient account of human sin, but that they identify progress with the irresistible march of either civilization or evolution. Such easy identification seems often to involve an insensitivity to moral evil. Thus Teilhard could write, again after Auschwitz (1951), 'When cosmogenesis is accepted, then . . . not only is there a solution to the problem of evil, but the problem itself *ceases to arise*.'[12] He could say this on the ground that 'in all evolution we have to reckon with failures and mistakes'. Such an attitude rightly provokes the 'protest atheism' of Ivan Karamazov. But to affirm the possibility of progress in what is truly human does not in the least entail this view. It entails only that there is a solidarity not only in sin but also in redemption. It entails trust in the promise that love is stronger than hate and life than death, which we receive in the life, death and resurrection of Jesus. It recognises the terror of history, but refuses to assess history solely in terms of its negative products. It discerns, for instance in the women's movement or in the programme to combat racism, small signs at least of the possibility of a more human future, and in these signs it discerns the pedagogy of God's Spirit realising a solidarity in redemption to break the hold of, and set people free from, solidarity in sin.

SOLIDARITY IN REDEMPTION

How does God redeem us and our history? The New Testament authors are all convinced that in Jesus of Nazareth God has acted decisively for human redemption, and the wealth of titles for Jesus and metaphors for his 'work' which they use represent their attempt to fathom this redemption in all its depth and complexity. Underlying all these titles and metaphors however is the conviction that fundamental to redemption is God's solidarity with his creation, what the writers of Israel extolled as God's *hesed*. This solidarity is presented in the synoptic gospels in the picture of Jesus as the Son of Man who had nowhere to lay his head, who refuses the temptations of power and glory and falls into line with the masses coming to baptism. For this reason the author of Hebrews remarks that we have a mediator who can help 'because he himself has suffered and been tempted', because like Moses he chose solidarity (Heb. 2:17–18, 11:25). In his letter to the Philippians, Paul gives us the beautiful, perhaps pre-Pauline, 'song of God's solidarity', which depicts Jesus again refusing to 'snatch at' or hang on to glory, but opting for the lot of the great majority of the Roman world, the lot of a slave, and dying the death which was reserved for them, crucifixion.

It is to Paul that we owe the most compact description of solidarity in sin and redemption, the phrases 'in Adam' and 'in Christ'. The realities, to which these formulae point, deeply exercised the minds of the Fathers of the Greek Church, who sought to express their perception of God's redeeming solidarity in two classical expressions, in the doctrine of the *homoousion* and in the doctrine that 'not assumed is not healed'. The *homoousion* was first introduced during the Arian controversy to assert Christ's true deity, but when the integrity of his humanity appeared to be challenged, some fifty or so years later, it was natural to apply it to his humanity also, and say that he was not only 'of one substance' with the Father but also with humankind, standing in a two-fold solidarity. The epigram 'not assumed is not healed' was also coined at this time (by Gregory Nazianzus), but both formulae echo similar sentiments to be found repeatedly in earlier theologians, especially Irenaeus, Origen and Athanasius. In these doctrines the Fathers tried to understand redemption not only as presupposing human solidarity but as *actually accomplished through God's solidarity with us*. In seeking to explain this difficult notion it is usually emphasised, in relation to Irenaeus' idea of recapitulation for example, that 'some kind of mystical identity' amongst human beings is implied, so that what happens in the one man Adam or the one man Jesus affects all. Alternatively, Athanasius may have presupposed a Platonic doctrine of concrete universals in which individuals partake.[13] According to this line of explanation the Fathers thought of redemption as 'divinisation' meaning a partaking of the divine nature and attributes. On these grounds this view of redemption has long been known as 'the physical theory'. This characterisation however, whilst corresponding to a genuine strand in patristic thought, misses the complex unity of the patristic view of redemption for which the incarnation stands at the heart of both the divine education and the struggle with the demons. As this point is central to our thesis the reasons for believing this may be briefly indicated.

In the first place the corruption from which human beings are rescued has an inescapably moral dimension and includes, according to Athanasius, the power of the lie, barbarism, war and fetishism (*De Incarnatione* 15, 50–2). Irenaeus likewise understands incorruptibility strictly in relation to morality: 'This, therefore, was the long suffering of God, that men, passing through all things and acquiring the knowledge of moral discipline, then attaining to the resurrection of the dead, and learning by experience what is deliverance, may always live in a state of gratitude to the Lord, having obtained from him the gift of incorruptibility, that he might love him more; for "he to whom more is forgiven, loves more" ' (*A.H.* 3.20.2). Thus whilst incorruption is not itself a moral state it is inconceivable without both the preceding moral discipline and the succeeding gratitude. In the same way 'deification' cannot possibly be understood as the primarily 'physical' gift of immortality. Expounding 1 John 4:13 Athanasius argues, 'because of the grace of the Spirit which has been given to us, in Him we come to be and He is us . . . by the participation of the Spirit we are knit into the Godhead; so that our being in the Father is not ours, but is the Spirit's which is in us and abides in us' (*Contra Arianos* 3.24). 'Deification' is a way of talking about the work of grace (ibid. 3:19) renewing the image in us, renewing us by bringing us into communion with God. This is expressed even more strongly by Irenaeus. 'What will be the effect of the whole grace of the Spirit which will be given to men by God?' he asks. 'It will make us like him and will perfect us in the Father's will; for it will make man in the image and likeness of God' (*A.H.* 5.8.1). This crucial moral dimension, to both the 'corruption' from which we need to be redeemed and to deification, means that redemption cannot be accomplished by any purely 'physical' act. Redemption itself must be a moral process, and it is here that the idea of divine education, and the struggle against the demons, comes in. The divine pedagogy is not an independent side theme to the main theme of the 'physical theory'. For Athanasius it is the incarnation itself, God's taking human flesh and mind, which is the heart of the divine education and the means of freeing human beings from 'corruption' (*De Inc.* 14). Summing up the first stages of his argument in *De Incarnatione* Athanasius can speak equally of Christ's incarnation turning the corruptible to incorruption, renewing God's image in human beings, rendering the mortal immortal, teaching us of the Father, and destroying the worship of idols (*De Inc.* 20). In a later work he speaks of the purpose of the incarnation being that 'sin might be completely expelled from the flesh and that we might have a free mind' (*Contra Ar.* 1.56). The solidarity of God with the creature, tersely expressed in the *homoousion*, far from arising from a 'physical theory' which thinks in non-moral terms, may in fact be regarded as arising from the very logic of the process of education.

In seeking to understand this liberating pedagogy, an analogy from many Third World liberation movements may be helpful.

These movements are engaged in liberating people from forces of corruption and death, forces which make people objects of the power of Mammon, and which dehumanise people through every kind of social, political and sexual exploitation. They work not by supplying aid but through what Freire calls a 'pedagogy of the oppressed', adult education which makes people aware of the non-necessity of their situation, and which changes the situation by initiating a critical solidarity which will eventually lead to political and social liberation. Because this solidarity challenges power and privilege it also commonly leads to liberation only through suffering. The analogy is helpful in two ways: both in understanding the redemptive function of the incarnation, but also in understanding the redemptive function of the process as such.

If we begin by asking about the function of solidarity in this analogy we note that it is of the essence of these movements that a liberating pedagogy cannot be conducted from a safe distance beyond the struggle. In fact it can only be conducted from a position of complete solidarity with those who are oppressed. The force of this 'only' is a moral and practical one: those who take up 'people's struggle' from a safe distance evoke nothing but cynicism. This provides us with a clue in the search for an answer to the question how the solidarity of God in the incarnation is itself redemptive. To paraphrase Stendahl, the only excuse for a God who does not manifest his solidarity with his suffering creation in the most concrete way is that he does not exist. But it is precisely in this way that Irenaeus and Athanasius understood the incarnation, as an act of redeeming solidarity at the heart of the divine education. Athanasius faced the question, 'Why an incarnation?', 'Why all this messy blood?' (Ted Hughes). He answered that, whilst God logically 'could' have redeemed humankind without it, only redemption through incarnation was 'fitting' (*Contra Ar.* 2.68). Not assumed could not have been fully healed; it would have been a piece of magic, a failure on God's part to take its history seriously. It is precisely the cross, however, which teaches us with what astounding seriousness God does take this history. Our first step then, in seeking to understand how God's solidarity is itself redemptive, and how this is related to a redemptive education, is to note that without solidarity redemptive education is not possible. Solidarity is the necessary presupposition of any liberating pedagogy.

In order to go deeper into the understanding of how God's solidarity actually helps us, it will be helpful to compare the image of divine education with other metaphors and analogies for God's redemptive work, and this calls for a note on how these function. In the first chapter we noted some of the classic New Testament metaphors for Christ's work: the metaphors of redemption, of sacrifice, of justification, each of which relates to a particular aspect of the human situation 'bound under sin'. In understanding what the New Testament authors are saying here it is essential to remember that we are dealing with metaphors. Metaphors have many uses but they may perhaps be understood as essentially a form of recommendation: Think of it like *this*, then perhaps you will understand.[14] As such they do not offer explanations but invite reflection. They cease to be useful as soon as they are no longer treated as metaphors, but as if they were descriptions of actual states of affairs, and this has happened time and again with the great metaphors for redemption. Thus in the period from the second to the eighth or ninth century the New Testament language about 'ransom' was reified into the story of Christ's barter with or deception of Satan. The details of the metaphor were often allegorised so that, for instance, Christ's humanity was supposed to be the 'bait' and the cross the 'hook' which caught the devil. Anselm's exposition of the atonement began from a protest against the absurdities of this account. Again, it is very commonly believed that Christ's death actually was a sacrifice, as opposed to the language of sacrifice offering a vivid and illuminating way of looking at Christ's death. Again, Protestantism has often forgotten that 'justification' was a metaphor and treated it as the record of a heavenly transaction of indeterminate status which 'imputes righteousness' to the believer. This failure to treat metaphor as metaphor arises out of the desire to do justice to the 'objective' nature of what happened on Calvary: the idea that what happened there was simply a very inspiring example is rightly rejected as inadequate. All the same, the nature of metaphor as an invitation to reflection must be respected, and with that caution we shall attempt to understand the 'objective' element in the educational analogy by a comparison with these other great metaphors.

Our argument begins with the assumption that because human beings are historical creatures the solidarity in sin in which they find themselves locked is an historical reality, and therefore redemption too must take an historical form. (In case it should be objected that this is to start with an anthropological *a priori*, note that we have already established that we learn the true seriousness of the historical process from the cross.) What role do the cross and incarnation play in this redemptive process? Paul offers us a vivid image by which to understand this: here is the court room, the Judge, the accused – but to the astonishment of all the Judge himself goes to the dock and takes sentence on himself. The punishment we, the accused, ought to have received was borne by him and we are now freed. Insistence on taking this vivid picture literally has led to the immorality of substitutionary theories of the atonement, and the idea that the Son had to die to bear the 'punishment' for sin. But Christ is our representative, not our substitute, and if Christ's death were really a punishment what would this say about the moral order of the universe? It seems more helpful to follow the suggestion of the metaphor that when the Judge is judged in our place our pretensions to act as the judge of others are radically undermined. This is not to turn an 'objective' event into a subjective, because without the cross this cannot occur. In the same way, according to our analogy, the Educator becomes the educated, he who has no need of education stands alongside the millions in the darkness of oppression and despair, in solidarity. This means, as Moltmann has pointed out in another context, that the oppressed and despairing are no longer alone, they are no longer God-forsaken, and this is a ground for hope. It is precisely by instilling hope and courage, by creating faith (the movement by which the objective becomes subjective) that solidarity helps.

Next we could take the metaphor of the cosmic battle. In terms of our analogy Christ's death on the cross is the moment when the powers which seek to destroy human beings, blessed by religion, are exposed for what they are. 'Church' and State can and do claim absolute loyalty, but the person who stands beneath the cross refuses to worship idols because their false claims have been once and for all exposed. Just so in Freire's 'education for critical consciousness' the forces which exploit and oppress the poor are exposed and so robbed of their principal strength, which is the myth of their necessity. Here too the cross stands inescapably at the head of the redemptive process, for without it there is no exposure.

A third metaphor we can compare the educational analogy with is that of sacrifice, which is the metaphor most usually understood in literal terms. To discuss this theme fully would require a book in itself, but we can suggest reasons for insisting on the metaphorical character of this language in four points from the New Testament and one from anthropology. First, alongside those Old Testament texts which speak of sacrifice as a divinely ordained means of dealing with sin, there is also a prominent and important strand which protests that obedience is better than sacrifice (1 Sam. 15:22), that mercy (*hesed*) and knowledge of God is more desired by God than burnt offerings (Hos. 6:6), that the true sacrifice of God is a broken spirit and that by contrast God has 'no delight' in animal sacrifice (Pss. 51:17, 40:6), and which speaks of righteousness or joy as sacrifices (Pss. 4:5, 27:6). This tradition is quoted by Jesus three times in the gospel records (Matt. 9:13, 12:7; Mark 12:33), and it seems highly likely he agreed with it. Paul too speaks of our lives being a living sacrifice (Rom. 12:1) or of the tokens of support from Philippi as 'a sacrifice acceptable and pleasing to God' (Phil. 4:18). Hebrews, which is usually appealed to to support the literal view, in fact thinks more clearly of the offering of obedience than any other book in the New Testament, and the author quotes Psalm 40:6ff. to make the point (Heb. 10:5). Thus we find a comprehensive and profound reinterpretation of sacrifice within the Bible, taken up by Jesus and Paul. Is it likely that Jesus thought of his death as 'literally' a sacrifice, seeing that he identified with this tradition? Defenders of the literal view turn to the language about blood and about expiation, but this too is not unambiguous. When Paul or the author of Ephesians talks of 'redemption through blood' or being 'justified by his blood' (Rom. 5:9), what seems to be in mind is the Hebrew identification of 'blood' with 'life': 'blood' here is a terse way of referring to the outpouring of life to the uttermost, rather than a reference to a particular sacrificial theory. Thus Paul says that Christ reconciles all things to himself, 'making peace by the blood of his cross' (Col. 1:20); a little later he speaks of Christ 'cancelling the bond' against us, nailing it to the cross (Col. 2:14). Both metaphors are a way of saying: on the cross God once for all dealt with human sin. Neither metaphor is meant to be taken literally (apart from Christ, only the titulus was nailed to the cross!). Again, let us take the language of being 'cleansed by the blood'. It is important in this connection to look at all the uses of the verb *katharizo* (to cleanse) in the New Testament. Ephesians speaks of a cleansing 'by water and the word' (Eph. 5:26), and in the gospels we repeatedly see Jesus cleansing lepers simply by speaking a word (e.g. Mark 1:42; Luke 7:2ff.). John too speaks of cleansing through the word (John 15:3) and depicts Jesus cleansing the disciples through example and service (John 13:10). When the first letter of John therefore speaks of our being cleansed by his blood, my suggestion is that here too no particular theory of sacrifice is in mind but that the reference is to the totality of Christ's self-offering. This brings us finally to the four occurrences of either *hilasmos* (1 John 2:2, 4:10) meaning a means of appeasing, propitiation or expiation, or *hilasterion* (Rom. 3:25; Heb. 9:5) meaning place of expiation, or expiatory. These words are notoriously difficult to translate: recent versions have adopted 'expiate' or 'expiation' instead of propitiate, because the latter suggests appeasing a vengeful deity, but the roots of 'expiation' likewise lie in the Latin *piare*, to appease. Two points may then be noted. First, the use of these unusual words seems intended to have the sense of 'means of dealing with sin' rather than to carry the freight of a specific theory of sacrifice. Thus Romans 3.25 means: 'God set forward Christ as a means of dealing with sin.' Second, in the Septuagint *hilasmos* is used to mean 'forgiveness'. If *hilasmos* is a means of dealing with sin is there any other means than forgiveness? The word from the cross recorded by Luke, 'Father, forgive them for they know not what they do' (Luke 23:34), may not be historical, but it is certainly a profound commentary on what happened on Calvary. It is not that Christ's death is the price of forgiveness (1 Cor. 6:20, 7:23 cannot be used in this way) but that, bearing the brunt of human wickedness, Christ forgives it even in its execution, and it is this forgiveness itself which is liberating. The 'means of dealing with sin' of Romans 3.25 and 1 John 2:2 is forgiveness. This cannot be pronounced from afar by a divine 'Uncle' who smiles benignly at the pranks of his children, because the innumerable crosses of human history are not pranks. It can be pronounced only from that cross which stood in the midst of other human crosses, as the cross of Christ stood between those of the two criminals, from a position of solidarity with the tortured.

To these New Testament considerations we should add the insights of the French anthropologist and theologian René Girard, who demonstrates in his great book *Des Choses cachées depuis la fondation du monde* how sacrificial theory in all cultures has represented a rationalisation of collective violence. Far from the New Testament condoning this violence, he argues, in Jesus we have the truth of all the violence which went before at last made explicit (again the theme of exposure), and therefore the end of all legitimated sacrifice – and this necessitates a total change of view, a spiritual metaphorphosis without precedent in human history.[15]

If we now turn back to our analogy we observe first that a long list of martyrs already attaches to those groups which have, over the past thirty years, attempted 'education for critical consciousness' among the poor. To expose, for instance, the illegalities of a landlord or a politician or perhaps even a drugs company is to threaten them and this commonly leads to counter-threats and often enough to murder. (This is a prominent fact of contemporary life which can be documented by even a small degree of exposure to the problems of the poor in the Third World.) The murdered teacher-activist, we can say, gave his or her life for the liberation of the oppressed, and in this sense their death was a 'sacrifice' for others. Analogously Christ was crucified not in a case of mistaken identity, as many contemporary accounts of the gospel seem to imply, but because he was correctly sensed to be dangerous by the powers of imperialism, nationalism and religion. If Pilate said, 'I find no harm in him,' he crucified him all the same. We should also not underestimate the importance of the fact that the heart of Jesus' preaching was, according to Jeremias (who was no liberation theologian), 'good news to the poor'. Christ's death was then a 'sacrifice' which resulted from his solidarity with the poor and despised, and it helps us, as all such sacrifices help, by instilling courage and creating faith, the determination not to be defeated by the powers. (Thus far the *homoousion* of the Council of Constantinople of 381, of one substance *with us*, will take us. At the end of the chapter we will take up the significance of the fact that Christ was not simply another martyr, but the Son of God himself.)

We can now turn to Girard's thesis, according to which Christ's death is indeed that offering of the Son to Moloch 'according to the abominable practices of the nations' (2 Kings 16:3), not by the Father, but by human beings worshipping the hypostasised image of their vengeful and destructive selves. Here we have the real problem of so-called 'natural theology', that if God is made in the image of man the result is Moloch, or Kali the goddess of destruction. The sacrifice of the Son of God to this idol reveals the utter horror of such practices and finally puts paid to that myth of divine violence which is used to rationalise human violence. As such it is the foundation for the 'alternative education' of the Spirit, which seeks to create an order based on forgiveness rather than violence, on weakness rather than strength. (For a very profound commentary on this theme of the sacrifice to the idols of national pride, and the sacrifice of the Christ which demands an end to this, see the poetry of Wilfred Owen, especially 'The Parable of the Old Man and the Young', or 'At a Calvary Near Ancre':

> The scribes on all the people shove
>   And brawl allegiance to the state,
> But they who love the greater love
>   Lay down their life; they do not hate.)

Another aspect of this analogy could be illustrated by Gandhi's use of *Satyagraha* in the Indian Independence struggle. *Satyagraha* (truth force) was the use of non-violence as a weapon, bringing moral pressure to bear on the oppressor by turning violence on the self. Gandhi's biographer, Louis Fischer, describes it as follows, drawing on Gandhi's own words:

> Satyagraha is peaceful. If words fail to convince the adversary perhaps purity, humility and honesty will. The opponent must be 'weaned from error by patience and sympathy', weaned, not crushed; converted, not annihilated. Satyagraha is the exact opposite of the policy of an eye-for-an-eye which ends in making everybody blind. You cannot inject new ideas into a man's head by chopping it off; neither will you infuse a new spirit into his heart by piercing it with a dagger. Acts of violence create bitterness in the survivors and brutality in the destroyers; Satyagraha aims to exalt both sides.[16]

Gandhi himself spoke of *satyagraha* as 'practising the Sermon on the Mount', and almost every word in the above description is illuminating for the atonement. In particular it would seem that the idea that God's righteousness demands that sin be punished (rather than forgiven) would be an application of the policy of 'an eye-for-an-eye'. For the purpose of our analogy we can note that *satyagraha* was in fact a massive educational campaign aimed both at the Indian public and at British public opinion. This educational campaign rested on Gandhi's moral authority, and in particular his attempt (however flawed) to identify with the Indian masses. Analogously the divine education rests on the solidarity of the Son. Redemption, we have argued, means humanisation, human fullness, the restoration of wholeness, and this is possible only through forgiveness (cf. Luther's identification, *tout simple*, of grace with forgiveness). The divine education is therefore education in love and forgiveness: the syllabus we find in the Beatitudes, or 1 Corinthians 13, or Galatians 5. But where would this education be without the cross? It would have the cogency of a pop song, 'love' as a sentiment costing nothing, instead of what, through the cross, we know it to be – forgiveness 'costing not less than everything'. There is simply no pedagogy without this supremely costly forgiveness, and the solidarity which alone makes this possible is thus the heart of the divine education.

We can now turn to another aspect of the analogy with education for critical consciousness, which illuminates this time the *process* rather than the foundation of the process. Suppose a people oppressed by a corrupt and tyrannical regime, and a sudden intervention by a 'friendly' power which instals a new and much more benevolent government. What has been achieved for the people concerned? It is true that in the short term more human conditions may very well obtain – but the people themselves have learned nothing in the process of transition. It is the insight of the liberation movements we have mentioned that solutions imposed 'from above' are never in a true sense liberating. In such a process people are ultimately patronised and so demeaned. The point of education for critical consciousness is that people become the subjects of their own history, discover their need for liberation, and then effect it. *The process itself is an essential part of the final liberation.* Some of the great historical failures of revolution, such as the Russian revolution, may be traced to the fact that the vast majority of the people never underwent this education, a failure which facilitated eventual control of 'the Party' from above down. This offers us an analogy

– a partial correspondence, though with a greater degree of unlikeness – to God's work of redemption. For the New Testament the cross is unique – but not isolated. The redemption once for all effected there is real-ised in the process of human history through the education of the Spirit. Redemption does not happen over the heads of the creature but involves them, assumes them into responsibility, and it does so by creating a subversive movement, a solidarity in redemption. This does not mean that people are their own saviours or liberators – here is the disanalogy – but it means that God's work of redemption is effected through the toil of human history, by treating human beings as 'fellow workers' (1 Cor. 3:9). The gospel of the incarnation is not the gospel of a divine avatar, of a Paternal General installing a 'friendly' regime. The purpose of God, as we discern it in Christ, is that human beings should become fully human, grow from the image to the likeness, and this could not be helped by action 'from above' which failed to involve them. The gospel of the incarnation is that God is alongside human beings, in solidarity (*hesed*) with them on the long road to freedom, that they are not alone on that road, and that the road is going somewhere. The description of the fellowship of the road, what we have called a redeeming solidarity, occupies chapter 6 following, the description of the 'economy' of the Spirit.

It is commonly said of the theme of atonement through education that it cannot offer an account of what took place for us once for all *pro nobis* in its relation to the ongoing work of the Spirit *in nobis*. Since this account is essential for what follows, it will be as well to give a resumé of the preceding argument. We began from the observation that the central formulae of patristic theology think in terms of a redemption effected by a solidarity with us on the part of God's Son, and we noted that this theme should not be separated from the themes of divine education and the cosmic battle but that all three should be read together. To help understand this patristic argument we have resorted to an analogy from contemporary political practice, the exercise of education for critical consciousness. We have stressed the limitations of what can be expected from an analogy: no 'explanation' of the salvation wrought in Christ can ever be expected. Every precious thing in our experience is a 'mystery', and this event more than all. Nevertheless it is a bright not a dark mystery (to use John Cowburn's terms), a rational mystery which may be illuminated if not fully understood by analogies. In understanding the relation of cross and incarnation to the succeeding divine education we have then sought to make the following points: The incarnation is that expression of the divine solidarity with us (the *homoousios* of the Council of Constantinople of 381), without which no redemptive education is possible. The divine education does not proceed on the human model, 'Do as I say, but not as I do', for God is 'the Holy One in the midst of us'. Because he is holy and loving, he enters into total solidarity with our misery and despair and hopelessness, not being defeated by it but triumphing over it, and this solidarity is, as it were, the 'moral authority' of the divine education. Secondly, in the patristic theology, the battle with the powers cannot be rigidly separated from the divine education. Likewise, according to this analogy the exposure of the powers on the cross is the central moment in the divine education. When the Holy Spirit leads us into the truth of Christ he does so by convicting the world of sin, righteousness and judgement (John 16:8; the text is explored further in chapter 5). It is this exposure which liberates us from the idols of death. Again, without the exposure of the cross, there is no divine education. Thirdly, cross and incarnation establish the manner, quality and direction of the divine education. It establishes the *manner* of redemption as the refusal of all arbitrary and tyrannical power, showing that the new order is established 'by kindling the light of compassion and solidarity among those who live on the night-side of society, in the darkness of poverty and humiliation'.[17] The establishment of solidarity itself is shown to be liberating, not only on the social and political level but in the deepest sense of creating a society where human beings may be more open to each other and learn to forgive one another. Relatedly it reveals the mode or *quality* of redemption, for the solidarity of the Messiah who takes the form of a slave is marked by love, which denies the power established by repaying evil with evil. The solidarity we see in Jesus introduces a new perception of what is meant by 'power politics', revealing, as Paul Lehmann has it, the weakness of power and the power of weakness. This in turn suggests a whole new reading of history, which is usually written and read as the history of the mighty but which, if the gospel be true, is silently subverted and is more truly the history of 'those of low estate'. Again, God's solidarity in Christ reveals a specific *direction* in redeeming solidarity. God sent his Son to redeem the world, rich and poor alike, but his love is not a generalised benevolence, a sort of divine sunshine. According to Jesus' parables God may be for the rich man, through Lazarus, and for the Pharisee, through the tax-collector. People put themselves 'beyond redemption' by arrogating the place of God, by assuming the role of judge and lord. By coming as the one who is judged, and as the servant, Jesus unmasks such pretensions and shows the way of relationships not based on judgement and a society not based on domination. God is for all therefore, but from a specific direction, from below, from the position of the non-person and the despised. Again, how should we know this manner, quality and direction of the divine education without cross and incarnation? We could not; and so again we find these 'once for all events' at the root of the ongoing work of the Spirit. In all these ways we are but trying to explicate the relation between Christ and the Spirit so profoundly reflected upon in the 'farewell discourses' of John (chs. 14–17), passages which, in speaking of the Spirit leading us into the truth of Christ, suggest the practice of divine education. Alternatively, this may be regarded as an attempt to understand the relationship between 'objective' and 'subjective' aspects of the atonement. As Moberly said, these are mutually correlative terms. The atonement was objective that it might become subjective and become personal experience by belief, contemplation and love. Therefore, he said, we need a doctrine of the Holy Spirit in explicating the atonement. Understanding education in deeply personalist terms, and yet with that political dimension without which this easily becomes romanticism, we maintain that both these poles of the atonement, objective and subjective, can be – not satisfactorily, for that applies to no theory, but illuminatingly understood according to the model of education for critical consciousness.

To close this chapter we can perhaps turn to the first *homoousios*, the formula of the Council of Nicaea, which asserted that Christ was 'of one substance with the Father'. The revelation of the manner, quality and direction of redemption in Christ constitutes a permanent question to every human system, forestalling the illusion that we may have reached our goal at any particular moment in history. In this sense it is the incarnation itself which is the 'eschatological proviso', the challenge to all partial and provisional realisations of authentic human community, and in this sense 'realised eschatology'. It frames this challenge with final and convincing power, because it is truly *God* who takes the form of a slave.[18] Were the announcement of the power of love and the power of weakness the proclamation of a paradoxical social programme, based perhaps on the perception of the self-destructiveness of evil, then this could only be good news to the powerful who could continue to rejoice in the nihilism of wanton destruction. But it is the Lord of life and death who is a servant, whose lordship qualifies every other. When the lords of this world despise and challenge the power of solidarity in love, compassion and weakness they are not challenging an abstract principle but the inner rationality of creation, for it is this inner rationality, God's Word and Wisdom, which takes flesh in Jesus. In all specific acts of solidarity with the poor through which we seek to let God's will be realised on earth, we are not doing something 'noble' but bringing ourselves into line with the deepest rationality of the whole cosmos. It is this which is the ground of hope in the long struggle with those powers which seek to take a short cut in the historical process through every manner of domination, giving way to the temptation which Jesus rejected. Because this hope is hope in the living God, and not in an abstract principle or programme, there remains hope also for the victims of the terror of history who died, 'not receiving deliverance'. To say that there is hope also for the dead is not to relativise the importance of the redemptive process, making God into a kindly Conjurer who sees that everything is 'all right in the end', but to assert that the rationality of the cosmos extends to history, that despite its cruelty and suffering it is a rational and redeemable process, the sphere of the operation of God's love. In the self-effacement of love, God draws back and allows the creature freedom, expressing the power of his love only in solidarity, only in the crucified Jew. But the mystery of redemption is the infection of human history with the power of the hope this engenders and the strength of this solidarity, and this is the pedagogy of the Spirit.

4

The Spirit and the Kingdom – I

According to the biblical witness God is active in human history, proclaiming and making real his righteousness in that history, 'mighty to save' (Isa. 63:1). God is engaged with his creation, and in this engagement he is not concerned to offer an interpretation of reality, as if salvation might be obtained by contemplation, but his purpose is the transformation and renewal of creation from within. The incarnation is the focal point of this engagement and activity of God. Just as, according to Paul's metaphor, God in Christ is both Judge and accused, so according to the image of a divine education Christ is both Educator and educated. It is the letter to the Hebrews which above all emphasises the significance of the fact that Christ himself undergoes the education of the human race – 'For because he himself has suffered and been tempted, he is able to help those who are tempted' (Heb. 2:18). Therefore, 'Although he was a Son, he learned obedience through what he suffered; and being made perfect he became the source of eternal salvation to all who obey him' (Heb. 5:8–9). Becoming subject to discipline and death, Christ seals the value and hopefulness of the historical process in the face of what must otherwise be a very justified scepticism. It is God's act of solidarity which is the ground of that 'hope against hope' which is for Christians the motive for action towards the creation of a more human world. But God's engagement cannot be understood only in terms of the incarnation. That engagement begins with creation and includes not only Israel but the nations. To speak of this continuing engagement of God the biblical witness uses the language of 'Spirit'.

THE MEANING OF THE WORD 'SPIRIT'

Perhaps more than any other word in the vocabulary of faith the word 'Spirit' tends to vagueness. It was partly in reaction to Hegel's talk of Spirit active in universal history that Marx elaborated the thesis of historical materialism. Marx's thesis is that the whole 'superstructure' of society, 'morality, religion, metaphysics, all the rest of ideology and their corresponding form of consciousness' must be understood strictly in relation to socio-economic realities – the organisation of the means of production and the resultant organisation of society into classes. As such it is a hermeneutic discipline specifying rules necessary for the proper understanding of cultural constructs such as religion and philosophy. Thus, where Hegel used 'Spirit' as the key to understanding historical process, Marx preferred to talk of different modes of production and the class structure, and regarded this as a necessary 'demystification' of history. Recently the Old Testament scholar Norman Gottwald has used this historical hermeneutic to astonishing effect to illuminate the period of Israel's origins recorded in the book of Judges.[1] His thesis and method has been highly suggestive for this chapter and the next, but to admit this calls for a clarification. Disconcertingly Gottwald follows Marx not only in his historical method but in his atheism, and he seems to imply that the latter follows from the former. Need we accept that, if we wish to understand the word 'Spirit' (for example) strictly in relation to socio-economic realities, we must end up with it as an account of what Gottwald calls a 'socio-servo mechanism'?

Like Marx Gottwald wishes to dismiss 'the distorted, alienating line of tradition which absolutizes and falsely projects the traditional religious models into eternal idols and spectres of the mind'.[2] Whilst talk of God's engagement as Spirit might have been useful for the tribes of Yahweh, it is intolerable for modern man, 'fuzzy nonsense' which tends to isolate us in our private souls, cultivate mood and sentiment in place of vision and passion, instil resignation in the name of sweetness and sacrifice, persuade us to accept the unacceptable, and confirm our fixation towards the past and venturelessness towards the future.[3] The echo of Marx's critique of Hegel's *Philosophy of Right*, in which the famous description of religion as 'the opium of the people' occurs, is unmistakeable. Marx followed Feuerbach in understanding 'God' as the projection of the human shadow on the mists of history, a sort of metaphysical Brocken spectre. The word 'God' has a referent, he would say, but the referent is a purely human reality (Gottwald's 'socio-servo mechanism'). There is no transcendent being to whom we can pray, who is enaged in the historical process and who will, 'at the end of history', wipe the tears from every eye. To believe in such a being neutralises the protest against suffering and robs it of its transformative power.

Marx is quite right: if God does not exist, then religion, with all its talk about Spirit, is an illusion we are better off without. But the Marx who arrives at this conclusion is Marx the petit-bourgeois social democrat, Marx the nineteenth-century rationalist, convinced once and for all by what Barth called the 'offensive triviality' of Feuerbach's arguments that God did not exist. Feuerbach's conclusion that all theology was anthropology owed nothing to historical materialism: Marx developed historical materialism out of his critique of Feuerbach, because he saw that he worked exclusively on the level of ideas. In the elaboration of his thought he continued to presuppose atheism, not least because much of the religion he saw around him was indeed a theological justification of injustice, but in no way is atheism entailed in his method. That theological ideas, like all other ideas, should be understood in relation to their socio-economic context is a proper and necessary demand. This is quite different from the thesis that they may be *reduced* to a function of socio-economic conditions. Behind that thesis, espoused by Gottwald, is the tendency to elide historical and metaphysical materialism, an elision Marx avoided. Metaphysical materialism is the thesis that an exhaustive account of reality can be given in terms of the constituents of this universe. Like any other metaphysic it is a cultural construct which needs to be understood against its social and economic background. It does not 'follow' from historical materialism, and the view that it does may be found to rest on extremely dated assumptions about the nature of science and verification. To accept the hermeneutics of historical materialism does not mean accepting the shallow rationalism of the nineteenth century. To the extent that this hermeneutic claims to be exhaustive it transcends its bounds, for any hermeneutic which is genuinely historical must be open to the random and indeterminate factors of human behaviour, and therefore to the possibility of transcendent factors within history. With that caveat the historical materialist method may be used to try and help understand the word 'Spirit'.

Marx believed that religion was opiate because he believed that God did not exist, but the argument would be equally cogent if by 'God' was meant merely an 'impersonal, immanent and rational orderer of the universe', such as David Hume is said to have believed existed.[4] Religion is a dangerous distraction, either if Feuerbach, Marx and Freud are right in understanding 'God' as a projection of human consciousness or equally if 'God exists but does not wish to get involved'. If religion, and talk of Spirit, is not simply a distraction from the real business – seeing the hungry are fed and not sent away empty, for example – it must be because the God who is worshipped relates to the real and that relationship *makes a difference*. It is the function of language about Spirit to make precisely this point, to direct attention to God's redemptive engagement with his creature.

One good reason for the use of historical material method at this point is that the word 'Spirit' is not only vague but also extremely slippery, and if meaning is in the use (which we can accept just for the sake of argument) then the meaning of the word may not be taken for granted. In many languages, including Hebrew and Greek, a more or less systematic ambiguity attaches to it – a witness to the elusiveness of God's presence. Thus for instance the Hebrew word *ruach* can mean simply the confidence and self-possession of a person: when the Queen of Sheba saw Solomon's wisdom and magnificence 'there was no more spirit in her' (1 Kings 10:5) We read of a 'spirit of jealousy' (Num. 5:14) and a 'haughty spirit' (Prov. 16:18), which are purely psychological observations, whilst Isaiah speaks of God sending a 'spirit of judgement and burning' (Isa. 4:4), of confusion (19:14) and of deep sleep (29:10) on a nation. The same passage may sometimes use the one word *ruach* to refer to God's Spirit, the human spirit, and the wind (Ezek. 37:1, 5, 9). This terminological inexactness has proved a rich source of theological confusion. The root meaning of *ruach* as wind, or even 'snorting through the nose' in the Akkadian as we are told, has suggested to some contemporary writers a connection between Spirit and the subconscious, as though this was the privileged field of the Spirit's operation. This is of course in more or less deliberate reaction to the patristic and medieval connection between Spirit and reason (which we saw in Origen). Again, exposition of the doctrine of Spirit has suffered more than most doctrines from the application of a simple evolutionary perspective. Thus we are presented with a picture of the crude, violent and sensational inspiration of Judges which is slowly ethicised and attached more to interior and spiritual renewal in Ezekiel, and which finally climaxes in the complete other-worldliness of Jesus and Paul. Yet another source of confusion has been the influence in biblical interpretation of non-biblical ideas of Spirit, especially those derived from Stoicism of spirit as an immensely rarefied matter pervading all things, and Platonism, with its contrast between body and soul, the latter of which has been only too easily identified with 'spirit'. Of course, both in Wisdom of Solomon and in Paul, Greek ideas exert an important influence, but to recognise this should not be to deny the distinctiveness of many aspects of biblical thought. Finally, comparative religious studies have suggested that Spirit is an especially religious reality, so that if we wish to talk about Spirit we must talk about religion. But neither ecstasy, nor immanence, nor religion and piety is especially the concern of the biblical language about Spirit where this is used to denote God's operation within human affairs. This becomes clear when we resist the temptation to thematise the biblical material which speaks of Spirit but rather, as far as possible, try to read it in its historical context.

'SPIRIT' IN PRE-MONARCHICAL ISRAEL

The earliest biblical texts which speak of the Spirit come from the pre-monarchical situation when, according to Gottwald's very plausible thesis, disparate groups of *ḫapiru* bands, peasants and liberated slaves are coming together around the Yahweh cult to form 'Israel'. Gottwald argues that these groups constituted a radically egalitarian culture which first threatened and to some extent took over from the Canaanite city princes, against whom most of the struggles recorded in Judges were directed. Although Judges has been edited by the Deuteronomic school, the references to Spirit do not seem to belong to this stratum but come from the early tradition. It is important to notice that in this tradition all but one of the texts speak of the Spirit being bestowed in times of emergency or crisis for the tribes. The exception is Judges 14:6, when the Spirit enables Samson to tear the lion to pieces, but the same story speaks of a Spirit-inspired raid on Ashkelon. The fact of ecstasy in no way stands in the foreground, and it is therefore a very dubious procedure to discuss these texts under the heading 'the primitive Spirit', and to try to relate the stories first and foremost to the subconscious.[5] In these stories the Spirit always comes with a very concrete *purpose*, namely the liberation of the slaves and peasants who constitute 'Israel' in the struggle with the Canaanite overlords. The story of Othniel may serve as a paradigm for the use of 'Spirit' in these narratives: 'The Spirit of the Lord came upon [Othniel], and he judged Israel; he went out to war, and the Lord gave Cushan-rishathaim king of Mesopotamia into his hand . . . So the land had rest forty years' (Judg. 3:10). Freedom and 'rest' for Israel is not achieved by magical means but by ordinary people who are able to transcend themselves in the struggle for liberation – ecstasy is simply a sign of this transcendence. The Spirit comes on *people* – it is not primarily associated with holy places or objects. It makes them leaders in a struggle ('deliverers', which is the meaning of 'judge' here) after which they resume their ordinary role (Judg. 8:23) – there is no question of permanent endowment with the Spirit. These 'charismatic leaders' (Weber) are taken from and remain with the people; Gottwald remarks that Israel remains the subject of these stories, rather than their being an account of 'great heroes'. The occasional nature of the Spirit's coming is linked to the anti-centrist and egalitarian political set-up of Israel at this period (1 Sam. 10). There are reasons for thinking that this egalitarian political background accounts for the fact that we have a greater depth of reference to the Spirit in these narratives than at any time until we come to the exilic period. In these texts it is through men, and women, who become leaders of the people, and in the struggle for freedom, that God is discerned to 'make history', to create his people and give them the land. 'Spirit' language is a way of expressing this discernment. It is at the heart of Buber's 'active history'.

THE COMING OF THE MONARCHY

In the struggle against the Canaanite kings 'Israel' could hold its own but this situation changed with the invasion from the sea by the Philistines, who settled on the coast and who brought with them an iron-age technology that Israel lacked (1 Sam. 13:19). The crisis caused by this situation led to the demand for 'a king like all the nations', a gloomy description by the Deuteronomist of Israel's experience of monarchy. The two books of Samuel and the story of Solomon's reign describe the transition from a federation of tribes where leaders were thrown up as and when needed to the centralised army, bureaucracy and cultus under Solomon, and in this transition 'Spirit' language plays an important role. In these books we find side by side both a royal ideology and an 'alternative history' (compare 1 Sam. 8:10ff. and 1 Sam. 10; 2 Sam. 7 and 1 Kings 8). According to the royal ideology Spirit is now channelled through the king, and linked to the ceremony of anointing (1 Sam. 10; 16:13). Whereas in the old tribal federation the tribes gathered at a variety of regional centres for the great cultic festivals, first David and then, decisively, Solomon centralise the cult in Jerusalem and validate it with a myth of divine presence (1 Kings 8:30), so that the divine presence is now located in a place rather than with the people. Whereas the 'Mosaic' covenant which derives from the tribal federation was with the whole people, the royal house now speaks of a covenant with the house of David, and so the Spirit is now mediated 'for the good of the people'. Of course it is not possible to be completely cynical about the royal ideology. Just as Joseph's betrayal by his brothers was the means of the salvation of Israel, so the royal ideology was transformed and became the preparation for Christ. Nevertheless we need to be aware of the presence side by side of official history and alternative history in these texts. The depth of the old tribal traditions showed itself in many ways. It led to the revolt under Absalom; it forced David to abandon his planned rationalisation of the army when he was trying to get away from the old tribal levies (2 Sam. 24); it led to a stubborn resistance by the people to the centralisation of the cult at Jerusalem; and finally, with the old tribal cry 'To your tents, O Israel', led to the break up of David's empire (1 Kings 12:16).

In the stories of the birth of the monarchy the position of the prophetic bands with whom 'the Spirit of the Lord' is associated is worthy of note. Their connection with Samuel may indicate that in tribal days they fulfilled a political as well as a cultic function. In 1 Kings 18 they appear as advisers to the king, and perhaps this was a rationalisation of their earlier role. If so this is another instance of the connection between 'Spirit' and the affairs of the nation.

'SPIRIT' UNDER THE MONARCHY

Despite the relative greatness and importance of Solomon's reign the narratives do not suppress a critical note (1 Kings 11). Solomon, and many of the kings of both northern and southern kingdoms after him, aspired to a despotism similar to that which prevailed amongst Israel's neighbours. The need for a standing army, chariot cities, ostentatious building projects and a large bureaucracy meant both forced labour, land appropriation and high taxation. The end result of this was a widening gap between rich and poor, and mass poverty. No longer could the oppressors of Israel be identified with the Philistines, but they were found within her borders and worshipped the same God. In this situation two things are very striking: one is a marked decrease in language about Spirit; the other is that when it appears Spirit is often associated with the critique of injustice. Thus it is the Spirit who 'transports' Elijah, the fearless critic of Ahab in his ruthless expansion of crown land (1 Kings 18:12). The same king is eventually destroyed by following the advice of prophets who, according to 'a prophet of the Lord', speak at the prompting of a lying spirit sent by God (1 Kings 22:21–3). As far as Ahab is concerned the prophet who, it transpires, has 'the Spirit of the Lord' (22:24) 'never prophesies good concerning me, but evil' (v. 8). Conflict with the institutional prophets who pander to the king likewise inspires the oracle we find in Micah, perhaps spoken during the reign of Ahaz (about whom we learn that 'He even burned his son as an offering' (2 Kings 16:3). Whereas the prophets who cry 'Peace' in the face of injustice will be disgraced,

As for me, I am filled with power,
  with the Spirit of the Lord,
  and with justice and might,
to declare to Jacob his transgression
  and to Israel his sin. (Micah 3:8)

Isaiah too considered that God had closed the 'eyes of Israel', which were its prophets, sending upon them 'a spirit of deep sleep' (Isa. 29:10). Jeremiah is the most scathing of all. Perhaps because of the institutional prophets' claim to be inspired by *ruach* he scarcely uses the word at all, except in judgement:

They have spoken falsely of the Lord,
  and have said, 'He will do nothing;
no evil will come upon us,
  nor shall we see sword or famine.
The prophets shall become wind [*ruach*];
  the word is not in them.' (Jer. 5:12–13)

Speaking of the day of Yahweh's future Isaiah prophesies that 'the Lord of hosts' will be 'a spirit of justice' to those who sit in judgement (Isa. 28:6). The famous warning that the Egyptians on whom Judah relies for military aid are 'men and not gods' and their horses 'flesh and not spirit' (Isa. 31:3) must also be read in the context of the earlier warning about this defensive treaty:

'Woe to the rebellious children,' says the Lord,
  'who carry out a plan, but not mine;
and who make a league, but not of my spirit,
  that they may add sin to sin.' (Isa. 30:1)

No abstract opposition of flesh and spirit may be read from Isaiah's words. Judah should trust in the 'God of justice' (Isa. 30:18), but their preference for every kind of injustice (Isa. 1) leads them instead to rely on military treaties of their own devising.

If the oracles in Isaiah 11 and 32 are indeed from the first Isaiah, it is at this point that the contradiction between present experience and the promise and demand of Yahweh forcibly throw up a new vision of Yahweh's future. The same Spirit which prompts the critique of existing injustice is associated with a forthcoming rule of righteousness and peace:

> For the palace will be forsaken,
> the populous city deserted . . .
> until the Spirit is poured upon us from on high,
> and the wilderness becomes a fruitful field . . .
> Then justice will dwell in the wilderness,
> and righteousness abide in the fruitful field.
> And the effect of righteousness will be peace
> and the result of righteousness, quietness and trust for ever.
> (Isa. 32:14–17; cf. Isa. 11:2f.)

Here, as in Judges, the coming of the Spirit is associated with rest (*shaquat* – Judg. 3:11, 3:30; Isa. 30:15, 32:17).

Many of the stories in the Pentateuch were probably put down during the monarchy, and the story of 'revolt in the desert' in Numbers 11 comes from these old traditions. The story pictures Israel in the wilderness after the flight from Egypt. The struggle for liberation has not proved easy and has resulted in hunger and privation. The *nephesh* (AV: soul; RSV: strength) of the people is exhausted – they have lost heart (11:6). As far as they are concerned, well-fed slavery would be better than the privations of struggle (11:4–5). According to the story, Moses had been given the Spirit 'to bear the burden of the people' – and, in view of the upshot of the story, a veiled reference to royal claims to do the same may be suspected. However this may be, Moses goes to God with the same complaint as the people, perhaps hoping for 'superhuman' strength to 'bear the burden'. God's answer however is not in terms of any supernatural endowment whatever but in terms of a different leadership pattern (i.e. the leadership pattern of the tribal federation), distribution of 'the Spirit' on seventy elders, conferring on them responsibility to rule. Interestingly, even this is not the end of the story, for the Spirit falls on two men not amongst the elders called to the Tent of Meeting, and this provokes a vigorous protest from the newly empowered elders. To the demand that their 'prophesying' should be stopped, Moses replies, 'Would that all the Lord's people were prophets and the Lord would put his spirit on them all' (11:29). Whether this climax of the story looks back, as we know the prophets often did, to the earlier period before the monarchy can only be guessed at. Certainly it thinks of a time when 'the burden of the people' will be the responsibility of all, and precisely this is the gift of the Spirit. Like the much earlier 'fable of the trees' (Judg. 9:7ff.), the story looks like a critique of the monarchy which implies support of the earlier more democratic pattern. It is this story which is taken up by Joel after the exile, and is again used by the early Church to explain the significance of the new era inaugurated by Jesus.[6]

Again in Numbers, the story of Balaam speaks of the Spirit of God inspiring a prophecy in wholly political terms, of Israel's forthcoming dispossession of her enemies (Num. 24:2ff.).

In the use of 'Spirit' language thus far we can see two trends. First, at no point is the Spirit concerned with 'purely religious' realities, but rather this language speaks of God's guidance of and intervention in secular political activities, and in particular the establishment of justice. On the other hand this same language is wide open to abuse by powers which seek to validate their position by claiming divine sanction. From Micaiah ben Imlah to Jeremiah we find the prophets of justice set against the establishment prophets, and both claiming inspiration by the Spirit. Jeremiah indeed finds the currency so debased that he does not use it. Nevertheless the '*ruach* YHWH', the Spirit of the God of justice, could not forever be abused in this way, and Spirit language again comes to the fore at the time of the exile.

THE EXILE

As the power of Babylon rose, the position of independent Judah became more and more precarious. A first group of leaders was deported in 598 BC, and finally in 587 Jerusalem fell and there was another deportation, though the bulk of the population remained in Palestine. This collapse obviously had drastic implications for the royal ideology. The kings who were the 'guardians' of the people disappeared into exile and obscurity. The temple which had been the guarantee of God's presence was looted and fell into ruin. What then remained of the covenant with David? And if that was abrogated did it mean the same for the covenant with the whole people? As the monarchy tottered the Deuteronomic school had already offered a thoroughgoing reinterpretation of Israel's history which preferred to look back beyond the monarchy to the Mosaic covenant. In different ways all of the writers of the exile, and of later periods, take up this work of reinterpretation. Ezekiel could still look forward to the restoration of the monarchy, but we find in the work of the so-called Second Isaiah an astonishing reinterpretation of rule through service, the climax of which is to be found in the 'Servant Songs'. Here the old royal ideology receives its most thorough transmutation, raising themes which are taken up by much later reinterpreters of Israel's history, Jesus and Paul. This ideology had sought to control and channel the working of the Spirit – just as the church hierarchy was to seek to do many centuries later. Its collapse led to a new outburst of 'Spirit language' unmatched since the time of Judges, and unmatched thereafter until after the death and resurrection of Jesus (which was also the subversion of an ideology which claimed control of the Spirit). In a period of despair and the collapse of established certainties, Ezekiel and Second Isaiah preached a message of hope and renewal to the exiles, and to do this they used language about 'Spirit'.

The story of Ezekiel's 'call' is framed in terms of the Spirit: 'the Spirit entered into me and set me upon my feet' (Ezek. 2:2). What for? To proclaim first a message of judgement and then of hope and national renewal which would be accomplished through God's Spirit. Perhaps taking up the thread of Jeremiah's prophecy, Ezekiel thinks of a new covenant with the whole people:

> A new heart I will give you, and a new spirit I will put within you; and I will take out of your flesh the heart of stone and give you a heart of flesh. And I will put my spirit within you, and cause you to walk in my statutes and be careful to observe my ordinances. (Ezek. 36:26–7)

National renewal depends on the fact that all respect the rights and freedom of all, as Torah requires. Ezekiel envisages this situation as being brought about by the Spirit. More poetically and more vividly he expresses the same hope in the vision of the valley of the dry bones (Ezek. 37). The people are 'dried up' because their hope is lost (37:11) – hope or vision is the 'soul' of a people. God's word through the prophet breathes new hope in them, the Spirit brings them back to 'life' – it restores the corporate forms in which community life is expressed – and eventually back to the land. As before, this work of the Spirit gives the people rest, here spoken of in terms of a covenant of peace (Ezek. 37:26).

The vision of the Second Isaiah is wider still. For him (or her – we should not jump to conclusions) 'Spirit' is a designation of the God who is creator of all things (Isa. 40:13), and it is in this rooting of all ultimate power in the Creator that he finds hope. For this writer, the Spirit renews not only Israel (Isa. 44:3) but is given so that servant Israel may 'bring forth justice to the nations' (Isa. 42:1). It is this text which later becomes decisive for Matthew's understanding of Jesus, and perhaps even for Jesus' self-understanding.

In 539 BC Babylon fell to Cyrus, and Israel came under Persian rule for the next two hundred years. The Persian policy was against deportation, preferring to collect tribute and levies of forced labour from client states. Hence in 538 Cyrus decreed that the Temple might be rebuilt, and a small group of exiles returned the next year and began work. The troubled state of the empire meant that this work went slowly – the city walls were the first priority – and the new Temple was only consecrated in 515. It is in this interim period, with a community in both Babylon and Judah, and some intercourse between the two, that Third Isaiah, Zecharaiah and Haggai prophesy. It should be noted that, whilst the rebuilding of the temple figures as a matter of the utmost importance to a Haggai or an Ezra, Judaism finally survived the total destruction of the temple in AD 70 with scarcely a tremor. This was due not only to the emergence of the synagogue structure, from this period, but also to the continuation of that rethinking of what God's self-giving to history really entailed which we have already seen. Torah and its exposition came to be more important than Temple, and it was here that God's work as Spirit was located.

The 'Third Isaiah' (Isa. 56–66) continues reflection on the connection between the Spirit and the New Covenant (Isa. 59:21), but in the tradition of the Isaianic school sees the Spirit as the inspiration of a messianic age of justice and peace (Isa. 61:1–2). Longing for a new act of deliverance and for 'rest', the prophet discerns the Spirit as the moving force of the exodus:

Where is he who put in the midst of them his holy Spirit,
who caused his glorious arm to go at the right hand of Moses,
who divided the waters before them . . .
Like cattle they go down into the valley,
the Spirit of the Lord gave them rest [*nuach*]. (Isa. 63:11, 14)

Here 'Spirit' means both God in his redeeming initiative, leading the people, and also 'God in the midst', giving courage and hope for the venture of liberation. Once again we observe the connection between the Spirit and 'rest', which we must understand in terms of peace and freedom. The connection between the exodus and the leadership of the Spirit seems to have become a theological commonplace at this time, both Haggai, more or less in this period, and Nehemiah, later, making the same connection (Hag. 2:5, Neh. 9:20). Another connection, which had been commonplace since the days of the prophetic bands gathered round Samuel, was that between the Spirit and prophecy. What we now find is a looking back to what was spoken 'through the former prophets' (Zech. 7:12, Neh. 9:30), where Spirit is seen as the agent of God's warning and instruction. God speaks now through what was spoken then, and thus we find here the origin of the connection between Spirit and Scripture. At the same time these prophets look forward to the new age when the Spirit will fall on all, thus fulfilling the desire of Moses as expressed in the story in Numbers – a hope which reflects the uncertainty which attached to the leadership of the nation at this time (Joel 2: 28–9).

It was in this period that the priestly redactors edited the ancient Israelite traditions in which an emphasis on the work of Spirit in creation is very marked (Gen 1:2; Job 26:13, 27:3; Ps. 104:30). The connection of the Spirit with creation is already clear in Second Isaiah, and doubtless lies behind the prophetic message of the re-creation of Israel through the Spirit. The stories about the craftsmanship of Bezalel, which was inspired by the Spirit, belong to the priestly source, and likewise see the Spirit active in creation, though this time in human creativity (Exod. 31:3, 35:31). Noteworthy too, from this time, is the connection of Spirit with God's presence (Ps. 51:11, 139:7–8) – a connection which later became taken for granted. Here 'Spirit' means God not only as encountered in the historical process but as encountered in *my* experience. Pietism has always reversed this order (first my experience then, possibly, God in the historical process), which is certainly a mistake, but on the other hand the biblical witness clearly thinks of God not only as the Lord of history but also as the Lord of my history, and in this experience the Lord is the Spirit.

THE SELEUCID PERIOD

Persian rule, under which Haggai, Zechariah and Joel prophesied, was paternalistic and allowed a certain autonomy to the Jewish state. Ptolemean and Seleucid rule was far more oppressive, and the absolute state, epitomised in a 'divine' ruler, came into conflict with the sentiments of the majority of Jews outside of Jerusalem. Israel suffered not only political but cultural oppression worse than at any time in her history. This oppression perhaps accounts for the fact that many people believed the Spirit was 'quenched' at this time. At the same time the contact with Greek culture which this period brought was by no means a wholly negative experience. In particular it seems to have stimulated an interest in the ancient Wisdom traditions of Israel, which led to the editing of these traditions and to the production of new works in the same genre.

The roots of ancient wisdom seem to be twofold. There is on the one hand the proverbial lore which is related primarily to village or tribal life, and which enshrines many observations relating to how such a society can work successfully, and what destroys it. On the other hand there is evidence of an international Wisdom, centred on the royal courts of the ancient Near East. In Israel this first flourished under Solomon, who drew on the wisdom of Egypt, Babylon and Edom. These two traditions, the rural and the courtly, were then woven together and become the subject for further reflection in the introduction to Proverbs (Prov. 1–9), probably written at this time, and the other post-exilic Wisdom books. In both streams of tradition there is a primary reference to the wise government of affairs – many commentators draw attention to the deeply secular character of the Wisdom literature. The same emphasis is found in later reflection. Thus the author of Proverbs 1–9 makes personified Wisdom say: 'By me kings reign, and rulers decree what is just; by me princes and nobles rule, all just judges' (Prov. 8:15).

Sirach has advice for kings and magistrates (Ecclus. 10:1–5), and the Wisdom of Solomon considers that 'A multitude of wise men is the salvation of the world, and a sensible king is the stability of his people' (Wisd. 6:24). The relevance of this to our theme is that the wisdom for this proper conduct of affairs is given by the Holy Spirit: 'Who has learned thy counsel, unless thou hast given wisdom and sent thy holy Spirit from on high?' (Wisd. 9:17). Although the Christian tradition from the beginning used Wisdom language to speak of Christ, we see here its close affinity to language about Spirit. Like the Spirit, wisdom is identified with craftsmanship (Wisd. 14:2), creation (Prov. 8:27–31) and, as we have seen, with 'politics' in the broadest sense, the proper arrangement of human affairs.

Wisdom was from the beginning, needless to say, an educational tradition. The scribes thought of God instructing people through Wisdom, but this instruction involved also a search for wisdom. As Childs has put it, 'the search for wisdom emerges in a dialectic between its being the gift of God which is given and an acquisition which we actively pursue'.[7] This dialectic is of the essence of the divine pedagogy, illustrating once again the way in which God makes history, changes reality, through men and women, co-opting them as fellow workers whilst at all times remaining their free and sovereign Lord. Thus God 'works' through that human quest for given regularities and orders which has issued in the achievements of modern science and technology; he 'works' in the quest for a more just society, for truly human patterns of behaviour. Science, technology, the political order become demonised when the first part of the dialectic, God's self-revelation, his self-gifting, is ignored, when dialogue becomes an intra-human monologue.

At the same time as these reflections on Wisdom and the Spirit were elaborated there was another and very different movement of thought emerging, it would seem, from the situation of oppression. Just as Third World nations today are often swamped under the impact of the Coca-cola culture so Israel reeled under the sometimes forcible imposition of Greek cultural mores (2 Macc. 4:9–10). Whereas during the exile Spirit language was used to preach a message of hope, under this oppression it simply went 'underground'. 'When Haggai, Zecharaiah and Malachi, the last of the prophets, died, the Holy Spirit departed from Israel', runs a rabbinic text. This view finds poignant expression in Maccabees where the stones of the defiled altar of sacrifice are stowed away 'until there should come a prophet to tell them what to do with them' (1 Macc. 4:46). Simon Maccabeus too is apointed only 'until such time as a prophet should arise' (1 Macc. 14:41). Psalm 74 may well come from this period, lamenting as it does that 'there is no more a prophet; none among us knows how long' (74:9). A mood of pessimism traced a decline in the presence of the Spirit: whilst in the time of the patriarchs all pious and upright men had the Spirit, it was said, later this was restricted only to kings, priests and prophets, owing to the sin of Israel. After the death of Malachi, however, only the *bath quol*, the echo of the voice, remained.[8] John the Baptist and Jesus come therefore to a situation thirsty for Spirit, where 'Spirit was not yet given' because the Messianic age had not yet come. Paul's understanding of the Gentile mission on the other hand, which Luke gives symbolic expression to in the story of Pentecost, is the story of the reversal of this trend, as the Spirit is poured first on Jesus, then on disciples, and then on the maid-servants and menservants of Corinth, on the Gentiles.

REVIEW

God is not idle but active, engaged in redemption, and the language which speaks of this engagement is the language of 'Spirit'. But what does this language mean? Whilst this chapter makes no pretence to have given a complete or balanced account of 'Spirit' in the literature of Israel, yet one consistent thread can be discerned running from the stories of Judges (which must have existed orally in the tenth century BC) to the book of Wisdom, written a hundred or so years before Christ. In the prophetic tradition (which includes the historical books in the Hebrew canon) the Spirit always comes to liberate, to bring rest or peace, and to judge, or establish righteousness. In the Wisdom tradition it is the Spirit which enables wise government in village, tribe or kingdom. The priestly tradition emphasises the connection between the Spirit and all forms of 'life', which includes a better future in this tradition as for the prophets. 'Spirit', says Eduard Schweizer, 'reaches its goal only when it becomes identical with the "word" ', but this is a word neither of pious preaching nor of religious ecstasy but the word with which Yahweh 'hews' Israel (Hos. 6:5) and which hastens to an historical fulfilment (Isa. 9:8). 'Spirit' language certainly indicates a reality which is beyond human control, which cannot be manipulated, and yet this 'stranger Spirit' is 'poured upon' (Isa. 29:10), 'clothes' (Judg. 6:34) and 'leaps upon' (Judg. 14:6) human beings so that they become filled with it (Exod. 31:3) and have it within them (Isa. 63:11). The Spirit is only a stranger in that it refuses to be domesticated by royal cult or theology. If it is 'wholly other' to human beings as the Spirit of the holy God, all the same it determines them in such a way that God makes history through human beings. It is this Spirit, and this area of experience of which we are speaking, when we speak of the redemptive education of the Spirit. 'A real humanist', says Freire, 'can be identified more by his trust in the people, which engages him in their struggle, than by a thousand actions in their favour without that trust'.[9] The God who cannot become a human possession nevertheless trusts himself, and the future of his world, to his creature, in this as in the incarnation revealing what Barth called his 'humanity'. The experiences which led Israel to speak of God in terms of *ruach* reveal the dialogical mode of God's working, they reveal him as 'the God of hope', the God who hopes, as well as the God who is the goal of all hope. Ezekiel recognised in the Spirit not only the giver of life but the giver of new life, the power of the future, which is not 'any old' future but a future of justice, righteousness and peace for all. 'Revelation' likewise, in so far as this is an appropriate name for God's speaking through the Spirit, is not epiphany but the word as a prophetic judgement which comes with a task and an historical promise and summons. The Spirit is connected therefore not accidentally but deeply and essentially (though of course also not solely) with politics, history, rule and order, with freedom, justice and a new society – what Jesus, quoting Isaiah 61, refers to as 'the kingdom'. It is towards this goal that the pedagogy of the Spirit is directed.

5

The Spirit and the Kingdom – II

'If I by the Spirit of God cast out devils,' said Jesus, 'then is the kingdom of God come upon you' (Matt. 12:28). Similarly we read in John's gospel that only one who is born of water and the Spirit will be able to 'enter' the kingdom of God (John 3:5). The profound connection between Spirit and kingdom indicated by these remarks partly explains the curious fact that, whilst in the synoptic gospels Jesus repeatedly speaks of 'the kingdom', the word 'Spirit' as a reference to God scarcely occurs a dozen times there. Conversely, the word 'kingdom' only occurs ten times in Paul but the word 'Spirit' more than one hundred times. Of course, the New Testament accounts for this difference in terms of the event of Pentecost, the new gift of the Spirit which followed Jesus' death and resurrection. On the other hand both 'kingdom' and 'Spirit' speak in different ways of God's 'kingly rule', and this connection indicates the direction in which we have to look to understand the meaning of language about Spirit in the New Testament.

SPIRIT IN THE SYNOPTIC TRADITION

There is nothing in the external situation which justifies the new confidence in the coming of the Spirit which we find in the tradition about Jesus, a fact which warns us that the historical materialist hermeneutic must not be taken in a reductionist way. Concepts and ideas must always be understood in relation to their environment, but if the Scriptures be true there is always the possibility of the inbreaking of a qualitatively new factor into history, something we find in both the resurrection and the new experience of Spirit connected with that.

Since 63 BC Palestine had been under Roman rule, less oppressive than Seleucid rule but still bitterly resented by the majority of the population. Whilst the upper classes (Herod and the Sadducees) collaborate with Rome in order to preserve a modicum of power and independence, the middle classes (which included many Pharisees) and the lower classes (the *am ha'aretz* – people of the land) long for the end of Roman bondage. Into this situation comes Jesus as Messiah with a message scandalous in some respects to all. He is not a quietist who can be used by the Sadducees to keep the masses quiet, much as fundamentalist preachers are used by right-wing regimes in Latin America today. But neither is he a Zealot singlemindedly determined to overthrow the Romans, and thus he falls foul of nationalist elements in the middle and lower classes. Good news to the poor is the heart of his teaching, but it is not the good news of relief and development programmes, of popular handouts, but the good news of a specific discernment of the hand of God at work in history, the power politics of the God he calls 'Father' who blesses the poor and meek. It is in this context that we have to understand the synoptic language about Spirit.

Mark begins his gospel with a threefold reference to Holy Spirit. In the first place John the Baptist contrasts his own baptism with a coming baptism of one 'mightier than I' who will baptise with Holy Spirit (Matthew and Luke add 'and with fire'). Then Jesus is baptised and the Spirit descends 'like a dove', and the voice from heaven says, 'Thou art my beloved Son; with thee I am well pleased.' Finally, the Spirit 'drives out' or 'expels' (*ekballei*) Jesus into the wilderness where he is tempted by Satan (Mark 1:8–13). These three references are a sort of trumpet-blast announcing Jesus' presence. The one 'mightier than I', the 'coming one', is the Messiah coming to inaugurate the messianic age when Spirit will be poured out and Israel will be purified 'with fire'. The voice at the baptism may be citing Psalm 2:7, an enthronement psalm, in which case it refers to Jesus' 'induction into the eschatological office of the Son of God' (E. Schweizer). Matthew however seems to take it as referring to Isaiah 42, because he later quotes this passage in full:

> Behold, my servant whom I have chosen,
> my beloved with whom my soul is well pleased.
> I will put my Spirit upon him,

> and he shall proclaim justice to the nations.
> He will not wrangle or cry aloud,
> nor will anyone hear his voice in the streets . . .
> till he brings justice to victory;
> and in his name will the Gentiles hope.
> (Matt. 12:18–21; Isa. 42:1–4)

Allusion to this passage, and this Spirit, at the baptism, is of the first importance. In this case too Jesus' commissioning to messianic office is involved, but to a very specific understanding of this office. On the one hand Jesus is to 'proclaim justice to the nations', but on the other hand he does this as the servant whose voice is not heard in the streets. This is the very opposite of the messianic expectation of the Zealots, a fact underlined both by the temptation stories and possibly by the imagery of the dove and the wild beasts. It is the Spirit which 'drives' Jesus out to the wilderness where he faces the truth of his vocation. Should he attempt to inaugurate the kingdom of God by using the power of the 'rulers of this world'? This satanic temptation, later repeated more or less unwittingly by the disciples, he rejects. The messianic age which Jesus brings has more in common with the covenant of peace with Noah, which the dove announced, or with the peace with the animals promised in Isaiah (Isa. 11:6–7).

The story which Luke tells about the beginning of Jesus' ministry in the synagogue in Nazareth is, in the same way, a trumpet-blast which acts as a prologue for what is to follow. Given the scroll to read Jesus finds the text from Isaiah 61:

> The Spirit of the Lord is upon me,
> because he has anointed me to preach good news to the poor.
> He has sent me to proclaim release to the captives
> and recovery of sight to the blind,
> to set at liberty those who are oppressed,
> to proclaim the acceptable year of the Lord.
> (Luke 4:18–19; Isa. 61:1–2)

Jesus announces, 'Today has this scripture been fulfilled in your hearing.' There is no way we can be sure that the story actually happened, or whether it is one of Luke's inspired reconstructions.

At the very least we see in terms of which Spirit the early Church understood Jesus. This is not any old spirit which rests on Jesus, perhaps the spirit of the 'life divine', or a spirit of ecstasy. It is the Spirit of Jubilee, the Spirit of the God who makes all things new, who fulfils the messianic promises, who has good news for the poor at his heart.

The birth stories of Matthew and Luke, where 'Spirit' likewise figures prominently, must be understood in the same perspective. Matthew's announcement that Mary was 'found to be with child of the Holy Spirit' follows immediately on the genealogy, where Mary has been put in line with Tamar, Rahab, Bathsheba and Ruth. The point of this list may be that these were all Gentiles, and therefore that Gentiles are included in the promises. But Mary is no Gentile and in that case she is odd woman out. It seems more likely therefore that we are supposed to know the stories of these ladies, none of which were too genteel, and that Mary's strange pregnancy should be understood in the context of the grace of God which works precisely through such people, contrary to every human expectation. In Luke, on the other hand, the Holy Spirit who 'overshadows' Mary, in an even clearer allusion to the creation story than in Matthew, is also the Spirit coursing through Zechariah, Elizabeth, and Simeon, not a 'pietist Spirit' (Fison) but a Spirit of exultation in the new age of salvation which is dawning when, as Mary herself says, the mighty will be put down and the lowly exalted.

The saying about blasphemy against the Spirit which is found in all three synoptic gospels is usually understood to refer to the deliberate calling of good, evil. Here too, however, we should read the story in a wider messianic context. When messengers come from the Baptist to ask Jesus whether he is really Messiah, he refers them to the messianic signs promised in Isaiah (Matt. 11:2ff.). The Messiah has come and is announcing himself in ways which ought to be clear to those who read Israel's Scriptures. When these signs are ascribed to the power of the devil, Jesus remarks that in rejecting God's new order it is God's Spirit which is rejected and blasphemed, for it is his Spirit which – as in both birth and baptism stories – ushers in the new age (Mark 3:29–30).

From the 'Q'/Wisdom source comes the tradition according to which Jesus thanks the Father, according to Luke 'in the Holy

Spirit', that 'these things' – the good news of the kingdom – have been hidden from the wise and understanding and been revealed instead to the *nēpioi*, the unlettered and ignorant ones. In exegeting this pericope attention has always tended to focus on the question of Jesus' self consciousness, but the point of the story seems much more to be that here a very distinctive knowledge of the Father is announced, which is good news for the non-person and for those groaning under burdens. Given the echo of the description of Wisdom here, we can scarcely fail to think of Paul's description of the dialectics of divine wisdom in the letter to Corinth, where he likewise thanks God for a community which consists mainly of those of humble status (1 Cor 1:26ff.). Again we see in this pericope both the connection of the Spirit with the transvaluation of values which comes with Jesus, and with his radically different pattern of messiahship.

The Spirit is only mentioned on two other occasions in the synoptic tradition. It is promised to the community in time of persecution, so that it will empower them to witness 'before governors and kings' (Mark 13:11; Matt. 10:20). Again we think of the Spirit-inspired – and politically dangerous – confession, 'Jesus is Lord,' in Paul. Both Matthew and Luke close their gospels with a reference to the Spirit (which Luke refers to as 'power from on high'). In understanding Matthew's 'great commission' to baptise and preach the gospel 'in the name of the Father and of the Son and of the Holy Spirit' it is important not to become suddenly a-historical and read fourth-century doctrine into the first century (assuming the text is original). The reference to Spirit here must be read in the context of the first, eleventh and twelfth chapters of Matthew which make quite clear what Spirit it is we are dealing with. What is commanded here is essentially the messianic mission to the nations of Isaiah 42, and it is the messianic Spirit which inspires it.

Radical form criticism assumes that the gospels are the creation of the post-Easter community, which faces us with a problem. The density of reference to Spirit in Paul especially, but also in John, must reflect a massive fact of experience. If the gospels were a *free* creation of the community one would expect to hear more about this crucial fact. But the Spirit is mentioned as little as it is because it is part and parcel of the gospel of the kingdom, the announcement of God's subversion of the powers from below, of justice for the nations and good news for the poor. Jesus and Paul shared this same gospel, but Jesus preached it in terms of 'the kingdom', a fact which our documents preserve for us, and Paul in terms of 'the Spirit'. At the same time the Spirit in the synoptic gospels is never a spirit of piety and moral conformism but, as is clear from both Mary and Jesus' 'cry of joy' (Luke 1:46ff., 10:21ff.), the Spirit of the overturning of the established order, in which the last come first. It is this Spirit which, beginning with Mary and Zechariah, and then from Jesus, once more courses through Israel, from the one to the many, the Spirit of the messianic announcement.

'SPIRIT' IN ACTS

Luke's second volume is often taken as a demonstration of Loisy's thesis that Jesus preached the kingdom, but what came was the church. In particular it is suggested that the gospel of the kingdom is replaced by a gospel of individual sin and forgiveness. These suggestions are not encouraged by Luke's treatment of the theme of Spirit, and that for two reasons. In the first place the story of Pentecost undoubtedly occupies the central place in everything that Luke says on the subject in his volume two. Consistently with the Nazareth proclamation, Luke understands this event in terms of the prophecy of Joel when the dream of Numbers 11 is realised, and when those for ever denied a voice (even maidservants!) 'prophesy'. This outpouring begins the realisation of the new age – what Luke tells us in the list of nations who understood what was said, is his version of what Paul puts more compactly in Galatians 3. From this moment the scattering and confounding of the nations which began at Babel is reversed and the new humanity, where there is no distinction, is inaugurated. Further, the outpouring has concrete results in terms which had been dreamed of in Torah. Deuteronomy had envisaged that in the Jubilee year all would open their hand to the poor brother so that 'there will be no poor among you' (Deut. 15:4). Luke echoes this as he tells us that the Jubilee sharing of the community of the Spirit meant that 'there was not a needy person among them'. The story of Pentecost must not then be understood primarily as a story of religious ecstasy and of the empowering of Christian witness, though it is doubtless also both those things. Rather, the fundamental continuity with the gospel is maintained: it is the messianic Spirit which empowers the community and the new humanity which begins to emerge.

In the second place the thesis of 'early Catholicism' is discredited by Stephen Smalley's demonstration that in Acts the ideas of Spirit, kingdom and prayer regularly go together.[1] Thus, prior to Pentecost, the risen Lord speaks with the disciples concerning the kingdom, and they ask whether at this time the kingdom will be restored to Israel; the answer to this is that, whilst it is not for them to know times or seasons, the Holy Spirit will come upon them. This occurs after a time spent devoting themselves to prayer (Acts 1:1–24). This same threefold pattern can be discerned in the account of the early community (4:24–31), of the appointment of the Seven (6:2–6), of the Hellenist mission (8:12–24) and in Paul's farewell at Ephesus (20:22–36). Smalley therefore discerns a threefold structure in Luke's thought at this point: for Luke, God guides the course of redemptive history through prayer. Prayer is 'the means by which the dynamic power of God's Spirit is historically realised for the purposes of salvation' (or, as we could also say, it is an instrument of the divine pedagogy). But God's principal answer to prayer is the gift of the Spirit (Luke 11:13). At the same time the concepts of Spirit and kingdom are extremely closely interlinked: 'The rule of God is brought in and exercised by the Spirit of God through both the incarnate and the exalted Christ. In terms of the present/future tension in the idea of the kingdom, the presence of the Spirit is the *already* of the kingdom.' This confirms the point that the idea of Spirit in Acts is consistent with that of Luke 4:18ff., that it is the messianic Spirit with which we are dealing.

The book ends with Paul speaking 'night and day' about the kingdom of God and trying to convince the Jews about Jesus, 'both from the law of Moses and from the prophets' (Acts 28:23). Against this background, the message of the kingdom, and the dawning of the new age in the experience of the Spirit cannot possibly be reduced to a 'purely spiritual' forgiveness. The new thing is that 'this Jesus whom you crucified' is the fulfilment of God's promises, announcing a complete revaluation of ideas of those who constitute the community through which God works, and of priorities in this community which is bound to issue in the kind of results seen in the first community in Jerusalem.

'SPIRIT' IN THE PAULINE LETTERS

The letters of Paul have been used as quarries for doctrine for so many centuries that it is difficult to get back past doctrinal formulations, for instance on the Church or sanctification, to recover the freshness of Paul's thought, the sparks flying as the new 'stone' of Christ is dashed against the enduring stone of the law. As with the Old Testament books the best way to do this is to set them as far as possible in their context. Whilst Paul refers to the Spirit in all of his letters the most important discussions are to be found in the letters to Corinth, Galatia and Rome.

We know more about the Corinthian congregation than any other of Paul's congregations, and Walter Hollenweger has used this to present a vivid narrative reconstruction of the letter.[2] Corinth had been destroyed by the Romans and then rebuilt, and was therefore a 'new town'. It was a busy port and notorious around the Mediterranean for its red light area. We know that the small church there consisted of both Jews and Gentiles, and included some people of substance such as Erastus, the city treasurer (Rom. 16:23). On the other hand it included a majority of poor people, perhaps those Paul refers to as 'Chloe's people', and these two groups had many antagonisms. When the congregation assembled for the supper of the Lord the wealthy had already been taking their ease for some time, perhaps enjoying a glass of wine. Chloe's people turned up hungry after work, with their lunch packets containing food guaranteed to offend traditional Jewish susceptibilities, and proceeded to eat greedily. Whilst the wealthy group found this intolerable the other group made accusations of drunkenness (1 Cor. 11:21). The poor group evidently shared some of the life-style of pagan Corinth: the women wore their hair down, and men and women from this group spoke noisily in tongues at assemblies, consciously or unconsciously registering their presence in the midst of their educated 'betters'. The upper group find this freedom to be chaos, and furthermore level serious charges of immorality against the lower-class group. The latter meanwhile complain of being 'humiliated'.

In this context Paul spoke of the Spirit. Whilst the strict Pharisee who remains in Paul cannot abide immorality, and whilst he stays in the house of Gaius, one of the wealthy members (Rom. 16:23), Paul has some surprising things to say.

Right at the beginning of the correspondence Paul makes clear what he means when he speaks of Spirit. The Spirit searches the 'deep things of God' and, taught by the Spirit, Paul 'interprets spiritual truths to those who possess the Spirit' (1 Cor. 2:13). Paul contrasts the 'spiritual' with the 'unspiritual' or 'natural' (*psychikos*) man. The distinction refers back to the discussion of God's wisdom and power in the cross, and cuts across both groups in the congregation. The natural or unspiritual person is not just someone who is immoral but anyone who trusts in worldly ideas of power and wisdom. The Spirit on the other hand is the Spirit of God's folly and weakness, which are the 'depths' of God revealed only through the Spirit and impossible of perception by the worldly wise (1 Cor. 1:18ff.). Paul draws a direct connection between this nature of God revealed by the Spirit and the nature of the community the Spirit creates, which consists largely of the unlettered, the weak, the non-influential, the low and despised, through whom Paul sees God working 'to bring to nothing things that are' (1 Cor. 1:26ff.). This identification of the work of God with the calling of the illiterate, ill-mannered and none-too-savoury members from the Corinth dock area must have been a matter for much uncomfortable reflection for Gaius, Erastus and their set. Against this background we appreciate the revolutionary significance of the remark that 'by one Spirit we were all baptised into one body – Jews or Greeks, slaves or free – and all were made to drink of one Spirit' (1 Cor. 12:13). The Spirit is, as the seventeenth-century Puritans said, a great leveller. Paul does not advocate a programme for the release of Christian slaves, because in his view this would not reflect the radical nature of redemption in Christ. That radical nature is seen more in the fact that Gaius's people and Chloe's people, free men and slaves, Jews and Greeks, are 'one body' in the Spirit of the crucified. If the rich come into the movement of Messiah Jesus they stand in line with one who 'took the form of a slave', and so they cannot refuse solidarity with the slaves around them. 'Do you despise the church of God and humiliate those who have nothing?' Paul asks the rich and literate members of the congregation, who will probably read the letter to the whole gathering (1 Cor. 11:22). Paul does not advocate a class war, but, reflecting on the wisdom of the cross, sees in the Church a solidarity in the Spirit which in the assembly eliminates the deepest divisions of the Roman world, between slave and free, a solidarity which must have dangerous consequences for the powerful and the 'things that are', and which is the 'first fruit' or 'advance token' of God's new world where such distinctions are no more but God is all in all. No more than Jesus was Paul interested in a Zealot revolution, in a rising of slaves. But in a world built on slavery, whose navy and merchant marine depended on slaves for the galleys and whose big estates were worked by slaves, Paul's identification of the working of God in history above all with the illiterate group at Corinth was a deeply subversive statement, serving notice, as he said, on the powers (Col. 2:15).

Whilst Paul therefore saw a fundamental significance in the calling of the non-persons of Corinth, he otherwise laid about him evenhandedly between the complaints of the two groups. As far as Gaius and Erastus were concerned the free manner of Chloe's people, and especially the women, who were very brazen compared with their own quiet and retiring wives and daughters, amounted to licence, and they could point to specific instances of immorality. In the name of the Spirit of holiness Paul utterly repudiated such behaviour. What if they did come from the Corinth slums? They were not supposed to behave like everyone else, because we learn from Christ that the body is the temple of the Spirit: 'You are not your own; you were bought with a price' – words which slaves would understand only too well (1 Cor. 6:19–20). On the other hand, Chloe's people felt that they were being met with a rigid moralism which condemned them, and Paul was severe on that also. He points out that 'the letter', hectoring in the name of a strict morality, or homilies by the moral minority on what the new religion meant, 'kills' (2 Cor. 3:6). Moralising is no use. It constitutes a kind of veil between human beings and God, screening God's truly gracious purposes. The new religion is not letter but Spirit, and the Spirit removes the veil so that 'where the Spirit of the Lord is, there is liberty' – another difficult morsel for Gaius and his friends (2 Cor. 3:17). In both letters Paul is at pains to emphasise what this freedom amounts to. It does not mean licence, but nor does it mean confusion: 'God is not a God of confusion but of peace' (1 Cor. 14:33). It means respecting the gifts of each, so that in all manifestations of the Spirit they should 'strive to excel in building up the ecclesia', which is not identical with the Church as we have come to know it but the community springing from the 'new Adam', the first fruits of the new humanity (1 Cor. 14:12). The climax of Paul's description of how the gifts of the one body complement each other is his impassioned description of the real nature of love, which challenges both groups in Corinth: not boastful, or arrogant or irritable like the Gaius group, nor jealous or rude or resentful like the Chloe group, but bearing, believing, hoping and enduring all things (1 Cor. 13:7). In this experience of the new community, quite different from anything else to be experienced in Corinth, those who assemble for the supper of the Lord experienced life in the Spirit as a down-payment (*arrabōn*) of Christ's future (2 Cor. 1:22).

When we turn to Galatians we again meet a divided community, but as far as we can discern from this correspondence the problem is much more that a group of Jewish Christians with whom, by training and upbringing, Paul would most naturally associate himself, are treating Christianity as a kind of reformed Judaism and insisting on circumcision, keeping special feasts, and reverence for angels. At the heart of Paul's rejection of this view is Jesus' conflict with the Pharisees as we have this in the synoptic gospels. Jesus welcomes and accepts outcasts and sinners and in that way changes their situation, vindicating the righteousness of God, renewing people, fulfilling the Spirit of the law against a legalistic reading of the letter. To treat Torah legalistically is to make it a burden, according to Jesus (Matt. 23:4), and for Paul it is to make men slaves – here again it is very likely that some at least of the recipients of the letter were slaves themselves. The Spirit of the Son, on the other hand, teaches people to pray the Jesus prayer, 'Abba' Father, and makes them not slaves but sons. Again, the radical conclusions Paul draws from 'the one baptism' are truly astonishing in their context: 'As many of you as were baptised have put on Christ. There is neither Jew nor Greek, there is neither slave nor free, there is neither male nor female; for you are all one in Christ Jesus' (Gal. 3:28).

In the new community the deepest and most immovable divisions of the Roman empire are overcome – not only slavery this time but patriarchy! It must again be stressed that Paul does not make these statements as a social revolutionary. Had he challenged the Roman empire in the name of the principle of equality or of human rights he would occupy but a small page in the history books. But he went here and there establishing small communities in which he proclaimed that in the unity of the messianic Spirit neither slaves nor free, nor even male or female existed any more, and this went further than any manifesto. In Corinth we see the limitations of Paul's principle that there was 'no male or female': the combination of his inherited prejudices and the situation at Corinth where sacred prostitution was rife leads him to some fairly patriarchal pronouncements. But this did not dim his perception of the new creation, the new humanity begun through the Messiah. Just as Jesus himself had treated women on a par with men, Paul saw that 'in Christ' no distinction could be made. As in the Corinthian correspondence, Paul is led to a description of behaviour in the new society, behaviour 'led by the Spirit'. On the one hand there are works of the flesh, which include not only licentiousness and drunkenness but 'strife, jealousy, dissension, party spirit'. The 'fruit of the Spirit' on the other hand is 'love, joy, peace, patience, kindness, goodness, faithfulness, gentleness, self control,' the mark of humanity in the new age (Gal. 5:22).

Scholars have differed in understanding Romans as a letter written primarily to Jews or primarily to Gentiles, and many have taken it as a 'general letter' lacking a specific context. But it would be very surprising if the ecclesia in the chief city of the empire consisted exclusively either of Jews or Gentiles, and the discussion makes plain that tension between the two groups, especially over food habits, is found also in Rome (cf. Rom. 14). In this connection Paul warns that 'the kingdom of God is not food and drink but righteousness and peace and joy in the Holy Spirit', where the connection of righteousness and peace made by prophet and psalmist (Ps. 85:10; Isa. 32:15–16; Mal. 2:6) must surely be in the background. Throughout the letter Paul writes with the Scriptures of Israel uppermost in his mind. Therefore, when he talks of righteousness and peace in the Holy Spirit, it is not in the least unlikely that he has the promise of Isaiah in mind, that the Spirit will be poured down so that

justice will dwell in the wilderness,
and righteousness abide in the fruitful field.
And the effect of righteousness will be peace,
and the result of righteousness quietness and trust for ever.
(Isa. 32:15–16)

In any event the Spirit in this letter is very much the Spirit of hope for God's future: 'May the God of hope fill you with all joy and peace in believing, so that by the power of the Holy Spirit you may abound in hope,' says Paul winding up his argument (Rom. 15:13).

This theme he expands at length earlier in the letter. Christians, he says, have the 'first fruits' (*aparche*) of the Spirit (8.23). This means to be under the law of the Spirit of life, rather than under the law of sin and the flesh, where 'flesh' means every attempt to live without God, especially the attempt in the name of grace to live without grace, religion. Self-justifying life like this is bound to be destructive, according to Paul, because it means either a godless disregard of the truly human which we see in Christ, or it condemns us to forever acting as the judge of others. Because in Christ there is a 'new Adam', the beginning of a newly restored humanity, the vision of what human beings ought to be in sonship and freedom and openness to God, and because the Judge is judged in our place, we are freed from this wretched alternative. But what is experienced now is only the first fruits of freedom, freedom to hope. The Spirit of God or of Christ (Paul speaks of both in the same breath in Romans 8:9) does not make us quiescent and satisfied with the way things are, but makes us 'groan inwardly', intercedes within us 'with sighs too deep for tears' for the promised future for the whole creation. It gives us courage for the toil of overcoming evil with good through revolutionary patience and solidarity with the lowly (12:12, 16). In this Spirit of hope Paul can urge submission to the authorities, confronting the weakness of power with the power of weakness and rejecting both the 'self-justifying legitimacy that ends in the tyranny of order and a self-justifying rebellion that ends in the tyranny of anarchy'.[3] Beyond both of these is the debt to the neighbour by which the State is itself judged and which is fulfilled in the 'kingdom of God', the situation where God's will as expressed in Torah and in Jesus is concretely recognised (Rom. 13:8, 14:15ff.). The Spirit is what realises the first fruits of that new situation amongst men and women, a realisation which is a token for the whole of creation.

The topic of Spirit in Paul is usually discussed under such headings as 'Sanctification', 'Flesh versus Spirit', 'The Spirit of Unity' and so on. Such a treatment can be illuminating in its own way, but it often fails to root Paul's theology of Spirit clearly enough where it belongs – in his reflection on what God is doing in the crucifixion of Jesus. The fact that in Christ God took the form of a slave and died the death of a slave was revolutionary in a world built on slavery and for a community which included slaves among its numbers. When Paul talks about Spirit, he speaks of the Spirit of this God and this Messiah. When he talks about the first fruits or earnest of the Spirit, he is talking of God's initiating his messianic rule in a way unacceptable alike to strict Jews or educated Greeks. Paul's gospel is that God has begun the new creation, and if you want to see it you can – in the new community where slaves must not be humiliated and indeed where slavery ceases to count. Everything that is said about holiness and unity and countering the flesh is said from this standpoint. The uncomfortableness of this message, its scandal, has often been evaded by turning Paul into a theologian concerned mainly about concepts, or a revivalist preacher announcing an act of God comfortably over the heads of human beings and evoking nothing but a new moralism. Paul's vision is much broader: nothing less than a new creation, and the emergence of that situation which he, like Jesus, calls the kingdom, where human beings can be and remain human.

JOHN

There is no scholarly consensus about the historical context of John's gospel. Syria has long been accepted as a possible alternative to Ephesus, and recently Klaus Wengst has made a strong case for putting John in the kingdom of the second Agrippa in Transjordan, somewhere between AD 80 and 90, around the time of the consolidation of Judaism at Jamnia, and in dialogue with that movement.[4] This suggestion also illuminates the references to Spirit in the gospel.

The dialogue with Nicodemus (John 3:1–21) follows the first of

Jesus' 'signs' at Cana, and the demand of 'the Jews' for a sign to validate his authority after the cleansing of the Temple. The Pharisee Nicodemus comes to Jesus and refers to the signs which show that 'God is with' Jesus. Jesus at once starts talking of the kingdom of God, and when Nicodemus is perplexed refers him unequivocally to the tradition of Israel which he is supposed to know. Jesus' kingship, and therefore the kingdom of God, is to be realised through the crucifixion (John 3:14). His kingdom is therefore 'not according to the standards of this world' (John 18:36). The context of this discussion could well be dialogue with that pharisaic group which still, after the destruction of the Jerusalem temple, looked for an earthly kingdom and which later supported the Bar Kochba uprising. In a dialogue dense with 'Old Testament' allusions Jesus refers to the need of birth of 'water and the Spirit' to enter the kingdom of God, which also recalls the synoptic demand that people must become 'as children' to enter the kingdom. The whole dialogue turns on God's strange work in saving human beings through the cross and on the judgement and salvation which comes through that event. It is the Spirit alone, according to John, which can enable a person to see God at work here. The discussion is therefore very close to the understanding of Spirit in 1 Corinthians, chapter 2, which likewise proceeds from the crucified Christ. Birth 'from above' or 'anew' (*kat'anothen*) is the perception of God's working 'from below', a birth which is a new creation and which cannot therefore be guaranteed by any amount of study of Torah.

Another correspondence with Pauline thought is to be seen in the dialogue with the Samaritan woman (John 4:4–42). Paul refers to a situation, already in the process of realisation, where there will be no Jew and no Greek, no male and no female. Here these divisions are overcome in Jesus' discussion with a woman who is a Samaritan, and Jesus looks to the time when all who worship God will do so 'in spirit and in truth'. The statement that 'God is Spirit' is not to be understood as a metaphysical statement, but in the context of what immediately follows. The woman says, 'I know that Messiah is coming' – she understands the reference to Spirit quite specifically as the Spirit which will empower the Messiah, as prophesied by Isaiah, and therefore worship in spirit and in truth will be worship in the messianic age of peace and justice. Jesus accepts what the woman says as the correct interpretation of his words: 'I who speak to you am he' (v. 26). God will be worshipped neither in Samaria nor Jerusalem because the Messiah on whom the Spirit rests will bring forth justice to 'the nations', 'and the coastlands wait for his law' (Isa. 42:4). Against those who have withdrawn and who draw the boundary around Israel ever tighter, John asserts that in Jesus the messianic age has dawned, and the Spirit of that age breaks down not only narrow boundaries of race but even fundamental distinctions between male and female.

The saying of John 7:38–9 should be understood in the light of these two dialogues. Jesus refers to 'the Scripture', 'out of his heart shall flow rivers of living water,' which John tells us referred to the Spirit. But which Scripture is Jesus referring to? Zechariah (14:8) spoke of living waters flowing from Jerusalem, but the reference seems more likely to be to a series of Isaianic texts. Thus the second Isaiah spoke of a time when God would

> pour water on the thirsty land,
> and streams on the dry ground;
> I will pour out my Spirit upon your descendants,
> and my blessing on your offspring.

a promise which ends with the Gentiles taking the name Jacob-Israel to themselves (Isa. 44:3ff.). A later prophet in the same tradition promised that

> If you take away from the midst of you the yoke,
> the pointing of the finger, and speaking wickedness,
> if you pour yourself out for the hungry
> and satisfy the desire of the afflicted, then . . .
> you shall be like a watered garden,
> like a spring of water.
> whose waters fail not. (Isa. 58:9–11)

When Jesus spoke of rivers of living waters flowing from the believer he was speaking of the Spirit, says John. Later he tells us that 'The Spirit had not yet been given, because Jesus was not yet glorified' (7:39). The Spirit proceeds from the cross where God's glory and attractive power are manifested. Only through the cross will Jesus draw all people to himself (John 12:32). Only after this event is the messianic age truly inaugurated. The living waters which flow from the believer are the waters of the messianic age, waters which bring life because they spring from the crucified Messiah, powerful in weakness, poured out in a life which, like the life of Jesus himself, is given for the hungry and afflicted. Only life like this is 'a spring of water whose waters fail not'.

For John there is no doubt whatever that there is a task for the disciples in the future: 'He who believes in me will also do the works that I do; and greater works than these will he do, because I go to the Father' (John 14:12). What enables these works is the Paraclete, the Spirit of the truth which is Jesus, the crucified Messiah. This truth, as Paul found in his work, 'the world cannot receive' because it is folly to Greeks and a stumbling block to Jews. Nevertheless it is only when this truth indwells the community that it can do 'greater works' than Christ. It is the work of the Paraclete – in the strict sense a pedagogical work – to enable the community to understand and enter into the work of God in Christ (14:26, another similarity with 1 Cor. 2). Naturally the peace which follows this gift is 'not as the world gives', the peace of compromise with the *status quo*, of turning a blind eye to evil, of flight into religious realities away from the raw facts of political torture and execution. Like everything else that comes from Jesus the peace he gives comes only through the cross, and it is this that the Spirit witnesses to (John 15:26).

In the dialogue with Nicodemus Jesus refers to 'the judgement, that the light has come into the world, and men loved darkness rather than light because their deeds were evil' (John 3:19). The theme of judgement is taken up again when the Greeks come to see Jesus, when it is referred to the crucifixion, and again in the Paraclete sayings. The Paraclete, says John, will convince, convict or expose (*elenchein*) the world in respect to sin, righteousness and judgement (16:8). The passage is a notorious *crux interpretum*, but it is clear that the conviction or exposure must be understood in relation to the earlier passages where it is the crucified Messiah who brings the world to judgement. In Ephesians the author uses the same verb to speak of the exposure of the works of darkness (Eph. 5:11, 13), and in Colossians it is the public exposure of the powers which is the means of Christ's triumph (Col. 2:15). It is quite possible therefore that John intends both senses, convict and expose, to be understood here. The Spirit of the Crucified judges 'the ruler of this world' by exposing the weakness of power; he convicts men of sin because they insist on relying only on these power structures and refuse to trust in the power of weakness, which is at the same time the righteousness of God, the way in which he keeps faith with his creation by bringing salvation. It is deeper into the mystery of the divine powerlessness, of the truth and help available there, that the Spirit guides the disciples (John 16:13). And it is this Spirit which both abides in Jesus (John 1:32) and which Jesus bestows on the disciples (John 20:22).

The author of the gospel of John is an ironist and dialectician whose meaning is always complex and many-layered and cannot be reduced to simple formulae. Nevertheless, throughout the gospel runs the theme of the redemption and judgement brought through the crucified Messiah. John is in debate with a humiliated and defeated people who are not cowed by their defeat but still dreaming of a kingdom which will end the domination of Rome. In this context John insists that the Messiah has already come, bringing a kingdom based on a refusal of 'the power of this world', of coercion and techniques of persuasion, moral and physical brute force. He writes from the perspective of the new age of the Spirit, the advocate of the crucified Lord, the Comforter and Counsellor of the community. Criteria for discerning this Spirit are twofold: one is confession of 'Jesus Messiah come in the flesh' (1 John 4:2) with which we can compare Paul's confession (likewise inspired by the Spirit) that 'Jesus is Lord' (1 Cor. 12:3). What is important in these confessions is not the confession as such but that the *crucified* is Lord and Messiah – it is the impossibility of *this* confession which makes it possible only through the Spirit. The second criterion is that only 'he who loves is born of God and knows God' (cf. 1 John 4:7; cf. John 3:7). As in Paul the gifts of the Spirit are given for a unity in love, so in John Jesus' prayer for the community which receives the Paraclete is that 'they may become perfectly one . . . that the love with which you have loved me may be in them and I in them' (John 17:23, 26). The work of the Spirit is for both Paul and John the creation of a new type of community based on the new values and priorities, which derive from the crucified Jesus.

THE MEANING OF LANGUAGE ABOUT SPIRIT

The biblical witness which speaks of that reality which we designate 'Spirit' covers a span of more than one thousand years, a time of great changes socially, politically and economically, and also in Israel's understanding of God. All the same, there are certain constants in the experience which compel people to speak of 'Spirit'. In the first place, language about Spirit witnesses to the fact that *history cannot be reduced to the history of men and women.* Encountered in the lives of men and women is an Other, what Schweizer calls 'the Stranger'.[5] There is an aspect of experience which cannot be reduced to the psychological or the sociological, something qualitatively different. This strange aspect was recognised equally in the possession of the Judges, in the critique of the prophets, and in the life, death and resurrection of Jesus. All these were human realities, but human realities shaped by and responding to a power beyond them. Spirit language is then, in the second place, the recognition that the Other, the Stranger whom we call 'God', *makes history through men and women.* 'Spirit' speaks of God's presence to and within historical process, but a presence only discerned through action like that of the Judges, analysis and warning like that of the prophets, and through a life lived for the outcast like that of Jesus. To speak of Spirit is to refuse not only an absolute separation of God and creature, but also an absolute identity. God remains God and the human remains human, but God accomplishes his purpose only through his presence and promise to men and women. Thus to speak of Spirit is also to speak of a *specific directedness to human history.* From Judges to Paul the Spirit is always discerned to bring freedom. God makes history, but not history in general with all its slavery and oppression, as though history in itself might be revelation, but he gives a direction to history. To speak of the Spirit is to speak of *the openness of history,* to deny that it is controlled by iron laws, and to assert that its future may be infinitely better than the present. Within history God is the Creator of hope, the source of all generous visions, of all human openness. He inspires dreams of 'justice', 'peace', 'love', 'fellowship', dreams of a society where the rule of God will be realised. 'Spirit' language speaks of God revealing himself as merciful, gracious, longsuffering and loving, and this revelation, grasped little by little and set down in this situation and in that, inspires hope for human behaviour which is likewise compassionate and loving. For Paul and John 'Spirit' is discerned especially in Jesus of Nazareth, the man whose humanity is sustained by his faith and prayer, and who has hope even for such unlikely characters as Zacchaeus. Jesus is 'bearer and bestower of the Spirit' as he is 'the man for God and man for others'. What the birth stories seek to tell us is that he who is most totally shaped by the Spirit is he who is most truly human. This establishes criteria for talk of the Spirit. Where is the Spirit to be found? Both Paul and John answer without hesitation – in what humanises, what makes for life, for the establishment of truth in community, for mutuality, for shared responsibility, for freedom. The Spirit who inspires and creates behaviour and situations which are really human is not limited to Israel or Church, but in that tradition, sacramentally for all human traditions, the true trend and direction of the Spirit is discerned. God works for the freedom and openness of all, for the situation 'where all may be fully human because all are fully human', not through the exercise of totalitarian power, no matter how subtle, but through the power of weakness, through the cross. In the power of this Spirit God shapes the open future. To speak of the quality of this work of God Paul coined a new word – grace.

THE HANDS OF GOD

At the beginning of chapter 3, God's engagement with human history was said to have a twofold shape, which Christians speak of in terms of Christ and Spirit. Since the meaning of the word 'Spirit' may not be taken for granted, it has been necessary to review the witness of Scripture to this aspect of God's reality. The question may now be asked as to the relation of this twofold engagement. The problem may be stated as follows: If God's work as Spirit is a work of genuine involvement, what need is there of incarnation? What does the incarnation add to this already creative and redemptive work? On the other hand, if it needs incarnation to give real depth to God's involvement how are we to understand his work as Spirit? Does it imply that as Spirit God is not truly engaged? The first question leads to the relativising of what happened in the incarnation, the assimilation of the 'Christ event' to many other marvellous and profound human stories. In this way Christ easily becomes but one prophet, avatar, teacher or guru amongst many. The second leads to allegations of arrogance on the part of the Church and of underestimating God's work in other religions and cultures. The problem is not academic but is one of the major issues wherever Christians meet members of other religions in a situation of dialogue. Can it be resolved? What is the relation of the work of God in Christ and his work as Spirit? The question of God's work in other religions will be considered in chapter 9; here the question of the relationship of God's twofold engagement falls for consideration. And just as, to understand the role of the incarnation in the divine education, recourse was had to the fundamental patristic concept of the *homoousion*, so here we turn to another patristic concept, that of the divine 'economy'.

Irenaeus – incidentally, like Paul, a missionary theologian, preaching Sunday by Sunday in Celtic and sighing for his Greek mother-tongue – for whom 'economy' was a favourite term, liked to speak of Christ and the Spirit as the two 'hands' of God; both co-operated in creation (for it was to his 'hands' that God said, 'Let us make man in our image and likeness') but otherwise fulfilled different functions in the long process of the redemption of the human race. Irenaeus states this in many variations on the following formula: 'The Spirit prepares man for the Son of God; the Son leads man to the Father; the Father gives man immortality . . . The Spirit works, the Son fulfils his ministry, the Father approves' (*A.H.* 4:20.4, 6). Or again, 'The Father decides and commands; the Son carries out the Father's plan; the Spirit supports and hastens the process' (4.38.3).

The question of why God chooses to work in this way through his two 'hands' is not of course a question of necessity but a question of what God saw to be 'fitting', as Athanasius puts it. Because God saw this twofold redeeming work to be fitting, no independent redemption can be ascribed to either Son or Spirit but both must always be understood together – not the Son without the Spirit, as seems to be the implication of atonement theologies which centre exclusively on the cross, nor the Spirit without the Son, as seems to be often the case today with those who wish to start from the 'experience of God' in other religions. The profound mutuality of this work was nowhere stated more clearly than by John at the very beginning of the Christian tradition. 'All that the Father has is mine,' says Jesus in that gospel, 'therefore I said that he [the Spirit] will take what is mine and declare it to you' (John 16:15). To grasp this relationship we might borrow a term from Hosea and say that the work of the Spirit is the wooing of the human race, preparation for the Bridegroom, education in the art of loving. Both forms of the work of God share the same nature and direction.

Fundamental to our conception of the divine economy is what was called in chapter 1 the elusiveness of God's presence. The immediate presence of God means compulsion – it is incompatible with education. Hence Christ comes 'in the form of a slave', in humility and obscurity. In this act of humble solidarity we have found the ground of human hope, and in this way the incarnation stands at the heart of the divine education. The function of the Spirit is different, but this form of God's presence must also be understood to be elusive – resistant to royal or ecclesiastical ideologies and pretentious claims to work 'for' others rather than alongside them in solidarity.

This direction of God's work in solidarity is established once for all in the incarnation. Irenaeus understands the work of the Spirit as preparatory to and supportive of the incarnation. What this means, as we see it in the pages of the biblical record, is that God's Spirit woos, inspires and elicits men and women towards freedom, co-operation, righteousness and rest, towards the establishment of a human solidarity which could be described as 'in Christ', rather than 'in Adam' which is the mutual 'binding' of fear and distrust, solidarity in the Cold War and determination to keep the Third World as debtors rather than acknowledge them as partners. This is a work of education, and education has a goal – which is Christ and his kingdom. The two hands of God are not therefore 'uncoordinated', as if the left hand did not know what the right was doing; neither is it the case that the one might lack depth and other purpose, which would imply that God was not truly to be encountered in either one or the other. It is a question of economy, of fulfilling different though deeply related functions in bringing human beings to redemption. As Irenaeus puts it, writing out of his experience in Gaul, 'The Father supports Creation and his Word; the Word, supported by the Father, bestows the Spirit on all, as the Father wishes' (*A.H.* 5.18.2). The Spirit of Christ is bestowed on all – on Irenaeus' pagan Gauls, and today's Marxists, Hindus, Muslims, Buddhists and animists – and woos all to the measure, stature and image of Christ.

In the remainder of this book we turn to this economy of the Spirit – first to the question of the quality of the Spirit's work, and how it takes shape in history, which is the question of grace, and then to the role of sign, story and religion within this economy. Finally we ask about the role of the church in a history where God is to be found at work everywhere.

6

The History of Grace

Taking a hint from the Greek Fathers of the second and third centuries, and from Lessing, we are seeking to grasp what God is redemptively up to in human history through the image of a divine education. This involves a consideration of the related work of the two 'hands' of God, Christ and the Spirit. Having reviewed the scriptural witness to the Spirit's work we now turn to the crucial matter of the quality of that work, the stamp or brand mark of God's work in history which we call 'grace'. Beginning from the scriptural origins of the word we consider the relation of the concept of grace to that of education, and then follow the development of the 'mainstream' tradition from Augustine in order to contrast it with the account of grace in terms of attraction which emerges in Schleiermacher. Finally we ask about the way in which grace becomes history.

THE ORIGIN OF THE TERM 'GRACE'

It is from Paul that Christians have learned to use the word 'grace'. The use of *charis* (translated by Latin *gratia*, grace) in his letters is one of the clearest instances of what Barth called the *analogia fidei*. Barth maintained that the language we use of God is not based on an analogy of being, analogies from human fatherhood to Divine Fatherhood for instance, but suffers a divine take-over, a movement in which revelation commandeers language. Comparison of the use of *charis* before and after Paul, in the Septuagint for instance, on the one hand, and in the Apostolic Fathers on the other, illustrates how Paul wrenches the word out of its normal pattern of use and gives it a completely new content. Within two generations of Paul's death his understanding of grace had been lost, replaced by the old idea inherent in *charis* of a spiritual energy, 'a ghostly potency . . . not very different from the deifying *charis* of Greek mythology or the mystery religions'.[1] But a text is always there to resist its interpreters. Paul's understanding survived even the catastrophe of the Augustinian interpretation, surfaced in Luther, only to be submerged again, and then once again emerged in Schleiermacher and his disciples. For Paul 'grace' is the quality of the pedagogy of the Spirit, and history is interwoven with its signs. These we shall seek to understand in later chapters in terms of sacraments, story, and community.

With a pattern somewhat similar to the word 'Spirit', the word '*charis*' does not appear at all in Mark and Matthew, some twenty times in Luke-Acts, three times in John, but more than one hundred times in Paul! Paul was seeking a word which could express newness, freedom, initiative, mercy, love, righteousness, generosity, self-giving – all the things he found in Jesus. He turned not to one word only but to words like *dikaiosune* (righteousness or justification), *agape* (love) and *eleutheria* (freedom) as well. But characteristically he tries to sum up the way in which he is overwhelmed by the significance of Christ in the word 'grace'. In fixing on this word he was certainly influenced by the fact that the Seventy translators had regularly translated the Hebrew word *hen* and occasionally *hesed* by *charis*, though for the latter they preferred *eleos* (mercy) and *dikaiosune* – a significant fact in Paul's use of that word also. To these Hebrew words we must return. In secular Greek the word '*charis*' had overtones of charm, beauty, spiritual energy, or power. Paul took this word, kneaded it to its original clay and remoulded it. *Charis* in Paul's hands defies simple definition: it is a kind of impressionist rendering of Christ. 'You know the grace of our Lord Jesus Christ, that though he was rich, yet for your sake he became poor, so that by his poverty you might become rich' (2 Cor. 8:9). God's act in Christ, which is grace, is the nucleus around which the other meanings of the word revolve. Paul means by 'grace' the mode of God's initiative, in weakness (2 Cor. 12:9) and opposed to the wisdom of this world (2 Cor. 1:12). Grace is the power of God's love known in weakness and folly. It is the opposite of all strict reckoning of what is owing (Rom. 4:4), of the claim of good behaviour (Rom. 11:5–6), and therefore can be opposed to 'law', which is not Torah but a system based on merit and claim (Gal. 2:21, 5:4). It is the self-gifting of God which bears fruit in vocation and in specific gifts to do this or that in the believer (e.g. Rom. 1:5; 1 Cor. 1:4, 3:10; Rom. 12:3). Paul can talk of 'the reign of grace', which brings it into close relationship with the idea of the kingdom. It carries overtones of divine power, though what is meant by power is transvalued (1 Cor. 15:10). It can mean simply gladness (Col. 3:16), but always speaks of love in action (Rom. 6:1). Not the least remarkable aspect of Paul's usage is the constant use of the word in greeting and farewell: 'grace and peace' are for Paul the hallmark or quality of the new age ushered in by the Messiah. The bewildering variety of Paul's usage is irreducible, and this should warn us against trying too easily to define a 'concept' of grace – but undeniably everything focuses on the historical man, the Jew Jesus, crucified and risen, through whom God gives himself for the world.

To find out the cause for the new meaning poured into this old word we have to turn to the gospels. What Paul seeks to express in this one word is expressed in the Gospels in stories of healings, encounters with lepers, tax-gatherers and other outcasts, in the welcoming of children, in Jesus' serious discussions with women, in meals both large and small, and above all in Jesus' own stories illustrating God's love. These stories speak of the quality of mercy, as in the story of the Good Samaritan; they speak of God's initiative in seeking the lost, and of joy in heaven at finding them; they speak of great celebrations to which the outcast are bidden. Beyond this, Jesus' stories speak of grace because Jesus is not a puritan or a moralist. For him duty is not the 'stern daughter of the voice of God'. His parables are often mischievous, in the good sense. Jesus tells stories, about the unjust steward, or the wastrel son, or the 'churchwarden and the bookmaker' (Luke 18:9ff.), or the eleventh-hour labourers which are guaranteed to shock the moralistic of all ages. When Paul talked of a new order *kata charin* (according to grace) rather than *kata opheilema* (according to what is strictly due – Rom. 4:4) he is but summarising these stories. For Jesus God's love, which seeks the return to wholeness of all human beings, is subversive of all the ways by which human beings imagine they can 'bargain and huxter' with the Almighty. Jesus' stories tell of the mischievous, subversive, re-creative and joyful love of God. All of them assert in different ways that the Sabbath was made for man, exactly what Paul was getting at in his controversy with the legalists, though also in his discussions about the 'weak' and the 'strong' (Rom. 14:1ff.). The word 'grace' is not used in the gospels, because the reality of grace is seen and told in all these stories. It is Jesus' parables, and the stories of his encounters, which interpreted and made sense of his death and resurrection. Without them the event of resurrection would have been senseless and arbitrary. But then the resurrection retroactively interprets Jesus' death and life. Taken together, Christ's life and teaching and death and resurrection constitute one reality, 'grace', God's initiative for his threatened creation.

John uses the word *charis* in only three verses of his gospel, but in such a way as to sum up the Pauline meaning. It is the Word become flesh who is full of 'grace and truth' – in the man Jesus we see the depths of God's love and solidarity. If the story of Jesus is the reality of grace, then grace is a reality encountered in a human life, above all encountered in a human life given for others. But 'grace' always involves a 'plus', an abounding, a going beyond – expressed by Paul through his use of the intensive (Rom. 5:16–17) and by Jesus in a story like that of the Prodigal Son. For John the intensive of grace is indicated by 'glory'. In the man Jesus, who is the embodiment of the grace of God, we encounter glory – that which makes life rich and glorious, and not a dull or muddied affair. Grace is always fullness, and from the fullness of Christ human beings receive 'grace upon grace', gifts for the realisation of God's kingdom which are, in Jesus' words, 'pressed down, shaken together, running over'. As in Paul, this grace evoked by grace is opposed to law, to demand and reward, for the faithfulness of God, his truth to himself, goes beyond such considerations. But above all, as these verses at the climax of John's prologue make clear, grace is *God* encountered in the human historical act. It is the quality of God's presence to history.

John's phrase 'grace and truth' points us unmistakeably to the Hebrew words and stories which, as Luke tells us in the story of the walk to Emmaus, interpret Jesus (Luke 24:27). 'Grace and truth' echo the conjunction of Hebrew *hesed* and *emeth*. Paul's use of *charis* goes beyond the usage of the Septuagint but it represents, on the other hand, a unique concretisation and particularisation of a whole cluster of Hebrew words: *hen*, meaning gracious address to another, or favour; *hesed*, meaning loyalty, faithfulness, loving kindness; *emeth*, meaning truth or reliability; *tsedeq* and *tsedeqah*, meaning righteousness; and *raham*, meaning compassion. Paul is without doubt looking beyond the somewhat narrow use of *charis* in the Septuagint to this penumbra of words gathered round the covenant, the binding agreement between God and Israel. Through Paul all these words come to be considered under the one word *charis*, or grace. Every one of these words has a rich, concrete historical meaning – they are not in the least vague or abstract. Thus Jacob finds *hen* (favour) with the brother he had cheated in a meeting bound up in the closest possible way with his meeting with God; so 'grace' – God's self-giving to human beings, his encounter with us, his opening up of situations we close for ourselves – is mediated through human beings and historical situations (Gen. 33:8). Rahab shows *hesed* (kindness) to the spies and demands *emeth* (loyalty) in return (Josh. 2:12). *Hesed* is the quality of the love between David and Jonathan, which was 'wonderful, passing the love of women' (2 Sam. 1:26; 1 Sam. 20:8). For Jeremiah *tsedeq* and *tsedeqah* are equivalent to 'judging the cause of the poor and needy', and this is true knowledge of God (Jer. 22:15). For him the fearful thing about the Assyrian invaders is that they have no mercy (*racham*) (Jer. 6:23). All these words were applied to God: they describe his attitude to Israel, his love 'for better or for worse':

> For the mountains may depart
>   and the hills be removed,
> but my steadfast love [*hesed*] shall not depart from you
> and my covenant of peace shall not be removed.
> says the Lord, who has compassion [*racham*] on thee.
> (Isa. 54:10)

Yahweh's *hesed* demands Israel's loyalty. Hosea's basic complaint is that there is no truth (*emeth*) or mercy (*hesed*) in the land, but instead swearing, lying, killing, stealing – all the opposites of 'covenant' behaviour (Hos. 4:1). He looks forward to a new betrothal in *hesed* (in effect a new covenant) which will take fruit in behaviour marked by *hesed* (Hos. 2:19, 6:6, 10:12, 12:6). According to Jeremiah God practises *hesed* (justice and righteousness) 'in the earth' (Jer. 9:24). But he does so through his people (Jer. 7:5). This reflexive demand of Yahweh's *hesed* became known many centuries later as 'created grace'.

For the Old Testament writers this whole cluster of words becomes a fundamental character description of God. For example we read in Exodus 34:6: 'The Lord passed before his face and proclaimed, "The Lord, the Lord, a God merciful [*rachum*] and gracious [*chanun*], slow to anger, and abounding in steadfast love [*hesed*] and faithfulness [*emeth*]." '

The one word *charis* functioned in much the same way for Paul. Exegeting this same passage he speaks of Christians beholding with 'unveiled face' 'the light of the knowledge of the glory of God in the face of Christ' (2 Cor. 4:6) which shines through the ecclesia so that 'as grace extends to more and more people it may increase thanksgiving' (4:15). When Paul writes that the Lord 'said to me, "My grace is sufficient for you," ' what he means by grace is 'fundamentally the movement in love of God to man that takes effect in Christ', what the Old Testament traditions call God's *hesed*.[2]

EDUCATION AS A GRACIOUS PROCESS

The thesis of the present essay is that redemption takes the form of a divine education, and we have already noted that education necessarily involves process. There are no short cuts in education, no magical formulae which produce the desired result, which is human 'salvation', completion, conformation to Christ. But if education involves process, equally educational theorists from Plato to the present have realised that at its best it is a *gracious* process. As Simone Weil put it: 'The intelligence can only be led by desire. For there to be desire there must be pleasure and joy in the work. The intelligence only grows and bears fruit in joy . . . desire directed towards God is the only power capable of raising the soul.'[3] *A fortiori* this applies to the divine education, though this has not always been grasped in the church tradition. In the remaining parts of this chapter we shall seek to understand what is meant by speaking of the divine education as a gracious process, which will involve a critical dialogue with the tradition which derives from Augustine.

All the Hebrew words which Paul concentrates in the one word *charis* may be said to describe the fundamental openness to the other of God's love. 'Grace' describes the fact that God, though he lacks nothing in himself, nevertheless opens himself up to otherness. This 'otherness' is the whole created universe which is therefore posited on God's will to share his being, on grace. Grace is the presupposition of all created reality, what we have to think before we think creation at all. In a transferred sense creation *is* grace, in that it is the product of a free, gratuitous self-giving. At the same time 'grace' is not something God has, or gives, or uses. It is a way of speaking of the essential reality of God. It indicates that when Christians speak of God they do not speak of the Unmoved Mover of Aristotle, or of the Alone with the Alone of Plotinus, but of a God who is relationship in himself, essentially. As Buber said, 'In the beginning is the relation.' The God and Father of Jesus Christ is the 'living God' and 'life' means relationship. The sphere where there is no relationship, no calling and answering, is the sphere of death (Job 7:10, 21b). 'Grace' on the other hand signifies the freedom and openness of God's relationship to himself, what Christian tradition came to speak of as the relations of the three divine persons. It is from this fullness of living being that God creates, reconciles and redeems, and in terms of our image, enters into dialogue with and educates his creature.

Just as grace describes an attitude of radical openness, so 'sin' signifies the closing up of options, erecting of barricades, stopping of ears, closing of minds. It is the foreclosure of all genuine relationship, the refusal of people to be open to others, excluding, using and demeaning others on the grounds of sex, caste, class, race, nation and the will to hang on to what is mine and not yours. As Hosea describes it, it is the opposite of all loyal and trustworthy dealing (Hos. 4:2). This refusal of relationship grows like a cancer and is called by Paul 'the power of sin', the anti-grace reality. Sin, the opposite of grace, can thus be called 'the great refusal', the process by which situations become locked in ever tighter and more vicious circles, 'totalities' from which there is no escape. These situations are no figment of the theological imagination but constitute a description of much of human history. This fact presents us with a paradox which bears directly on the divine education. We speak of redemption as an historical process, though we have refused to identify history with redemption. When we look at history we see 'terror on every side', and yet a very influential line of thought has seen the divine education at work in this terror. But are we then justified in speaking of a pedagogy of grace?

From at least the time of the Deuteronomist Israel understood the sufferings of her history, the downfall of the northern kingdom, and the constant wars and invasions of Judah, not to mention the injustice of the rulers, as 'the chastening of the Lord' – they conceived them, in other words, as education. This reading of history continues into the New Testament. Thus the author of the letter to the Hebrews applied the words of Proverbs to a persecution which may have involved martyrdom:

> My son, do not lightly regard the
> discipline of the Lord . . .
> For the Lord disciplines him whom
> he loves,
> and chastises every son whom he receives.
> (Prov. 3:11–12; Heb. 12:5–6)

Throughout the centuries both Jewish and Christian communities have applied these words to themselves and understood the terror of history as education, as a chastisement for sin. But the experiences of Auschwitz, Buchenwald and Treblinka are so qualitatively terrible that they compel a questioning of this interpretation of history, a questioning which must then be applied to all the terrors Israel in particular has experienced, including those mentioned in the 'Old Testament'.

One way of understanding the interpretation of the terror of history as education is to see it as a refusal to let go of God's grace no matter how terrible the experience. The community takes to itself the confession of Job: 'Yea, though he slay me I will trust in him' (Job 13:15, AV). The language of 'chastening' arises out of a refusal to let go either God's existence or his goodness or his lordship of history. It says in effect: God is good, God is acting, therefore we must understand these experiences as somehow being for our benefit. But clearly, Auschwitz is not for anybody's benefit. How then are we to understand this talk of education through terror? As an instrument for causing death through torture the cross is a symbol of the terror of history, and it is therefore to the cross we must look for a response to this question.

In what appears to be an allusion to Gethsemane, and perhaps also to Calvary, the author of Hebrews remarks that Jesus 'learned obedience through what he suffered' (Heb. 5:8), language which is close to the idea of 'chastening'. And yet it is quite clear that we cannot understand the cross as God's affirmation of suffering and evil, as if the terror of history was part of the shadow which was necessary to appreciate the light, as Augustine and Aquinas later suggested. Nor may we understand the cross as either 'education' for Jesus nor, positively, for the human race. Rather, just as we saw that Jesus' death as a 'sacrifice' was the ultimate demonstration of the evil of that whole line of human thinking, so the cross represents the absolute rejection and refusal of the terror of history, the clearest possible expression that this is what God does not will. Only in such a deeply dialectical way may the cross itself be regarded as 'education', and this goes for all the rest of the terror of history. Again as we saw in the discussion of sacrifice, as an expression of what God does not will it is at the same time an expression of the deepest divine solidarity with the victims of the terror of history. But together with this refusal and solidarity there is also the demonstration of how such terror may be taken up and used redemptively. 'Father forgive them' is, as also emerged in the discussion of sacrifice, the refusal to be defeated by terror, to be corrupted into meeting hatred with hatred and fear with fear. This does not mean that we should regard terror as an opportunity for forgiveness (as the '*O felix culpa*' might perhaps be understood) but that, given the terror which results from the great refusal, God shows that he is not defeated by it and demonstrates how he deals with it. That demonstration of forgiveness may, perhaps, be regarded as education.

Despite their understanding of disaster as discipline, Israel never arrived at a gloomy idea of God. On the contrary, the psalmist confessed: 'In your presence is fullness of joy' (Ps. 16:11), and it is through this 'presence' that God's education proceeds. This means that, as Simone Weil said of education, the divine education is also a gracious process, that is, a process in which there is beauty, pleasure, desire and joy. It was therefore a sound instinct which led the early Christians to see in Christ the bridegroom of the Song of Songs. The sur-plus, the overflow of grace is precisely the beauty of God which causes joy, 'the only power capable of raising the soul'. Because of the terror of history this beauty was experienced in a highly paradoxical fashion: thus, the servant 'has no form or comeliness; and when we see him there is no beauty that we should desire him' (Isa. 53:2). If anything sharpening the paradox, Venantius Fortunatus in the sixth century sang of the cross, an instrument of torture, as 'the tree of beauty, tree most fair'. The belief that God is working in history and educating us through that history might easily have led to a Marcionite split between a God of wrath and a God of love, and yet neither Jewish nor Christian tradition ever let go of the beauty and attractiveness of God, his grace, and they continued to think of his education as a history of grace. The most profound meditation on this theme in the Christian tradition is John's gospel: Jesus, lifted up from the earth on the cross, 'draws all men to him' because it is there that the *doxa*, the glory and attractiveness of God, is seen (John 12:32, 7:39). To spell out the meaning of this paradoxical *doxa* would be a perilous exercise, but it obviously includes God's humility, his solidarity with the suffering (*hesed*), his faithfulness despite the great refusal, his mercy to those who show no mercy – all the attributes, in other words, of Exodus 34:6, known in their incarnation in Jesus, the glory of God shining in the face of Christ. The drawing of all humanity to Christ by this very paradoxical 'glory' is what is meant by the pedagogy of grace. We must now go on to see how the exercise of this attractive power may be conceived.

'GRACE' AND THOUGHT REFORM

It is an extreme irony that Augustine, whom the Church of the Middle Ages called the *Doctor Gratiae* in view of the intense concentration of his thought on grace, and who set the terms for discussion of the doctrine of grace for a thousand years, should have missed precisely this character of grace as a slow pedagogy which works by attraction and which suffers violence rather than imposes it. In all its terms, and especially in its christological focus, Augustine's doctrine of grace is 'biblical'. But the framework into which he fits the biblical doctrine – an inscrutable omnipotence, a psychologising account of God's working, the effect of the sacraments *ex opere operato* – throws the whole doctrine out of true. Paul's context was the

Jewish covenant, all the words which form the background to his use of *charis*. Deprived of this context the Lord of history becomes the Manipulator of history, the elusive presence an irresistible compulsion, a patient pedagogy a divine despotism.

The framework of Augustine's understanding of grace is the divine omnipotence. God's power bears directly on human will: 'God has men's wills more in his power than they themselves have their wills in their own power.'[4] 'Who will be guilty of such impious folly as to assert that God cannot convert to the good such evil wills of men as he wishes, when he wishes, and where he wishes.'[5] Since 'grace' is the name of God's will active to save, it obviously relates to this omnipotent power. Augustine understands the 'economy' of the exercise of this power in terms of predestination. There are those predestined to salvation and those predestined to damnation. He rejects any form of universalism on the grounds that it conflicts with the clear evidence of Scripture and undermines the moral fabric of the universe.[6] The question why one is saved and another damned is repeatedly referred to the secret judgement of God.[7] These issues provoke the question how God works (the mode of God's education), and Augustine has his answer: in a famous sermon he pictures God speaking to the sinner:

> That you should not commit adultery a tempter was absent: that a tempter should be absent, I brought it about. Place and time were lacking: and that these should be lacking, I brought it about. Suppose on the contrary that the tempter was there, and place and time were not wanting: that you should not consent, I terrified you. Acknowledge therefore *the grace* of him to whom you owe that you did not commit this crime.[8]

Here grace is brought into conjunction with a manipulative as well as inscrutable providence which in a later age came to be understood in terms of causality. Although Augustine does not apply the actual word 'irresistible' to grace, he says that it works in a way 'not able to be refused and not able to be overcome', which is the same thing.[9]

From Paul the Church had received the connection of grace with baptism. Deprived of Paul's covenant framework, two questions now combined to give this connection a completely different direction. First there was the question of the validity or otherwise of schismatical baptism, raised by the Donatist controversy. Cyprian had denied it was true baptism. Augustine preferred a distinction between a sacrament's validity and its efficacy. Schismatic baptism was valid, in his view, because it is always Christ who baptises through the Spirit, rather than the minister, but it was not efficacious because efficacy presupposes the bond of charity, and this the schismatics had broken. Since 'grace' was bestowed in baptism, this raised the question of grace which might not lead to salvation, and so led to the distinction between justifying and sanctifying grace, sufficient and efficacious grace, only the latter of which brought people to salvation. This parcelling up of grace inevitably divorced it from 'God's essence and his very self', as Newman correctly saw. A second question which led in the same direction was that faced by Augustine in his care for the church in Hippo. He saw many who had received Catholic baptism whose immoral lives clearly showed they were not bound for the heavenly city. Since they had 'received' grace in baptism, and since grace was irresistible, there must be a distinction, either quantitative or qualitative, in grace itself. The notion of grace which was 'congruous' to the merit of the sinner was an attempt to overcome the arbitrariness of the concept, but at the cost of firmly joining merit to the idea of grace. In Augustine we have the beginning of the distinction between created and uncreated grace:

> 'Grace' in Augustinian terminology means primarily the salvific will of God, operating partly by way of the providential arrangement of exterior circumstances, partly by the secret inspiration of good thoughts and the communication of interior spiritual vitality: by *a natural metonymy, it comes to mean the good thoughts and the spiritual vitality so imparted.*[10]

'Grace' then comes to mean something *in man*, an attribute of the recipient, rather than a description of God's meeting persons.

This Augustinian reading of grace is a catastrophe of the first order. In Augustine's own terms it is meticulously faithful to the letter of Scripture and disastrously unfaithful to the Spirit. Two crucial factors contributory to this are a tendency to Platonising exegesis, which concentrates on what Scripture has to say for the salvation of the individual soul, and the Hellenistic idea of *charis* as power which re-emerged after Paul in the Apostolic Fathers, and in Tertullian, the fount of North African Christian thought, took on overtones from Stoicism leading to an opposition of grace to nature, rather than to sin.[11] In this the character of grace as the openness of God's engagement with history as a whole, rather than with the individual soul, was lost sight of. It was particularly disastrous in view of its enormous influence on succeeding ages: Aquinas wrote the tract on grace in the *Summa Theologiae* with Augustine open on his desk, and Luther rejected Indulgences with the Bible in one hand and Augustine in the other, whilst Calvin, when challenged on a point of Augustinian interpretation in a debate with Roman Catholics, proceeded to quote Augustine for six hours from memory!

Aquinas' theology of grace dots Augustine's 'i's and crosses his 't's. As the source of grace, its 'principal cause', God is grace in himself. In this sense he is uncreated grace, by which is meant 'either the divine acceptance of us or the uncreated one who is given, the Holy Spirit'.[12] On the other hand, 'The grace of the Holy Spirit is a kind of interior disposition infused into us which inclines us to act rightly'.[13] Aquinas' focus is on this reflexive aspect, 'created' grace. 'When a man is said to have God's grace, something supernatural is referred to, issuing in man from God'.[14] This *quiddam supernaturale* is, first, God's moving of a person's mind to know or will something and, second, 'some habitual gift . . . infused by God into the soul'. In this sense grace is 'a kind of quality' which 'acts in the manner of a formal cause', the example given being the way possession of justice makes a person just.[15]

Aquinas' framework is that of nature and grace as two orders of reality supervening on each other. Human beings can reach their end, the vision of God, only by transcending their nature, for which they need the assistance of grace. This 'grace perfecting nature' language refers by and large to intellectual and moral processes, it is not subpersonal. For example, 'the human intellect cannot know more profound intelligible realities unless it is perfected by a stronger light, say the light of faith or prophecy; and this is called the light of grace, inasmuch as it supplements nature'.[16]

In the state of intact nature man needs a gratuitous capacity

> supplementing the capacity of his nature in one respect, namely to perform and will the supernatural good. But in the state of spoiled nature he needs it in two respects, namely, in order to be healed, and further that he may perform the good proper to supernatural capacity, which is meritorious. Furthermore, in both states man needs divine assistance so as to be moved by it to act well.[17]

Where the suspicion of a sub-personal conception of grace arises is in the idea of the sacraments as instrumental causes of grace, 'instruments of divine power'.[18] Everything then depends on how we understand a sacrament.

Aquinas followed Augustine in seeing grace as making history through its impact on the individual will. He also followed him in the connection with predestination – for him the damnation of the reprobate was conducive to the ordered whole of the beauty of the universe.[19] Such an idea of predestination effectively negates the significance of history as *human* history.

Luther too followed Augustine's teaching on predestination, but he does mark a return in many ways to a more authentically biblical conception of grace. In his reply to the doctors of the Sorbonne (1521) he defines grace as 'the favourable disposition of God towards us', 'God's favour towards us, the opposite of wrath'. On the lines of the *simul iustus et peccator* he speaks of the whole man being under grace and the whole man under wrath. Twenty four years later, lecturing on Galatians 1:3 he pronounces: 'Grace and peace – these two words embrace the whole of Christianity. Grace forgives sin and peace stills the conscience.' The connection between grace and forgiveness was absolutely fundamental for Luther, underlying his whole understanding of the connection between grace and the sacraments. 'In this Christian church, wherever it exists, is to be found the forgiveness of sins, that is a kingdom of grace and of true pardon'.[20] The connection with the kingdom is also characteristic: 'We are saved only when God reigns in us and we are his kingdom . . . when grace and virtue (that is, the kingdom of God) are perfected . . .'[21] In the same way grace is understood very strictly in relation to Christ, though not to the exclusion of the Holy Spirit: 'That little word "testament" is a short summary of all God's wonders and grace, fulfilled in Christ.'[22] The famous remark that 'it is the Word and only the Word which is the vehicle of grace' must likewise be understood christologically. Thus we see that Luther has taken an axe to the distinctions deriving from Augustine and reinstated an understanding of grace in terms of the forgiveness brought about by Christ, appropriated through faith and lived in the Spirit:

> Faith is a living daring confidence in God's grace, so sure and certain that the believer would stake his life on it a thousand times. This knowledge of and confidence in God's grace makes men glad and bold and happy in dealing with God and with all creatures. And this is the work which the Holy Spirit performs in faith.[23]

Nevertheless the tradition of grace as an infused divine energy, and there are enough usages in Luther to suggest that view also, ensured that Luther was unable to change the mind even of those Christians who appropriated his name to the Church and Lutheran orthodoxy returned to the medieval distinctions.

Calvin consciously did away with the medieval distinctions regarding grace, but his account of the divine pedagogy was built on the *praedestinatio gemina*, the twofold predestination to salvation or damnation. Thus,

> It behoves us to consider the sort of remedy by which divine grace corrects and cures the corruption of our nature. God begins his good work in us by arousing love and desire and zeal for righteousness in our hearts; or, to *speak more* correctly, by bending, forming or directing our hearts to righteousness.[24]

The language of love and desire is scarcely compatible with the language of what Robert Lifton called 'thought reform', the language of bending, forming and direction.

THE ATTRACTION OF GRACE

The immense weight of the tradition deriving from Augustine, its individualism, its focus on the will, its connection with predestination, makes it all the more remarkable that at the beginning of the nineteenth century Schleiermacher managed to strike a new line even here.

Schleiermacher's thought on grace is christocentric. Christ redeems us by assuming us into his fellowship.

> The original activity of the redeemer is best conceived as a pervasive influence which is received by its object in virtue of the free movement with which he turns himself to its attraction, just as we ascribe *an attractive power to everyone to whose educative intellectual influence we gladly submit ourselves*.[25]

His analogy is with someone who conceives a new idea of civil community (like Anselm taking up a political analogy, though this time with regard to the Spirit). In this case,

> what happens is that the idea of the state first comes to consciousness in him and takes possession of his personality as its immediate dwelling place. Then he assumes the rest into the living fellowship of the idea. He does so by making them *clearly conscious of the unsatisfactoriness of their present condition by effective speech* . . . everything resulting from this is the corporate life.[26]

The resemblance to the theory of education in Freire's *Pedagogy of the Oppressed*, which supplies the root analogy for the present essay, is striking. People are made conscious of the unsatisfactoriness of their present condition through 'effective speech' – this is the instrument of liberation. 'The influence of Christ . . . consists *solely* in the human communication of the Word, in so far as that communication embodies Christ's word and continues the indwelling divine power of Christ himself.'[27] This word calls into being a fellowship, and 'the continuance of that fellowship constitutes . . . *the essence of the state of grace*'.[28] Why? Because it is this human historical fellowship which mediates redemption: this community is the 'means of grace'. 'Being drawn into the fellowship of believers, having a share in the Holy Spirit, and being drawn into living fellowship with Christ – must mean one and the same thing'.[29] This is not a rationalistic reduction of the divine to the human, for Schleiermacher. For him Christ, the origin of the community, is at once 'under the law of historical development' and at the same time must be understood as the subject of 'a creative divine act'. In the same way the community is 'the supernatural becoming natural'. For him there is no spiritual influence but the presentation of a person in word and deed, and thus Christ must attract human beings to himself in this way. Attraction is a key notion. Schleiermacher speaks of an influence of a redemptive and *therefore* attractive kind. This attraction, this drawing people into Christ's fellowship through the community, is the pedagogy of the Spirit.

Commenting on Schleiermacher's *Life of Jesus* Albert Schweitzer remarked that 'nowhere . . . is it so clear that the great dialectician had not an historical mind'.[30] This would indeed seem to be the implication of his failure to understand the Old Testament as a preparation for Christ, and reckoning it on a par with the surrounding heathenism. Consonant with this is the near docetism of his picture of Christ as ideal man. Yet there is another side to Schleiermacher which seems to be an attempt to take the historical process with extreme seriousness as the medium of God's creative and redemptive purpose. His identification of the will of God with natural causation might be understood in this way, and certainly the balancing of natural and 'supernatural' in his picture of Christ, but above all his deeply immanent account of God's gracious working through the community. This account makes it clear that the doctrine of grace has no place for the celestial Stalin with his Gulag ready for non-party members. It cannot be framed in terms of the irresistible manipulation of the will. 'Grace' is essentially a qualitative word, a description of the mode of God's action, rather than a substantive. If Christ is its focus then it certainly speaks of an initiative of God, but an initiative of a certain kind, which finds its character description in the Beatitudes, or the hymn to love in First Corinthians, or in the 'Song of a Slave', or of God's solidarity, in Philippians. 'Patient, kind, humble, obedient' – these are a description of the quality of God's initiative, what makes it gracious. This initiative is at all times surprising and inventive beyond the schemes which humanity can dream up for God, but it can never be an initiative which rides people down. Schleiermacher rather offers us the analogy of the teacher to whose attractive power we submit ourselves.

This draws our attention therefore to the Word, to the Christian story, or as Schleiermacher calls it, the presentation of the person of Christ in word and deed. Here we once again come upon the deeply paradoxical character of the attraction of grace, for this 'presentation' is a story of death by torture. Some of the ways in which this terrible and attractive story may be conceived to change history will be the subject for reflection in the following chapters, but in essence it refers to the subversion of all accounts of arbitrary power. If this is the case, it illustrates how thoroughgoing was Augustine's misconception of grace, for which the connection between grace and this non-transvalued power was fundamental. Schleiermacher also offers us a picture of grace working as it were in the veins and capillaries of history rather than by manipulation. Only because it is personal, veiled, elusive, is this work of God actually gracious, because thereby it allows the other freedom, inviting rather than imposing response. Redemption, for Schleiermacher, is through education, and education is gracious process: both terms must be taken equally seriously. It is process because it requires a genuine response, which demands time and patience. It is gracious because 'the intelligence is led only by desire' and an education which does not work by attraction is no education.

This leads us now to the question of how grace takes historical form. Simone Weil teaches us that education involves attraction; she also teaches that both prayer and education consist in attention, in the case of the former a 'waiting on God'. But the patience of God which is grace suggests that this is a twofold process, not only a waiting on God but also (and we would not dare to say it but for God's revelation in Christ) a divine waiting on man. In this twofold waiting grace becomes history.

GRACE AND HISTORY

'Grace' describes the quality of God's redemptive initiative, an initiative which does not run out into nothingness but which takes effect in history. Nicholas Lash has pointed out that sin is not simply a moral category but an historical category which must be 'specified, rendered determinate, in the analysis and resolution of specific situations and circumstances, specific dimensions of human sinfulness individual and social'.[31] If 'sin' is a description of those vicious circles of greed, hatred and aggression in which human beings lock themselves, then 'grace' is the name for that initiative of God which breaks them open. It too, therefore, needs to be 'rendered determinate' in specific situations, a fact that Aquinas was getting at in his talk of 'created grace', and Schleiermacher in his account of grace working through the community. When we talk of grace we speak of something which happens in this world, as we might learn from John's identification of the incarnate Word with 'grace and truth'. But how is grace, the quality of God's mercy, his redeeming initiative, incarnated? Here we take up the theme of prayer and presence, which was raised but not pursued in chapter 1. And we have to note that, profound as was his grasp of the historical reality of grace, at this point Schleiermacher's rationalism failed him. For him petitionary prayer was impossible, and that in itself rules out a satisfactory doctrine of grace. Augustine and Aquinas are right by contrast to see a close connection between grace and God's providential action (though not to connect providence and predestination). What is this connection? For an answer we turn, as always in any discussion of grace, to Christ.

Christ is the 'Son of Man' and 'Son of God' only as he is the man of faith, the man who prays, the man who spends many of his days and nights 'waiting on God', seemingly without an answer. He does not withdraw from society to the desert, like Antony, but the story of the temptations and Gethsemane, which frame the beginning and end of the ministry, seem to suggest that it is in and through these periods of listening and waiting that God's initiative takes flesh in his historical life and death. Here we can find the reality of phrases such as 'God acts in history' or the designation of Israel's history as the history of God's 'mighty deeds'. The action of God is not the action of a *deus ex machina*, but gracious action which in turn waits upon and enables the action of men and women. In Jesus we have a clue as to how this comes about, for the periods of strenuous listening and waiting which the gospels record only make sense against the background both of his passionate involvement with his people, on the one hand, and his searching of their Scriptures, his passionate involvement with their tradition, on the other. Somewhere between these two poles, in this seemingly unimportant and empty space, God's grace, his renewing, liberative, redeeming initiative becomes flesh.

To assert this requires facing the question whether this 'waiting on God', in which grace becomes flesh, is illusory. When Marx called religion 'opiate' he meant that it encouraged flight from reality, and a cursory glance at any hymnal or the contents of any religious bookshop reveals the extent to which he was correct, the extreme sentimentality of so many 'religious' productions marking the depth of their divorce from reality. Sentimentality, however, is not spawned by the Bible: rather it is a flight from the rigours of the realism of that tradition of witness, which knows no supermen and precious few happy endings. Repeated failure is written stark across its pages, not only moral failure but failure ever to attain the promised 'rest'. Paul speaks for the history of Israel as a whole and for so many of the individuals known to us from that history in his account of his brief period of missionary work: five times the thirty-nine lashes, three times beaten with rods, once stoned, three times shipwrecked. It does not sound like the record of a man running away from reality. For secular parallels we have to go to the champions of the great national liberation struggles, men like Gandhi or Mao, who were also not noted for their flight from reality. What sustained Paul, Jesus, Jeremiah, Job, the whole 'cloud of witnesses' invoked by the author of Hebrews, was a passionate commitment to the shape of God's future, sustained by a many faceted experience of 'presence', which they called 'hope' or 'faith'. Faith, says the author of Hebrews, is the reality (*hypostasis*) of things hoped for and commitment to things beyond the present horizon (*pragmatōn elenchos ou blepomenōn*). All the heroes of faith died 'not having received what was promised, but having seen and greeted it from afar' (Heb. 11:13). Paul spoke of this future reality as 'the glory that is to be revealed' and said it was grasped 'by hope alone' (cf. Rom. 8:24).

Augustine spoke of history as the history of two loves, the love of God and the love of earth, but we can as well speak of it as the history of two realisms, two understandings of what constitutes 'reality'. There is the realism of the 'hard facts', of the established situation, which never fails to appeal to 'human nature as it really is', and which believes in *realpolitik*. When this kind of realism theologises, it likes to think in terms of individual sin and individual redemption.

The other realism, which is opposed to this, is the realism of faith or hope, which dares to dream realistically of God's future for men and women and for the whole earth, and to give its life for this dream:

> The lawyers have sat in council, the men with the keen long faces,
> And said, 'This man is a fool', and others have said, 'He blasphemeth';
> And the wise have pitied the fool that hath striven to give a life
> In the world of time and space among the bulks of actual things,
> To a dream that was dreamed in the heart, and that only the heart could hold.
>
> O wise men, riddle me this: what if the dream come true?
> What if the dream come true? And if millions unborn shall dwell
> In the house that I shaped in my heart, the noble house of my thought?
> Lord, I have staked my soul, I have staked the lives of my kin
> On the truth of Thy dreadful word. Do not remember my failures,
> But remember this my faith.

So Padraic Pearse who, like Jesus and Paul, paid for his faith with his life.[32] Realists of the first kind will always call this type of faith fanaticism, but what constitutes fanaticism can only be measured by the results a belief has for people. Enthusiasm is neither mistaken nor excessive if the result of such enthusiasm is a community which is more compassionate, more just and more hopeful. In fact,

> Hope alone is to be called 'realistic', because it alone takes seriously the possibilities with which all reality is fraught . . . Hope and the kind of thinking that goes with it consequently cannot submit to the reproach of being utopian, for they do not strive after things that have 'no place', but after things that have 'no place *as yet*' but can acquire one.[33]

The first realism appeals to the way things are and, in despair or as an ideological justification, assumes that in the nature of things they can never be any different. It is naturally the most convenient ideology for those in power. The promise of something better however calls this present into question, especially for those who have 'everything to hope for'.

Realism of the second kind is of course not the preserve of the Church or of religious people in general, for by 'faith' is meant not primarily belief in God but commitment to a more human future, the opposite of all despair and cynicism. Nevertheless the Jewish Christian tradition has understood prayer and worship as central to this kind of realism. The English novelist John Wain, in his autobiography *Sprightly Running* describes the task of an author as 'a matter of feeling and living at the required depth, fending off the continual temptation to be glib and shallow, to appeal to the easily aroused response, to be evasive and shirk the hard issues. It is a matter of training oneself to live with reality'.[34] Just so has the tradition understood prayer, as a schooling in the realism of hope. People pray, said Alan Ecclestone, because 'hunger for reality' takes hold of them.

> Prayer strives to penetrate through what to eyes of un-engagement must be baffling and repellent, too hard to understand, too cruel to endure, too meaningless to use, in order to discern the lines of the emergent work, the future of Man being shaped, and in order to engage the one who prays with what is wrought.[35]

Partial, difficult, broken as it is, prayer means bringing the real issues of life and death before God, to let the silence refract them, but more than that in the expectation of a word of presence which can enlighten the darkness of confusion, indecision and despair. In this waiting and reflecting, prayer and worship are concerned with looking beyond the appearance of things as they are, bound by all kinds of 'iron laws', to the way things might be in a more human future where such laws no longer prevail. Far from being opiate they constitute a check on evasion of the hard issues, on the day-dreaming which is hope's shoddy imitation and the complacence which stands in the way of change and growth. As we see them in Jesus, in the prophets, in people like Francis or the Hasidim, they are concerned with the perception, the vision, through which faith is substantiated, and hope gives birth to a new world. 'In Paris', said Chagall,

> I frequented neither schools nor teachers. I found them in the city itself, at every stop, everywhere. There were tradesmen in the market, the café waiters, the concierges, the peasants, the workers. Around them hovered this astonishing 'freedom light', which I had never seen elsewhere. And this light passed easily onto the canvases of the great French masters and was *reborn in art.*[36]

Those who pray likewise frequent neither schools nor teachers, but in faith discern a 'freedom light' hovering over the mundane and commonplace, over what Paul calls 'things which are not', and through their engagement this light passes on to God's canvas, which is human history, and what is born or reborn is a future in accord with the purposes of God. For believer and non-believer alike it is faith, but for the believer faith informed by prayer and presence, which is thus the midwife of a new world. It is the retort of reality in what R. S. Thomas calls the 'Laboratories of the Spirit'.

7

Signs of Hope

Human beings are sign-giving creatures: this is as much a definition of what it is that distinguishes humans from other animals as to say that they are rational creatures or creatures which play (*homo ludens*). Education in particular, and at all levels, proceeds through signs, from the correlation picture-word-reality through which young children learn to the complex algebraic formulae of relativity theory. In the education of the human race God does not spurn signs but reveals himself as a sign-giving God. For this reason reflection on signs (sacramental theology) has occupied an extremely important place in Christian theology since at least the fifth century, and some of the Church's most acrimonious disputes relate to the giving and interpreting of signs, the nature of which has been very variously understood. What are the 'signs' which God gives us to walk by, and how do they function in the divine education? Beginning from the distinction between sign and symbol we inquire into the meaning of 'sacrament' and follow the disputes over 'mere' signs and means of grace which mark different perceptions as to the mode of the divine education.

SIGNS AND SYMBOLS

Augustine is the father of both Protestant and Catholic sacramental thought. His Platonic framework led him to emphasise both a strong contrast between sign and thing signified, but also a necessary correspondence. Thus, on the one hand, he tells us that 'the reason that these things are called sacraments is that one thing is seen in them but another understood'.[1] Moses and Aaron ate the manna and did not die because 'they understood the visible food in a spiritual sense; they were spiritually hungry, they tasted spiritually . . . We today receive visible food, but the sacrament is one thing, the power [*virtus*] of the sacrament is another'.[2] On the other hand, 'If the sacraments had not a kind of likeness to those things of which they are the sacraments, they would not be sacraments at all. As therefore the sacrament of the body of Christ is, in a sense, the body of Christ, and the sacrament of Christ's blood is Christ's blood, so the sacrament of faith is faith' (i.e. the faith of the adult sponsor in baptism is the sign of the faith of the infant).[3] From the stress on the disconnection between sign and thing signified, the conventionality of the sign, its arbitrariness, which is to say its origin in an act of divine choice or will (*arbitrium*), all Protestant reflection has stemmed. Catholic thought on the other hand and the thought of theologians much influenced by Plato, such as Temple or Tillich, has looked more to the deep and necessary correspondence between sign and thing signified suggested by the Platonic metaphysic of sensible and suprasensible, so that the sign participates in eternal reality. From this tension we can derive a distinction between sign and symbol.

Theologians who believe in the analogy of being, who look therefore to the correspondence aspect of Augustine's thought, generally give priority to the concept 'symbol'. Tillich defines a symbol thus:

> As symbols the sacramental materials are intrinsically related to what they express; they have inherent qualities (water, fire, oil, bread, wine) which make them adequate to their symbolic function . . . A sacramental symbol is neither a thing nor a sign. It participates in the power of what it symbolizes, and therefore it can be a medium of the Spirit.[4]

The symbols Tillich refers to here all stand in very close relation to creation. There are more conventional symbols, such as flags and the devices of heraldry, which function in a somewhat similar way: these we could distinguish as primary and secondary symbols. The primary symbols such as water, bread, fire, etc., are taken up in all cultures the world over, as the anthropologist Victor Turner has indicated in his book *The Forest of Symbols*. They derive their depth and fascination from the fact that they seem to emerge from what Jung called the 'collective unconscious'. They belong to the world of myth, of correspondence between this world and the other world. Theologically they may be regarded as a response to what will be called in chapter 9 God's 'silent work'.

From the beginning, the tradition of Israel seems to have been aniconic. The introduction of symbols into the Jerusalem temple was the result of the need to assimilate the Jebusite cult and come to terms with the culture of Canaan. For good or ill this symbolic tradition was never fully domesticated in Israel: 'Myth, just because it is myth, is a way of thinking by means of symbols and images: but Israel fought with all the resolve she could command against the most important thing in all the mythic symbols which her religious environment offered her, namely, their capacity to serve as a means of revelation.' For von Rad, 'this awareness of the barrier which men erect between themselves and God by means of images is . . . Israel's greatest achievement'.[5]

By contrast Israel was from the beginning deeply concerned about *signs*. For the priestly writer both the stars (Gen. 1:14) and the rainbow (Gen. 9:13) were signs: the given orders and regularities of creation were read as signs of God's benevolence. More importantly the Deuteronomist spoke of the 'signs and wonders' which God performed in bringing Israel out of Egypt. Here historical events are read in the context of faith and prayer for salvation as demonstrations of God's redeeming purpose and activity. In the same way the early Church found their own lives full of 'signs and wonders' (e.g. 2 Cor. 12:12; Heb. 2:4). The prophets of Israel also gave their contemporaries 'signs'. Isaiah wrote the words, 'Spoil speeds, prey hastens,' on a tile before witnesses, and gave this name to his unfortunate child as a sign of what God would do through the Assyrians (Isa. 8:3ff.). Jeremiah bought a new loin cloth, wore it without shrinking it, and then hid it in rocks until it rotted as a sign of what was going to happen to Judah (Jer. 13:4ff.). Ezekiel drew a picture of besieged Jerusalem on a clay brick, put an iron plate before it and lay facing it as a sign of the same thing (Ezek. 4:1ff.). These signs were understood as being effective, as hastening the coming of the event they signified, and this tradition of sign-giving is presupposed in the gospels. The synoptic writers record that Jesus was asked to perform 'signs' which would remove all the ambiguity about his person. He rejected this demand as a temptation and said, 'No sign shall be given except the sign of the prophet Jonah.' The whole point of this was that Jonah gave no sign: the people of Nineveh repented merely at his preaching (Matt. 12:41). At the same time Jesus implied that people should be able to read 'the signs of the times'. When the messengers of John the Baptist come he refers them to the Messianic signs mentioned in Isaiah: Go and tell John what you hear and see: the blind receive their sight and the lame walk, lepers are cleansed and the deaf hear, and the dead are raised up, and the poor have good news preached to them (Matt. 11:5). John refers to these events as signs, '*semeia* in the Old Testament sense, special demonstrations of the character and power of God, and partial but effective realisations of his salvation'.[6] Finally, signs also refer to the eschatological events, the troubles preceding the end (e.g. Matt. 24:24, 24:30).

The Church has rightly perceived that the divine education proceeds through sign-giving, and the rehearsal of this sign-giving has been concentrated, following the example of Israel, in the liturgy. As in the Temple liturgy both signs and symbols are to be found, but these need to be understood in their proper order. Barth taught that creation was the presupposition of the covenant, and the covenant the meaning of creation, and in this way sign and symbol are also related. The liturgy necessarily and rightly employs symbols, for all creation is the 'product' of grace, the product of God's will to share himself, and likewise all human cultures respond to God's silent work. At the same time this response is partial, flawed, sinful, and the universal symbols reflect this in the fact that they can all without exception be used for good or evil, as much for Nazi rallies or black magic as for the Christian eucharist. We are called therefore – not to shun the symbols but to use them in obedience to and dependence on the divine sign-giving: there is an order. The subsumption of sign under symbol, as in Tillich, is contrary to the biblical perception of God's interaction with his world. God's grace is his *free* relationship with his creature (Exod. 33:19) in which he sets up signs of his rule. The biblical signs do not appeal to universal meaning, to any metaphysic of correspondence. In their concreteness they appeal not to an idea (myth) but to events. They are 'the moving of an instrument in the hand of God', they point to the reality of God's presence now and evoke faith and hope for the future. The symbols used in liturgy on the other hand are the means by which liturgy is dovetailed into the whole world of human culture. But symbols need redemption whilst the signs signify and hasten redemption. In the education of the liturgy we have not stepped outside the biblical world into the world of the mystery religions, with their chaotic appeal to the forest of symbols. We are in the world of the purposeful, historic sign-giving. Signs are of the *esse*, symbols of the *bene esse*. God uses both in his education but not both equally. The relationship is beautifully summed up in the story of Schleiermacher's death. His doctor had forbidden him wine, but he wished to celebrate the eucharist nonetheless. When he did so he partook only of the water, the family of the wine as well – for the reality is in the sign rather than the symbol.

SIGN AND SACRAMENT

When the Christian Church has talked about signs it has almost always talked about sacraments: the equation between the two was taken for granted for at least a millenium. But if we are to inquire into the role of sacraments in the divine education we must first discover in what sense a sacrament is a sign, and what sacraments signify. We begin from the rather devious derivation of the word 'sacrament' from the New Testament word 'mystery'.

The word 'sacrament' derives from the Latin word *sacramentum* which was used to translate the Greek *musterion* (mystery) in the early Latin versions of the New Testament. In the New Testament 'mystery' has a twofold reference. It refers first and foremost to God's act in Christ: 'To you is given the mystery of the kingdom of God,' says Jesus, 'but for those outside everything is in parables' (Mark 4:11). What is this mystery? It is what God is doing in Jesus, the breaking in of the kingdom, hidden from the many, revealed to the few. Somewhat similarly Paul tells the Corinthians: 'we speak the wisdom of God in a mystery [*en musterio*], that which is hidden, which God from all eternity foreordained for our glory' (1 Cor. 2:7). This wisdom *en musterio* is the cross of Christ, the significance of which is hidden from the worldly wise. In Colossians Paul can speak of Christ quite simply as 'God's mystery', 'hidden for ages and generations but now made known' (Col. 1:26). This mystery is not finished and done with but is the continuing secret of history, for the mystery is 'Christ in you, the hope of glory' (Col. 1:27). The confession of 1 Timothy sums up this witness: 'Christ indeed is the mystery of that which we worship [*tēs eusebias*]: he was manifested in the flesh, vindicated in the Spirit, seen by angels, preached among the nations, believed in the world, taken up in glory' (1 Tim. 3:16). The great mystery, or *sacramentum*, in the New Testament is then God's work in Christ. Derivative on this understanding, the phenomena which precede Christ's final return, the ingathering of the Gentiles (Eph. 1:9, 3:3, 9), the partial hardening of Israel (Rom. 11:25) and persecution (2 Thess. 2:7, Rev. 17:5) can all be described as mysteries. Nowhere does the word refer to baptism, eucharist, or any liturgical act.

Why *sacramentum* was chosen to translate this word, rather than the more obvious *mysterium* is not clear. T. A. Lacey hypothesises a colloquial sense for *sacramentum* no longer extant.[7] It may be that *mysterium* was suspect in the second century because of its connections with the mystery cults, whilst Jerome could use it in place of *sacramentum* in his translation at the end of the fourth century because these cults no longer presented a threat.

Neither *musterion* nor *sacramentum* are for certain applied to 'the sacraments', that is, liturgical acts performed by the Christian Church, before the end of the second century. Well into the fifth century both words maintain a great breadth of meaning. Thus in the East in the fourth century *musterion* can mean simply 'a secret' or the entire Christian faith or God's purposes in Christ, and Chrysostom uses it in an authentically Pauline sense to describe Christ's humiliation and crucifixion. Nevertheless it is in this century that the description of the eucharist as 'the holy mysteries' becomes quite general. For Cyril of Jerusalem, unlike his contemporary Athanasius, these mysteries are the living heart of his faith. We can catch the excitement in the lectures he delivered to catechumens in Jerusalem somewhere about the middle of the century. Once you have been instructed, he tells the catechumens, 'do not tell anything to an outsider. For we are entrusting to you a mystery, the hope of life to come'.[8] Baptism is 'divine' and 'life-giving' but in the eucharist are 'the more sacred mysteries'. After receiving communion, 'while the moisture is still on your lips, touch them with your hands, and sanctify your eyes and forehead and the rest of your organs of sense. Then wait for prayer, and give thanks to

God who has counted you worthy of admission to those great mysteries'.[9] Without a doubt the influence of the mystery religions is here very strong indeed. Under this influence the New Testament understanding of 'mystery' is eventually lost and everything is concentrated on these rites, so that the rites themselves become the mystery as opposed to the historical man Jesus of Nazareth. Of course this focus of attention is an attempt to grasp how what was done then becomes real for me now, but at the cost of the very great danger of Christianity becoming an epiphany religion, centred on the manifestation of the divine here and now, the intersection of the eternal with time – rather than what is indicated in the biblical witness, which is an historical movement, a pilgrim people, to whom signs are given for orientation.

The word *sacramentum* had in the second century two well-established meanings which are known to us. It meant both the security deposited in public keeping in a lawsuit – a sort of bail, and also the oath of loyalty sworn to the emperor by soldiers enlisting in the legions, which seems to have carried with it the impress of a brand. It is especially the second meaning which both Tertullian and Augustine take up, though both meanings suggest the idea of 'sign'. Where the East followed through the meaning of the word 'mystery', the West very quicky equated sacrament and sign. In a series of references which are more or less casual – a couple of letters, a sermon, a discussion of sacrifice in the *City of God* – Augustine reflects on the nature of sacraments, reflections which were to be rigorously quarried and systematised both by the Schoolmen and the Reformers. In general, he says, 'signs are called sacraments when they have reference to divine things'.[10] The classic Western definition of a sacrament as 'an outward and visible sign of an inward and spiritual grace' is approached most nearly in the *City of God*, where Augustine explains the Old Testament sacrifices as symbolising our efforts to be re united to God: 'A sacrifice is therefore the visible sacrament or sacred sign of an invisible sacrifice.' The sacrifice he has in mind is a moral one: 'This sacrifice the Church celebrates in the sacrament of the altar, which the faithful know well, where it is shown to her that in this thing which she offers she herself is offered'.[11]

Augustine was not precise in his use of *sacramentum*, and a wide range of meanings for the word can be found in his writings, but he also liked to speak of 'the few most salutary sacraments of the Gospel' or of the sacraments of the Church being, in contrast to the sacraments of the old law, 'very few in number, very easy to take note of, and most glorious in their significance'.[12] What exactly constituted a sacrament remained imprecise for many centuries. Hugh of St Victor spoke of thirty sacraments, whilst distinguishing seven principal ones. Lombard fixed definitely on seven, followed by Aquinas and then by the Council of Trent, which insisted on 'seven sacraments, no more and no less'. The Reformation narrowed down this number still further. Luther was at first inclined to speak of one sacrament (Christ) and three sacramental signs (baptism, eucharist and penance). Later he restricted the name of sacrament

> to those promises which have signs attached to them. The remainder, not being bound to signs, are bare promises. Hence there are, strictly speaking, but two sacraments in the church of God – baptism and bread. For only in these two do we find the divinely instituted sign and the promise of the forgiveness of sins.[13]

Here the agreement between the Reformers and the Council of Trent is perhaps more striking than the disagreement: sacraments remain, as Aquinas puts it, liturgical actions of the Church designed to perfect human being and remedy the effects of sin in the realms both of corporate and individual life.[14] The Church had to wait for a disciple of Schleiermacher to break open this obsessively liturgical reference. John Oman describes life itself as 'the one Supreme Divine sacrament' and the sacraments of the Church exist 'to express and, as it were, give the concentrated essence of the sacrament of life'.[15] For Oman all forms of human sharing and expressions of compassion, tenderness or love are sacraments. The church sacraments signify the sacredness of the everyday: 'They teach men not to use the sacred shrines as a shelter from the world but to make all things sacred and so, in the right way, to abolish the distinction between sacred and secular till the world is our possession as much as Cephas'.[16]

More recently both Karl Barth and Karl Rahner have in different ways gone back to the New Testament origin of the word 'sacrament'. Barth took up the hint from Luther's 'Babylonian Captivity of the Church' and proposed that the Church should return to the usage of the first century according to which 'the death of Christ is the one *mysterion*, the one sacrament, and the one existential fact before and beside and after which there is no room for any other of the same rank'.[17] Later he proposed that the incarnation is 'the great Christian mystery and sacrament besides which there is, in the proper sense, no other'.[18] The ground of his argument was that the incarnation is without analogy and that therefore language applied to this, such as mystery or sacrament, cannot be applied to the Church and its sacraments. Rahner, on the other hand, prefers to see a hierarchy of sacramental signs: Christ as the arch-sacrament, the Church as fundamental sacrament (sign of a sign) and the liturgical sacraments derivative on these. Somewhat differently and closer to Oman, he envisaged, in an essay written in 1970, the liturgical sacraments as signs of God's grace operative in the whole of human history. History he conceives of as God's 'terrible and sublime liturgy', and the point of the church sacraments is to reflect on this liturgy of the world, to celebrate and signify the fact that God is to be found in it, in all its superficiality, folly and hatred, but in its dedication, responsibility and joy also. Unless this connection between the liturgy of history and the church liturgy is made at the deepest level the church sacraments become 'empty ritual attitudinisings, full of unbelief'. The eucharist therefore signifies and celebrates the fact tht 'the world itself is already ceaselessly offering itself in rejoicing, tears and blood'.[19] The church sacraments are then 'signs', pointers, of 'grace' – the openness and fundamental hopefulness of human history under God's pedagogy despite all reverses.

MERE SIGNS

It is above all from the Reformation, and especially from the conflict between Luther and Zwingli, that the confusion as to whether the eucharist is a 'mere sign' or whether it is a 'real' presence derives. Zwingli insisted on the semantic sense of *sacramentum*: a sign cannot be the thing signified, he said, or it ceases to be a sign. 'The sacraments we esteem and honour as signs and symbols of holy things, but not as though they were themselves the things of which they are signs. For who is so ignorant as to try and maintain that the sign is the thing which it signifies . . .?'[20] Who indeed? Zwingli never meant for a moment to deny 'real' presence, but for him as a Platonist 'real' meant 'spiritual'. Luther however, fixing on 'the plain sense of Scripture', insisted that '*Hoc EST corpus meum*' must mean something different: 'Whoever read in the Scriptures that "body" means the same as "sign of the body" and "is" means the same as "represents".' The rhetorical questions about 'mere sign' and 'real' presence were hurled from side to side in the centuries which followed and the dust which was raised prevented anyone from seeing. Full of indignation John Oman said that to speak of 'mere' symbols was to set 'the working of omnipotence above the gracious personal love of our Father, which is the same as measuring a token of love by its material value'.[21] The notion of a 'mere' sign is indeed extraordinary, for we can have false signs, unhelpful signs, or misleading signs – but what would a 'mere' sign be? The confusion rests on different understandings of the real. Let us imagine a child learning the word 'banana': BANANA – picture of banana – but what is interesting is a real banana which fills the stomach and helps you grow. From this perspective (what Lonergan called the 'already out there now real') the word and the picture are 'mere' signs. The theology of 'real' presence obviously did not have this kind of reality in view, but looked rather to the correspondence side of Augustine's thought, the Platonic idea of type and antitype. To read the sacraments in terms of that metaphysic is, however, to impose a particular view of reality on the signs instead of allowing, what both the biblical writings and Luther suggest, that signs have their own mode of reality, 'reality as signifying' (Nicholas Lash).

To come at this distinctive reality it will be helpful first to take up an issue raised in the preceding section, the question of the number of sacraments. It has to be granted that if we adopt a perspective like that of Rahner's, thinking of the liturgical sacraments mirroring the liturgy of the world, it is highly artificial to apply this to all 'seven' sacraments. Rahner actually speaks only of the eucharist in this discussion of the 'sacramental event'; it could be applied to baptism, but not convincingly to marriage, ordination, etc. On the other hand, Oman's vision of the sacramental universe is likewise too broad – if anything can be a sacrament then nothing is a sacrament. Barth's return to the New Testament has the merit of underlining the foundation of any sacramental language, but does it do justice to the importance of sign-giving in the biblical tradition? Here Luther's definition of sacrament as 'a sign to which a promise is attached' is important. When he came to speak of baptism in the Large Catechism[22] he fixed on *God's promise as the specific reality of the sign*. This seems to be an authentically biblical perception, because in the Bible 'signs' are, in their positive aspect, signs of hope for a new and different future, which precisely in and through their sign reality advance this future. The question of the reality of signs is not one which needs to be answered by any metaphysic but in terms of a theology of history. It is true that, as Luther puts it, 'whatever God effects through us he does through . . . external ordinances', but these external ordinances (water, bread and wine, Jesus of Nazareth) are bearers of the promise and as such change the future. The reality of God's presence is the reality of the promise. The promises are the ferment (leaven) of human history, the means of divine education. Where the promise is found we would have to ask, in response to Barth's rigorously christocentric understanding of sacrament, whether the signs which the Church has always treasured should not be understood as he sought to understand Scripture, as a witness to God's self-revelation which is 'wholly the work of God and wholly the work of man'. In this way we speak of God's continued self-witness through historical material means, a witness which is wholly human, provisional and imperfect, but also wholly the work of grace – of God's free initiative in meeting, breaking open and challenging human beings. Scripture, Israel-church, and the sacraments as bearers of the promise can all be taken as witnesses, pointers (cf. Barth's favourite image of the pointing finger of John the Baptist in Grünewald's 'Crucifixion') to the one true sign of God's love and his ultimate promise for humankind, Jesus Christ. The 'reality' of the signs is then the reality of the promise of God which they signify, as Luther said. There is nothing more 'real' than God's Word, which called creation into being in the first place and which, spoken in the midst of human history, acts to recreate that history. This is the heart of 'reality as signifying' and it means there are no 'mere' signs.

John speaks of his gospel as a 'book of signs' (John 20:30), which may be understood in several senses. Fundamentally it is the record of those signs which attest the truth about Jesus; it is also the book which speaks of the Messiah who, when he is lifted up, becomes the eschatological sign which will draw all human beings, the sign for the nations (John 12:32; Isa. 62:10). At the same time it is a book of signs in the tautological sense that it is, like Plato's *Republic*, or the *Upanishads*, or Shakespeare, the product of the most fundamental of human signs, words. The function of signs in this sense is to explore the heights and depths of the mystery of the universe, a mystery of which persons are the centre. Liturgy is part of this sign world – alongside, for instance, poetry, philosophy, music or geometry. In terms of our earlier illustration it is not 'real banana', and the liturgy is fetishised if we pretend that it is, if we treat it as the most important thing in life, if we give it the place which can only be occupied by the struggle for peace and justice and a more human society. On the other hand, the material ('real banana') is not the sum of reality – there is a mystery to be explored and, along with the rest of the world of human sign-giving, liturgy takes us into this mystery. Unlike the rest of that world it is not primarily the result of human reflection on that mystery but a response to the heart of the mystery making itself known – to revelation. Signs which are based on the promises involve a re-presentation of the heart of the divine self-giving to history. Through this re-presentation, and through these human, material and provisional means, God's story is interwoven with the human story, our mystery is caught up into his mystery, and the purpose of creation as revealed in Christ – to explore and to realise the mystery of love – is furthered and deepened.

According to this perspective a 'mere' sign would be like the idle word which Jesus criticises, which fails to accomplish anything (Matt. 12:36). Applied to the liturgy it would be the question raised by the Sri Lankan theologian Tissa Balasuriyea: 'What would be the meaning of fifty-two masses celebrated in a year in a city if as a result of it there were no effort at bridging the immense gulf that separates the rich in their mansions and the poor in their shanties?'[23] A 'mere' sign would be the product of faith without works and 'faith by itself, if it has no works, is dead' (Jas. 2:17). But for that faith which is 'a living, busy, active thing', as Luther put it, the signs are witnesses to God's living and present reality, bushes which burst into flame, signs of hope for an historical journey.

MEANS OF GRACE

In concluding this consideration of the role of sacraments in the divine education we can turn to the description of the sacraments as 'means of grace', familiar to many from the General Thanksgiving of the Book of Common Prayer. The roots of this terminology are to be found in the connection Paul makes between baptism and 'regeneration', the effect that God's redeeming initiative known in the gospel and signified in baptism has for a person. Once grace came to be conceived as a spiritual force or energy then it was but a short step to thinking of the sacraments 'causing' or 'channelling' grace. Thus Augustine writes: 'A person begins to receive grace from the moment he begins to believe in God . . . but the fullness and evidentness of the infusion of grace depends on temporal junctures and sacramental rites'.[24] Aquinas could say that the sacraments 'actually cause grace' and are "instruments of grace". More cautiously Calvin said that the sacraments 'do not of themselves bestow any grace but they announce and manifest it, and like earnests and badges give a ratification of the gifts which the divine liberality has bestowed on us'.[25] For Schleiermacher it was the community which was the 'means of grace' to the extent that it made the influence of Christ present by telling his story and acting according to his precepts. This more immanent account of grace, rescued from the idea of power or energy, makes it clear that the question of means of grace is the question of how God is encountered in the confusion of human history, and of how he is able to draw this history to himself without overruling it or manipulating it.

Since Augustine one of the greatest theological puzzles has been the question of 'grace and freedom', the question of how human freedom could be reconciled with the divine rule. However, if our understanding of grace is anywhere near right, the question is wrongly posed. Grace is incarnate in Jesus, in the powerless and humiliated one, and only thus is it grace. Grace, as we see it encountering people in Jesus, is not in opposition to human freedom but creative of it, and it is here that we find the 'rationale' of the use of signs in the divine economy. The outpouring love and compassion of God which is grace needs 'means' precisely because its aim is to create freedom (Gal. 5:1). 'Signs' – under which we include not only 'baptism and bread' but, with Schleiermacher, the community – are the vehicle of God's 'elusive presence'. A redemption which worked by *force majeure* would not be gracious, and this would include any presence of God which was known 'directly'. Such a presence might cow but would not necessarily redeem – the devils believe, according to James, and tremble, but they do not yield themselves to the attractive power of grace (Jas. 2:19). In attracting the human race to himself God therefore takes the veiled form of the servant, his beauty known in a terrible paradox, and his ongoing redemptive work takes the form of sign and story as rehearsed by a fallible and broken community. These 'means' are of course profoundly ambiguous, but only so are they gracious – enabling of human freedom. Through these means God educates not 'for' the human race but through human structures, just as the Word was conceived in the womb of Mary. The function of story in the divine education we consider in the next chapter, and the function of the community in the final chapter. In this chapter we have seen that sign, story and community may be conceived both as gracious means and as means of grace. They are gracious means in their affirmation and use of the created material reality that we are. The Word became flesh, and that is grace. The Word is known also through bread, wine and water, the trivialities of human community, the inadequacies of human storytelling. This condescension is part of the very essence of grace. It is the signs rather than the symbols that do this, though the symbols also have their place. These signs arise from our engagement with God's engagement, they are a 'given'. Their origin lies above all in that experience of presence which we call the incarnation. They 'cause' or 'channel' or become 'means' of grace when they enable human beings to forgive, to enlarge their horizons so as to include others rather than exclude, to hope for a more human future and therefore to make sense of and to practise that apprenticeship in loving which we know as 'life'. They do this by pointing to and signifying, making present in the mode of sign, the attractiveness of Christ, the paradoxical glory of God's weakness and humility which is the ultimate demonstration of his grace. They are, as Calvin calls them, 'mirrors in which we may contemplate the riches of God's grace' where 'grace' is a summary description of Christ. As signs, not through any form of transubstantiation but precisely in their everydayness, transfigured by the promise like raindrops caught by the sun, they point to the presence of God amongst the bulks of actual things, hiding and revealing, their sign-character enabling freedom, inviting reflection, leading us beyond understanding and interpretation to the transformation of the real.

8

A Meal and a Story

The divine education, we have argued, proceeds partly through signs which, in their combination of both definite content and yet ability to invite further reflection, form fitting vehicles for God's elusive presence. Through the signs, which may perhaps be regarded as 'love tokens' (cf. Gen. 9:12), God woos or educates the human race (for 'the intelligence can be led only by desire') without constraint or compulsion. Chief amongst these signs are what Luther referred to as 'baptism and bread'. In a reversal of the usual practice baptism will be treated only after the eucharist, as a matter of the arcanum, the secret discipline which is primarily the concern of the gathered Christian community. The eucharist, on the other hand, is understood as rooted in a practice for which the paradigm is as much Jesus' meal with Zacchaeus as it is the 'last' supper. It is the sign of the gracious messianic invitation to 'the nations', an invitation extended to all, and as such takes its place in the economy of redemption.[1]

From the very beginning (as we see from Paul's letter to Corinth) Christians have focused their deepest theological and practical concerns in the eucharist. In the course of time it has therefore acquired as almost inexhaustible depth of meaning, but at the cost, sometimes, of lack of direction. The significance of the eucharist has been explained in many different ways – now as a mystic partaking of deity, now as a repetition of Christ's sacrifice, now as a preaching of the Word, now as a simple act of fellowship. Not all these understandings are compatible, and in deciding between them the practice of the Church has to be measured against the practice of Jesus. Accordingly, we begin this chapter with a description and analysis of that practice, from which we attempt to derive our own categories for understanding the eucharist, namely those of meal and story. To put this interpretation in perspective a brief account of the development of eucharistic theology is then attempted. This is the background to the account of how the eucharist, as meal and story, functions in the divine education.

THE ORIGINS OF THE EUCHARIST IN THE PRACTICE OF JESUS

For many centuries people believed that the origin of the eucharist lay in the fact that Jesus, on the night before he died, 'instituted' a rite for the Church he had founded, but the research of the past hundred years has cast doubt on this. Although description of the words at this meal as 'words of institution' is still commonplace, there seem good reasons for doubting such a view. Whilst Jesus is faithful to synagogue and (not uncritically) to Temple he seems to be the last man for rituals, unless it be the ordinary domestic rituals of grace before meals, washing the feet of visitors, greetings and farewells, which we know he paid attention to. At the same time New Testament scholarship suggests that the command to 'do this in remembrance' may not mean, as was long assumed, 'do this as a memorial rite' but 'when you do this, ask God to remember me'. But still, do what? To answer this question we have to look at four events or sets of events in Jesus' ministry.

(a) The table fellowship of Jesus

It is clear from the reports of both Jesus' friends and enemies that table fellowship was a matter of great importance to him. The element in Israel that was serious about the law evidently also took Jesus seriously – they sent delegations to meet him, and thought him worthy of debate and discussion – but they could not understand his extension of table fellowship to those who did not keep the law and even to traitors against the nation.

> And the scribes and the Pharisees, when they saw that he was eating with sinners and tax collectors, said to his disciples, 'Why does he eat with tax collectors and sinners?' And when Jesus heard it, he said to them, 'Those who are well have no need of a physician, but those who are sick; I came not to call the righteous, but sinners.' (Mark 2:16–17)

In Jesus' world, table fellowship was a sign of acceptance and close friendship. Jesus used it therefore as a sign of forgiveness and acceptance, a sign of what Paul later called 'the righteousness of God'. Just as Paul's use of *charis* refers to the quality of Jesus' encounter with people, so 'justification' summarises the experience of Jesus' fellowship meals, occasions on which God's faithfulness to his purposes in creation was demonstrated by putting the unrighteous 'in the right', forgiving and accepting them.

All the gospels, but especially Luke, record many stories of Jesus 'at table'. Luke puts the criticism of the scribes in the context of a meal at the house of Levi (Luke 5:29ff.). He tells of a meal with a Pharisee where the proper rites of welcome were omitted by the host, and performed by 'a woman who was a sinner' (Luke 7:36ff.). He tells many parables about wedding feasts, great banquets, the grace, or denial of grace, of table fellowship, celebration meals which were sacraments of forgiveness and restoration, the damnation incurred by the meals of the rich where the poor are ignored (Luke 14:7–24, 15:22–4, 16:19ff.). Jesus describes himself as having come 'eating and drinking', and it is scarcely surprising that he was accused of being 'a glutton and a drunkard' (Luke 7:34).

The meal with Zacchaeus (Luke 19:1–10) is in many ways the paradigm of all these stories. Luke introduces the story at the end of a long series of parables and other teaching about the danger of riches. We have heard the story of the rich man and Lazarus, and Jesus' stern warning that 'it is easier for a camel to go through the eye of a needle than for a rich man to enter the kingdom of God' (18:25). In this context Zacchaeus is introduced as 'a chief tax collector' and 'rich', and so we know how he should be understood and what fates awaits him – Zacchaeus is a man who has systematically 'camelised' himself. But Jesus brings 'salvation' to him (19:9), he restores his lost humanity – by inviting himself to dinner! By this sign of acceptance and forgiveness Jesus opens up someone who has been turned inwards in greedy acquisition, enabling him to return what he has extorted. Here table fellowship takes its place alongside teaching, healing and exorcism as one of Jesus' chosen means to accomplish his task – restoring humanity to wholeness. Table fellowship is part of the whole 'armoury' of redemption, a 'means of grace', a means by which God accomplishes his restorative and salvific purpose.

(b) The great feeding(s)

In addition to the stories centred on table fellowship there are also various accounts of one, or possibly two great meetings where the distribution of food was an important sign. The conclusion of John's account of this meal, that the people were about to come and take Jesus by force and make him king (John 6:15), alerts us to the meal's messianic significance, an anticipation of the messianic banquet promised in Israel's Scriptures, and spoken of by Jesus in his parables (e.g. Matt. 22:11ff.; Ezek. 39:18). At the same time, and precisely in view of this messianic significance, the evangelists see in the meal also a prefiguration of the eucharist. Thus Mark tells us that Jesus 'took', 'looked up to heaven', 'blessed', 'broke' and shared, and John elaborates this significance with his discourse on Jesus as the bread of life.

The rationalist theologian Paulus, as long ago as 1828, suggested that the true miracle at the feeding of the five thousand was that people were induced to share their lunch packets. Whilst it is clear that all the gospel writers view the incident as a miracle in the strict sense of a breaking of the 'laws of nature', the context of the discussion of the eucharist in Paul's first letter to Corinth indicates that this may not simply be a rationalist reduction. What provokes Paul's comments is a failure to share on the part of the congregation. In this story the disciples react to Jesus' request to feed the people by asking for money to go shopping in the nearby villages, but Jesus tells them to feed the people then and there. According to John it is a boy who first offers to share what he has brought with him, five loaves and two fish. In Paulus' reconstruction others in the crowd had brought food with them, but kept it concealed for fear that if the little they had brought was shared they would end up with nothing. The naivety of the child (incidentally an example of how, as Jesus often remarks, we can learn from children) puts others to shame, and sure enough when all share there is enough and to spare. If Jesus is the Messiah who refused spectacular signs, who expresses in his life and teaching God's confidence in his creature, and if the Messianic age is that situation 'where all may be fully human because all are fully human', could there be a more profound sign of this coming age than a mutual sharing of this kind and might it not be that this is in a much deeper sense the 'true' human miracle?

(c) *The meal on the night before Christ died*

It is in the context both of the regular table fellowship of Jesus and this great feeding that we must understand the meal on the night before Christ died. So much attention has been focused on this 'last' supper that it has become isolated and treated as if it were a unique event. Undoubtedly, the large place given to it in the synoptic records, its appearance in the Corinthian discussion, John's reflection on it in the sixth and thirteenth chapters of his gospel, all indicate the very great importance for the early Church of what happened at this meal. On the other hand it must be understood in the context of all the other fellowship meals of Jesus. The synoptic gospels represent the meal as a Passover meal, whilst John depicts it as happening on the night before the Passover. John has a theological motive for this, as he can then align the death of Jesus with the slaying of the Passover lamb. The case for the Passover dating, however, though strong, is not conclusive and we have to be content with the fact that, as Leenhardt said, paschal ideas were bound to be in the minds of those who attended the supper.

Of the four accounts of this meal those of Luke and Paul seem to stand together on the one hand, and those of Matthew and Mark on the other. Jeremias considers Mark the oldest text on account of its semitisms and the difficulty of some of its expressions.[2] All four accounts agree that Jesus 'blessed' bread before sharing it, and Luke and Paul's use of *eucharistein* rather than *eulogein* to describe this may well be intended to make clear to Gentiles what is meant by a Jewish blessing – which is thanksgiving. This thanksgiving, which accompanied every meal, was not a consecration prayer in the later sense but rather expressed a sense of the holiness and the givenness of everyday life. According to the Emmaus story Jesus was known by the disciples in this moment of thanksgiving, when the bread was broken and shared at the beginning of the meal. It seems likely therefore that this everyday thanksgiving, the giving thanks for the 'ordinary' blessings of creation, was invested by Jesus with particular meaning, that it was one of his characteristics, something which would immediately serve to identify him.

At the heart of all four accounts then comes a word of interpretation over the bread and over the cup which may be a reminiscence of Jesus' Passover *haggadah*, his retelling of the Passover story. According to Mark, Jesus says, 'Take, this is my body,' and 'All of you drink this . . . This is my blood of the covenant which is poured out for many' (Mark 14:22–4). The interpretation of these words has attracted volumes of print over the centuries and it is naturally only possible here to suggest what may be the possible meaning, taking the whole of Jesus' teaching and practice as the essential context for understanding.

In the first place Jesus, the teller of parables, the man of the messianic signs (Matt. 11:2ff.), in this critical hour again makes a parable and a sign out of the bread and wine which they are sharing. Bread and wine, body and blood, stand in parallelism. In Jewish thought 'blood' represented life (Gen. 9:4), whilst who a person was was not separable from their 'body' as it was in Greek thought. It seems then that in this piece of sign-giving Jesus is referring to his life which is 'given' for 'many'. A sacrificial and vicarious reference seems highly probable here. Jesus followed a man who had been executed (John the Baptist) and was by some confused with him; by others he was regarded as one of the prophets to whom Jewish tradition at the time popularly ascribed martyrdom (Luke 13:34). It is most probable therefore that Jesus expected his own violent death. Again, the Jewish world of the time attributed atoning significance to most deaths, especially those of martyrs, so it is not in the least implausible that Jesus attributed such a significance to his own forthcoming death. The 'many', to whom the Marcan text refers, seems to be a Hebraism for 'all' but, rather than meaning abstractly 'all humanity', it may mean 'for the Gentiles as well as for the Jews'. According to Jewish tradition there was no atonement for the Gentiles, and it may be that the Jesus who cleansed the Temple as a sign that it should be a house of prayer for all nations also makes his life offering for the inauguration of the messianic mission to the Gentiles promised in the Scriptures.

Also included in this final parable of Jesus is a word about the new covenant. At the very least we have to understand this as a reference to the new covenant promised by Jeremiah and other prophets, and thus as an act which inaugurates the new messianic age. Jeremiah's covenant has traditionally been understood in terms of 'inwardness, individualism and forgiveness of sins' (T. W. Manson), and this has coloured the understanding of the eucharist as the sacrament of an individual and spiritual religion. In 'Moses and the prophets', however, the covenant stood in the closest relation to the exodus and to the promise of a new kind of society. Thus 'Third Isaiah' can write, in a passage which we know was important either for Jesus or the early Church's understanding of him:

> I the Lord love justice,
> I hate robbery and wrong,
> I will faithfully give them their recompense
> and I will make an everlasting covenant with them. (Isa. 61:8)

According to Luke, it is by quoting the first two verses of this chapter from Isaiah that Jesus inaugurates his ministry in Nazareth. The heart of his announcement is the kingdom, and it would be surprising if, on such an occasion, when in a sign-parable he sums up the whole meaning of his life, Jesus had nothing to say about this. In fact reference to the covenant includes reference to 'the kingdom', for it is the covenant which ratifies the new age. In speaking of his 'blood of the covenant' Jesus therefore speaks of his life which is offered to the uttermost, even to the limits of death, for the realisation of the kingdom of the Father he announced.

According to Mark and Matthew there then follows Jesus' 'vow of abstinence': 'Amen I tell you, I will no longer drink of the fruit of the vine until that day when I drink it new in the kingdom of God' (Mark 14:25). Here again consecration to the realisation of the kingdom is very clear. On the one hand, Jesus here seems to make a final commitment to the way of the cross. On the other hand, Jeremias sees also in this vow a fast on behalf of the Israel which is about to reject Jesus, a final desperate attempt to throw himself into the breach and intercede for his people.[3] The 'eschatological' reference – the looking forward to God's act of vindication – is very clear, and perhaps this may be connected with the primitive prayer, 'Come, Lord Jesus' (1 Cor. 16:22; Rev. 22:20). From the first, stemming from Jesus' own words on this decisive occasion, the eucharist looks towards the breaking in of God's new order.

In the Luke/Paul tradition there then follows the command, 'Do this (*touto poiete*) in my remembrance' (1 Cor. 11:24; Luke 22:19), and the question is, 'Do what'? Jeremias argues that the phrase looks back to Old Testament usage and to the Passover liturgy, and that it is a request not for the disciples to remember (for how are they ever likely to forget?) but for them to petition God to 'remember' his people and his promises. Thus at the Passover the head of the family prayed for 'the remembrance of us, our fathers, the Messiah and your holy city Jerusalem'. In the same way Jesus asks his disciples to pray that God will remember his Messiah and the movement to the kingdom he set in motion. 'By coming together daily for table fellowship in the short period before the *parousia*, and by confessing Jesus as their Lord, the disciples re-present the initiated salvation work before God and pray for its consummation'.[4] Here Jeremias understands the command to 'do this' to mean the continuance of Jesus' table fellowship. For centuries it was understood to mean 'repeat these precise words' so that a eucharist would not be 'valid' if celebrated without them. Gregory Dix applied it to the fourfold action: take, bless, break and share. But the Greek text has 'this' (*touto*) not 'thus' (*houtos*) and it may also be that the injunction should be understood both in the light of Jesus' sign-parable, and of all his commands to 'do' rather than simply to hear. Jesus' words then mean something like this: 'I have given up my life for God's kingdom, for the poor, the marginated, and this broken bread and spilt wine is a sign of the breaking of my body for this doing of my Father's will. And you likewise who are my disciples – you must take you your cross, drink my cup, receive my baptism – for the realisation of this kingdom, for the liberation of people, their freedom, their dignity, their wholeness and growth and completion in humanness'.[5] Augustine certainly understood it like this as late as the fifth century: 'It is your mystery which is placed on the table,' he said in a well known sermon, 'You hear the words 'the body of Christ'; you answer 'Amen'. Be a member of Christ, so that the 'Amen' may be true'.[6]

The early tradition of the Church, which we have in Paul's letter and in the gospel accounts, seized on this meal therefore not because it saw in it the institution of a new rite for a new religion – there is no indication that the earliest Church thought of itself in this way. Rather, in the accounts of this meal the whole meaning and significance of Jesus, of the kingdom which he lived and died for, was seen to be expressed. It became an interpretative focus both for Jesus' life and teaching and for the significance of his death. As such it naturally had a quite decisive influence on the continuation of that table fellowship which played such a role in Jesus' ministry.

(d) The resurrection meals

'. . . God raised [Jesus] on the third day and made him manifest; not to all the people but to us who were chosen by God as witnesses, who ate and drank with him after he rose from the dead' (Acts 10:40–1). Reference to the meal Jesus kept on the night before he died as the 'last' supper is unfortunate because it ignores the evidence of Luke and John that Jesus ate with his disciples after the resurrection. For the early Church that supper was not the last but one of a continuing series, because the eucharist was understood as a meal in the presence of the risen Christ.

The Gospel of John records that Jesus shared a breakfast of bread and fish amongst the disciples, apparently without eating himself (John 21:9–15). In Luke's story of the supper at Emmaus Jesus is known in his familiar action of breaking bread (Luke 24:30, 35). To emphasise the non-spectral character of these appearances Luke represents Jesus as eating a piece of fish (Luke 24:42). These stories are often regarded as a theological reflection on the eucharist, but this seems to put the cart before the horse. The origin of the eucharist as a universal form of Christian practice is surely much more readily explained if there was some definite connection between table fellowship and the resurrection appearances, a connection which seems probable whatever the understanding of the nature of these appearances. Such a connection would account particularly for the joy of the early celebrations (Acts 2:46), which were grounded in the joy of resurrection.

The eucharist of the Christian Church is then rooted in the table fellowship of Jesus and in its varied expression in the great feedings, the paschal meal before the crucifixion, and in the resurrection meals. Jesus understood table fellowship as in itself a redemptive act, an effective sign, which restored dignity to outcasts and sinners, and so created the possibility for a new and more human life for them, a life based on openness rather than closedness, on grace rather than law. When he kept the Passover with his disciples he took up his reinterpretation of his messianic role and once again emphasised that what was true for him was true for his disciples. He had told them that they were to 'take up their cross': similarly, they were to 'do this' – follow in his steps, give their lives for others and for God's kingdom, and the meal, the breaking and sharing, was a sign of this following and giving. As in his lifetime this was to be both a sign and a creative means of the new community. The experience of the resurrection meals shed a vast and new light on what God had done and was doing in Jesus, and in that light the meal acquired new and universal dimensions. But, in the first decades at least, it could not lose the concreteness of all Jesus' practice, and it was not for lack of solemnity but for introducing class-division into the celebration and so denying its grace-giving character, that Paul criticised the Christians in Corinth. As Schleiermacher noted, the reality of the eucharist is to be found in Jesus' re-creative encounter with persons, his acceptance of them into fellowship, and his creation thereby of a new human community, and it is this 'glad encounter' which remains decisive for contemporary eucharistic practice.

FROM MEAL TO CULT: THE GROWTH OF EUCHARISTIC TRADITION

H. Lietzmann suggested that in the early Church there were two forms of eucharist, a joyful fellowship meal and a solemn recalling of the Lord's death, modelled more on Hellenistic practice. The thesis appeals to, among other things, the fact that in Acts Luke speaks only of the Church meeting to 'break bread' rather than to recall Jesus' death. But Paul uses the same language to refer to the eucharist in a context where bread breaking certainly recalls the Lord's death (1 Cor. 10:16). It appeals also to the distinction between *agape* (fellowship meal) and eucharist in later tradition, but here again the eucharist in Corinth was certainly celebrated in the context of a meal. At the end of the first century the *Didache*, or Teaching of the Twelve Apostles, still thinks of the eucharist in this context.[7] Meal and eucharist got separated some time in the second century, a change which Jungmann regards as 'perhaps the greatest change . . . in the whole history of the Mass'.[8] The thanksgiving prayers before and after the meal were now joined in one long prayer, and the fellowship meal followed after the eucharist. Athanasius still speaks of the meal; for Augustine at the beginning of the fifth century it is a charity meal. Thereafter it seems to drop quietly into obscurity.

A more fateful change than the separation of meal and eucharist, though this separation may have facilitated it, was the change in the understanding of the eucharistic sacrifice. In the second century the prophecy of Malachi regarding a 'pure offering' which would be offered 'in every place' among the nations (Mal. 1:11) was regularly applied to the eucharist. The church thought of the 'sacrifice' of praise and thanksgiving, and of obedience, on the lines of Romans 12:1. Late in the second century the apologist Minucius Felix glories in the fact that Christians have 'no shrines or altars'. 'Are not our minds and hearts better places to be dedicated to Him?' he asks.[9] Such a view is found as late as the fourth century in Eusebius of Caesarea, but it is in Cyprian, in the middle of the third century, that a priestly and cultic-sacrificial interpretation of the eucharist clearly emerges. In the eucharist we must do exactly as Christ did, he argues,

> For if Christ Jesus our Lord and God is himself the high priest of God the Father, and first offered himself as a sacrifice to the Father and ordered that this should be done in commemoration of him, then of course that priest functions rightly in the place of Christ who imitates what Christ did and offers in the Church the full and true sacrifice if he so begins to offer according to what he sees Christ himself to have offered.[10]

The cause of this change is a matter for speculation. Jungmann believes that it arose from countering the Gnostic emphasis on spiritual sacrifice which led to the contention that the eucharist was by contrast a 'real' sacrifice. Frend has drawn attention to the influence of native cults on North African Christianity.[11] For whatever cause, the inevitable result was that the eucharist rapidly became a matter of Christian cult. In place of the 'president' there is now a 'priest', understood on the levitical pattern, and altars were constructed following levitical instructions: 'the glorious history of the Christian altar had begun'(!). The appropriateness of keeping such a solemn sacrifice in a house is at least questionable, and so special buildings were required.

In the fourth century a further, and related, change can be marked in the Greek East. Here the eucharist is increasingly assimilated to the mystery religions. From the early emphasis on the joy of fellowship with the risen Lord there is a change to awe and fear. From the eucharist as the normal form of Christian worship for the assembly on Sunday, 'communion' becomes less and less frequent. John Chrysostom speaks about 'the terrible sacrifice', the 'shuddering hour' and 'the terrible and awful table'. One of the chapters of Basil the Great's *Shorter Rule* is entitled: 'With what fear . . . we ought to receive the body and blood of Christ'.[12] This feeling of awe led to a rapid decline in the frequency with which people 'took communion', the very idea of which marks a shift away from the *koinonia* of the Corinthian celebration. A Church council in the sixth century found it necessary to insist on 'communion' three times a year. In 1215 the Fourth Lateran Council ratified a long-standing practice when it declared once a year to be sufficient.

Another change which began in the fourth century can be traced to the new situation of the Church which began with the conversion of Constantine and was ratified when Christianity became the official state religion under Theodosius. The last great persecution occurred in AD 303–4, and right up to that time the Church was in no position to build great churches and conduct ostentatious liturgies. Once the emperor had become a Christian, however, there were new demands. It was obviously inappropriate to worship God in a poor building when the emperor lived in a palace. It was inappropriate to celebrate with humble vessels when the emperor supped off gold and silver. And so began the tradition of liturgical magnificence and the adoption of royal symbols into the liturgy to honour God the Sovereign of all.

These changes in the third and fourth centuries were decisive for what followed in the next thousand years. It was according to the logic of this theology that, in the thirteenth century, the laity were denied the cup, presumably lest a drop of the sacred 'blood' were spilt. Around the same time adoration of the consecrated wafer, the 'host' (from Latin *hostias* meaning sacrificial victim), replaced partaking at communion. Although the Mass was celebrated daily throughout Christendom its corporate dimension had been lost sight of; it became a form of priestly mediation, the most perfect form of intercessory prayer.

Many of the medieval protest movements took issue with these developments, and at the Reformation a certain restoration of primitive practice was effected. In some churches the altar again became a table and the building a *domus ecclesiae*, a meeting place for the faithful. Communion in both kinds was restored to the laity. But the late medieval emphasis on the death of Christ was not overcome – for Protestantism in general the eucharist remained a memorial of Christ's death for sin. The freedom of the early Church for the president to pray 'according to his capacity' was not recaptured. Both Luther and Calvin wanted the eucharist as the normal form of Christian worship on Sundays, but suspicion of the Mass as a piece of popery made this difficult. Calvin was overruled in this matter by the city council in Geneva, who allowed a celebration once a month and this, or an even less frequent practice, became the Protestant pattern.

In the Western churches a change in this situation began in the last century. In the Roman Catholic church the liturgical research which began with Guéranger contributed at last to the restoration of the cup to the laity, a change from Latin to the vernacular, increased lay participation, and a new emphasis on the importance of 'the Word' element. In the Protestant church the Anglo-Catholic and ecumenical movements and especially the rediscovery of the corporate dimension of Christian life, have all contributed to bring the eucharist once again back to the centre of worship. But this new-found centrality urgently raises the question of meaning. What are we doing when we celebrate eucharist?

THE PASCHAL STORY IN THE DIVINE EDUCATION

As we have seen, the significance of the eucharist has over the centuries been grasped in terms of various categories such as 'sacrifice', 'communion', 'real presence', each of which relate to a particular way of understanding God's redemptive action. In the first category the eucharist is obviously thought of as an act of vicarious sacrifice which is mirrored (Calvin) or repeated in the eucharist. The communion category – whilst a Schleiermacher might apply it mainly to the fellowship of the congregation – is more usually applied to God's continuing work through a mystical presence grasped through this particular sign. The Reformers on the other hand spoke of the eucharist as a '*verbum visibile*', and it is this category of Word on which we seek to build, understanding 'word' in the sense of story. As we saw, Jesus' 'last' supper was, if not a Passover meal, at least celebrated in a Passover context, and we know from the Quartodeciman controversy how important the Passover connection was for many early Christians.[13] The Passover is meal, sign and story: it is a meal in which the elements have an important signification, and are used as the jumping-off point for the telling of a story. The eucharist may likewise be regarded as meal, sign and story, and it is as such that it functions in the divine education.

G. von Rad taught a whole generation that if you wished to reconstruct Old Testament theology you had to do so by retelling the story. Story is the framework of the biblical record, even if it does not consist exclusively of stories, and Jewish theology has always had recourse to stories. The power of story was nowhere grasped more vividly than by the eighteenth-century Polish Hasidim, whose stories have been collected for us by Martin Buber. The following story comes to us from the rabbi of Rizhyn, one of the descendants of the founder of this Hasidic movement, the great Maggid:

> Once, when the holy Baal Shem Tov wanted to save the life of a sick boy he was very much attached to, he ordered a candle made of pure wax, carried it to the woods, fastened it on a tree, and lit it. Then he pronounced a long prayer. The candle burned all night. When morning came the boy was well.
>
> When my grandfather, who was the Holy Baal Shem's disciple, wanted to work a like cure, he no longer knew the secret meaning of the words on which he had to concentrate. He did as his master had done and called on his name. And his efforts met with success.
>
> When Rabbi Moshe Leib, the disciple of the Great Maggid

> wanted to work a cure of this kind, he said: 'We no longer have the power even to do what was done. But I shall relate the story of how it was done, and God will help.' And his efforts met with success.[14]

Human existence, says Freire, cannot be silent, nor can it be nourished by false words, but only by true words, with which people transform the world. 'To exist humanly is to *name* the world, to change it'.[15] In the Jewish Christian story God is given a *name*, and the community gathers itself around this name. Through this true naming, the telling of this story, the world is transformed. Like Moshe Leib's story, the story is an event, an effective word, it accomplishes something. It does this in the first instance by 'constituting' a people, the contemporary mode of Jesus' call of his disciples.

'In every generation let each man look on himself as if he came forth out of Egypt,' said the Rabbis, and it was the cult which made this a possibility. If we accept Gottwald's reconstruction of events in pre-monarchical Israel, it was around the stories of the escape of a small group of slaves from Egypt that 'Israel' first gathered itself. These stories gave Israel identity and a sense of historical direction. Writing of the Kalahari bushmen Laurens van der Post said, 'These people knew what we do not: that without a story you have not got a nation, or a culture, or a civilisation.' We may add: you have not got an individual either, and thus the saying of the Hasidim: 'God made human beings because he liked stories.' It is the story which gives a community identity and which therefore constitutes community. 'Stories' have immense power for good or ill, as the examples of the myth of the Aryan race or of White Supremacy or of Patriarchy testify. They are the bearers of ideology, the more powerful as less formalised and operating on subconscious levels. Now in the eucharist the Church retells and gathers around the story of what God has done for all human beings in Jesus. It gathers to hear the story (told in both word and sign) and goes out to tell the story. It is this story which makes us 'church', which gives us identity and purpose. *As such* it is not an idle but an active word, which 'makes history' (once again we note the proximity of our exposition to that of Schleiermacher). It calls into being an historical fellowship with a specific task – and this means that the story is not finished. The story told in the eucharist did not happen 'once upon a time, long, long ago' – it continues. 'The greatest story ever told' is not the story of Jesus, as is often said, but Jesus is the crucial part of that story. We could say that the story begins with the call of Abraham, though like the editors of Genesis we would then have to extend that back to include creation and the whole human story. In response to an experience of presence Abraham and Moses start a new story which according to the New Testament reaches a climax in Jesus' story. The story speaks of the reality, the mode and manner, of God's engagement with human history. Through the story, in the telling of the story, God's story is interwoven with ours so that our story becomes part of his 'without confusion, without change, without division, without separation' as Chalcedon said. As such the story itself, like the fellowship meal, is 'a means of grace'. It calls into being a community which does not exist for itself – as if the point was the creation of the Church – but which exists for others, for the 'exodus' of humanity from slavery, the long road to the freedom of all peoples.

It is at this point that we have to listen to the urgent question put by Asian theologians: 'What was God doing in our story prior to the coming of the gospel?' The question is important and a response will be attempted in the following chapter. In this context we can make just two points. In the first place, God cannot be the author of every human story without history itself being revelation, which would be to ascribe to God the evils of man. The human story needs redemption and the content of the 'good news' is that God redeems it by telling his own story, both a divine and a human story, in the midst of it. Secondly, and more fundamentally, there is the question of how people are constituted by stories. Who I am, and the identity of my community, is a question which in almost every case is answerable only in terms of a plurality of stories. Thus, to take just three examples, a Northern Ireland Protestant embraces in his or her 'story' Celtic, Angevin, Dutch, English, Reformation and biblical stories; a Tamil Muslim embraces Tamil, Indian, Dravidian and Muslim stories; whilst an Anglo-Indian Christian embraces Indian, British, regional and Christian stories. The importance of this is that to convert is not, as Gandhi thought, to lose my story and substitute another one for it; it is to add another chapter to an already immensely complex story. To become Christian is to put my Celtic, Germanic, African, Dravidian or Aryan story into another perspective, to recognise that 'roots' are not primarily a matter of blood and soil but of the story which makes me what I am. Story is far more fundamental than nation as the problem of 'minorities' all around the world very clearly illustrates. Of course there remains the question whether there are human stories which are mutually irreconcilable, so that this putting into new perspective cannot occur – Christian and Muslim stories for example, or even, as is tragically claimed, Protestant and Catholic. This kind of clash occurs when two stories both make ultimate claims, and it poses a problem for which there are no glib or easy solutions.

To anticipate the final chapter, a possible response is to begin with the recognition that whilst God does not tell every story the story that he does tell is about the 'Son of Man', a story which cannot be understood outside of the context of Israel and Church but which is not identical with those stories. With Schleiermacher, though against much New Testament scholarship, we recognise in the term 'Son of Man' the claim that Jesus is not simply the Messiah of Israel but the sign of the truly human in history. To that extent Jesus' story is open to all manifestations of the truly human. Conversely the extent to which exposure to the gospel has highlighted humanist and liberation themes in Hinduism, for example, is very remarkable and this invites a new understanding of how stories acquire different perspectives ('convert'). Jesus called his disciples, bearing witness to the good news he announced, 'the salt of the earth', and salt only works by being lost in the stew – a stew of pure salt would be unthinkable. In this way the gospel might (to mix our metaphors with truly Pauline abandon!) 'flavour', 'add a new perspective to', or become part of the story of a pious Hindu or Muslim without them becoming 'Christian', and through this process that which is adored (what is counted as ultimate) take on Christ-like shape. In any event the story of the crucified is clearly not the account of the *elimination* of all other stories, but of their *redemption* ('salting' or acquiring a new perspective). God's activity in the manifold stories of the human race is still very much veiled in darkness but is nevertheless grasped in essence in the story of Jesus' journey into the heart of darkness (cf. Mark 15:33; '*descendit ad infernos*', as the creed says) which is retold in sign and story in the eucharist. The light on the path of the divine and human story which is shed by this storytelling is a significant part of the Spirit's pedagogy.

Another point of great significance which relates to the constitutive story also derives from the Passover liturgy. Expounding Exodus 12:6 the Mishnah comments:

> After the second cup the son asks his father (and if the son has not enough understanding his father instructs him how to ask), 'Why is this night different from all other nights? For on other nights we eat seasoned food once, but this night twice; on other nights we eat leavened bread or unleavened bread, but this night all is unleavened; on other nights we eat flesh roast, stewed or cooked, but this night all is roast'. And according to the understanding of the son his father instructs him. He begins with the disgrace and ends with the glory; and he expounds from 'A wandering Aramean was my father . . .' until he finishes the whole section.[16]

The pedagogical perception of this passage is very remarkable. It is based on the understanding, which has kept Israel alive throughout the centuries against all odds, that a community survives when the children know its story. It reckons realistically with the fact that children are the future, and that therefore it matters which stories they learn and come to live by. The rubric makes it clear that even very small children are in mind, and the father is instructed to tell the story 'according to the understanding' of the child who learns, not through a lecture, but by participating in a celebration meal. In this respect the connection between eucharist and Passover is of the greatest importance. The exclusion of children from the eucharist in the name of greater solemnity and because it is supposed to be beyond their understanding is not only an ungracious act which introduces an unnecessary division into the body of Christ, but marks a fundamental misunderstanding of the eucharist's real nature. In the eucharist the community gathers to rehearse the story in word and sign. It gathers as the community of wayfarers at the table of the Risen Lord. As at Passover children learn by being included in this fellowship and through participation this story *becomes their story*. In that precise way the future of the

promise is already taking shape and in that way God's pedagogy is exercised. The importance of this point for any attempt to understand how God works in history cannot be overemphasised. And as a matter of justice it should be noted (as we have already noted at one or two points) that Schleiermacher clearly understood and expressed this.

'Church' then is the name for a story-telling fellowship. It is not, on the other hand, a 'literary circle' but, to borrow an image from the patriarchal stories of Genesis, a people which tells stories at the resting points of a journey. In these stories it reflects, questions, celebrates and finds courage. The stories are by no means exclusively or even primarily 'religious'. In the jargon of contemporary scholasticism they 'render an agent' – not 'the divine', but the living, passionate, jealous, wrathful, loving God. This means that the stories have a bias. They speak of a God who 'loves justice and hates iniquity' and who does both passionately, and the eucharist, as visible word, is accordingly a sign of hope and justice.

THE SIGN OF HOPE AND JUSTICE

'Sacrifice' has always been one of the key categories under which the eucharist has been understood. Bearing in mind our discussion in chapter 3 we shall attempt to reflect on this category, at the same time understanding the function of the eucharist in the divine education as a sign of hope and justice.

'Christ our Passover is sacrificed for us,' said Paul, 'Therefore let us keep the feast' (1 Cor. 5:7). De Vaux points out that Passover was a non-cultic sacrifice which did not have atoning power.[17] However, in view of the widespread belief in the atoning efficacy of death prevalent at the time of Jesus, it seems likely that Jesus understood his death in this way, and Jeremias believes that he looked to Isaiah 53 for such an understanding. But in this case we have to go on and recognise that, 'If a man despised and disfigured by suffering, and his death in slavery and his grave with the wicked can be explained as an expiatory sacrifice, this involves a *radical desacralization of sacrifice*'.[18] In other words, whilst the New Testament does not regard Jesus' death as 'literally' a sacrifice, as an offering for sin, nevertheless that death must certainly be regarded as an offering of life for others, and of this the eucharist is a sign. As we have seen, Augustine understood the eucharist in this way: 'God wishes *us* to be his sacrifice, and in the eucharist his sacrifice is consecrated'.[19] Luther too took up essentially this understanding in his *Treatise on the New Covenant*:

> We do not offer Christ as a sacrifice, but Christ offers us. And in this way it is permissible, yea profitable, to call the mass a sacrifice, not on its own account, but because we offer ourselves as a sacrifice only with Christ; i.e. we lay ourselves on Christ by a firm faith in His testament and appear before God with our prayer, praise and sacrifice only through him and his mediation.[20]

Thus the story which constitutes the community tells of a 'radically desacralized' sacrifice of the offering of life for others and calls for such a sacrifice from the community. To understand why this is so we must turn for a moment to the understanding of the eucharist we find at the end of the second and the beginning of the third century.

Prominent in the reflection on the eucharist which we find in Irenaeus and Hippolytus is the theme of the offering of the fruits of creation. Thus Irenaeus spoke of the Church offering 'a pure oblation to the Creator . . . an offering from his creation with thanksgiving', because Christ is 'the Word through whom the trees bear fruit, the springs flow, and the earth yields "first the blade, then the ear, then the full corn in the ear" ' (*A.H.* 4.18.4). According to this perception the eucharist is an affirmation of the goodness of creation – of matter and all its possibilities, of the bodily, the sexual. It teaches us that we cannot by-pass matter on the road to salvation but must go through it. It reminds us that matter is a gift and not to be abused but respected. What is offered in the eucharist is bread which gives 'life', a symbol of all that makes possible that fullness of human being which God intended in creation. But this is just the problem for the most obvious fact of the world situation is that this fullness of human being is not available to all.

From a very early period the Church added to Irenaeus' perception, that the eucharist is thanksgiving for the blessings of creation, the further perception that what is offered in the eucharist is the fruit of human work. Bread and wine do not fall from trees but are produced, they are the product of work, 'the fruit of human hands'. It is work which transforms the earth according to the Yahwist, and it is in work that human beings find dignity and purpose (Gen. 2:15). Not only the good gift of creation is offered but also the good gift of work, which in the second account of creation is part of the blessing and which enables human beings to bring their offering to God. But the story of creation is immediately followed by an account of a failure in the alignment of divine and human purpose, and one of the results of this is that human beings now find work not a blessing but a curse (Gen. 3:17f). The reason for this is not only, and not even principally, that work can be soul-destroyingly hard but that, as both the Deuteronomist and Marx put it in different ways, most people are alienated from their product. For them work is not a form of self-expression, the God-given means of human realisation, but 'toil', a weary scramble to fill a bag full of holes, to find the means of subsistence, in which the gift of time, the basic gift of a person's life, is squandered to no creative purpose. Writing in a situation where there was still the remnants of an independent peasantry, Deuteronomy saw the answer to this as the end of land alienation and the restoration to all of their patrimony, their own plot of land, so that each family might dwell in peace and security 'under his vine and fig tree' (Deut. 15; Mac. 4:4). Writing after the Industrial Revolution, Marx analysed this alienation in terms of the work relationship. People work not for themselves but for a wage carefully calculated to allow maximum profit to a few. The gap between time spent on the work and profit made on the product Marx called surplus value. In this 'surplus' (a bizarre parody of the sur-plus of grace) a person's time, their life, is taken away from them to create profit. In this situation the bread and wine of the eucharist symbolise not only the good gift of creation, and not only the product of work, but the product of *alienated work*. Through this alienation arises the gap between rich and poor. In practice the rich become rich only by appropriating the fruit of other people's work as their own: ' "Rich" as a biblical category means not simply the sinner but the structural, historical, economic sinner; that is, he who enjoys, consumes, utilises the product of other's work as an instrument of domination over them.'[21] The Argentine theologian Enrique Dussel, from whom the above quotation comes, has developed the implications of this for the eucharist through the story of the first priest of the Spanish 'New World', Bartolomeo de las Casas. Bartolomeo was ordained only after serving twelve years as master of a slave plantation. When he came to celebrate his first mass he found his text to be Ecclesiasticus 34:18f:

> To offer a sacrifice from the possessions of the poor
> is like killing a son before his father's eyes.
> Bread is life to the destitute,
> And it is murder to deprive them of it.
> To rob your neighbour of his livelihood is to kill him,
> And the man who cheats a worker sheds blood.

As he reflected on his text Bartolomeo realised that the bread which he was about to offer in the eucharist was the fruit of Indian toil, of slavery. In terms of his text it was offering a sacrifice from the possessions of the poor, and therefore equivalent to murder. In order to offer the eucharist he had to deprive the Indians of the fruit of their labour and so it was stolen bread, the bread of death, which was placed on the altar as the eucharistic offering. But the bread of death cannot be offered to the Lord of Life. The god who delights in such offerings is not the Lord of life but a fetish, whom the Old Testament calls 'Moloch', Jesus calls 'Mammon', and Marx calls 'Capital'. To worship the fetish is idolatry and idolatry is not eucharist. 'Fetishistic worship offers the idol stolen bread, the blood of the poor; eucharistic worship offers the Father of goodness the bread of justice, the bread that has satisfied hunger.' But if the bread of the eucharist is the bread of justice, can we ever celebrate the eucharist, since we are all, willy nilly, caught up in the structures of injustice, which is what we mean by our 'solidarity in sin'? As is well known, the answer of the Bolivian priest and revolutionary Camillo Torres was that we cannot: he forswore the eucharist and went to the hills to join a guerilla band, looking forward to the day when he could once again celebrate in justice. The story of Bartolomeo, however, suggests a different possibility. Paradoxically, that worship which wishes to abolish 'human sacrifice', the destruction of human life in the name of rationalised greed, itself requires a sacrifice – but of a 'radically desacralised' kind. Those who wish to offer the eucharist, to place the bread of justice on the eucharistic table, have first to oppose the fetish, to interpose their body between it and the poor, as Dussel puts it. It is this which Jesus does in offering his life 'for many'. This too the priest Bartolomeo de las Casas did. On the occasion referred to he refused to celebrate the eucharist but took ship back to Spain to obtain a charter for the Indians. On his return he gave the rest of his life to the struggle for their rights, and this meant he was able to go back to the eucharist. The 'sacrifice' of life offered for others is what is demanded of a eucharist in which we do not eat damnation to ourselves, as Paul says, but share 'the bread of justice, the manna from heaven, bread kneaded in . . . commitment to the interests of the poor, to the development of more just economic structures, the practical conditions that make it possible to offer the eucharistic bread, the "bread of life" '.[22]

This enables us to turn once again, and finally, to the question of the role of the eucharist in the divine education. Education, according to Freire, happens not in word only, nor in action only, but in action–reflection. The eucharist is, for Christians, the central moment and focus of the process of reflection. In the eucharist the community is called into being, the liberating story is told, and the sign of the sacrifice of life for others re-enacted. Signs, we have said, form an important part of the Spirit's pedagogy. This sign, by which God educates his community, is a sign both of justice and of hope. It is in the first place, as we have tried to explore in the preceding section, a sign of justice. The offering of bread and wine speaks not only of the goodness of the created order but, as the bread is broken and shared and the cup passed around, signifies that the blessings of creation are to be shared by all. The very act of sharing calls into question the divisions of the community, between rich and poor, male and female, black and white – just as it did in Corinth. Paul went straight from his discussion of the eucharist to his discussion of 'the body', in other words to the discussion of a new order in which there was no place for individualism, for competitive class structures or any other divisions (1 Cor. 12:25–6). It constitutes therefore a protest against injustice. To share in the eucharist is to refuse the great refusal and opt for a more open lifestyle. Every celebration is a protest against the misuse of the gifts of creation, and an opting out of the structures of death, a 'No' to everything which dehumanises us. The eucharist is therefore, as Samuel Rayan puts it, 'a deep act of subversion'.

But in the biblical witness, as Barth insists, the 'No' never exists independently of the 'Yes' and the 'Yes' is always far clearer and stronger than the 'No'. The eucharist is rooted, as we have seen, both in the Passover, which is the feast of freedom, and in the restorative celebratory meals of Jesus. And so if the eucharist is a sign of justice it is at the same time and more emphatically a sign of hope. It not only teaches us what is wrong with the world but shows us the way in which God is putting it right. It is unfortunate that many liturgies still remain essentially a 'memorial' of Christ's death for sin, which gives the liturgy a backward-looking and introspective perspective. But the eucharist commemorates not the death of a martyr, but the death and resurrection of the Lord of life. As a sign of justice it is not a call to grim determination, the sort of sign we are only too familiar with from the 'ennobling' civic art of the Victorian and, later, the Fascist and Stalinist periods. Into the struggle it brings the note of celebration, for without celebration struggle becomes inhuman. The eucharist may be regarded as the story-telling of people on an historical journey, but it is also their feast. The gospel (the Christian story) is not education for justice for its own sake but education for *life*, and therefore for justice. The purpose of the struggle for justice is to remove all that hinders and diminishes life. One day ('in the kingdom') the struggle for justice will be over, but the celebration of life will never be over. And so the celebration reminds those on the road of where they are going, reminds them they are not alone, reminds them that life is stronger than death and that beyond the grave is resurrection. This celebration, stemming from adoration of the God who is life and relationship, beauty and joy, punctures the inhumanity of self-righteousness with which 'struggle' can so easily be invested. If it does not relativise the struggle for justice, it relativises us and our particular struggles. Grounded on the Messianic call of Jesus to table fellowship it is at the same time grounded on the acceptance and forgiveness of that fellowship, a forgiveness which both proceeds from the celebration (cf. Jesus' call to Zacchaeus) and makes the celebration possible (for without forgiveness there can be no celebration). Like the story this Paschal meal shapes the future by giving content to the present tense of redemption. Meal, sign and story are in this way, as Aquinas called them, channels for the working of God's Spirit, instruments in the divine education.

Through them we experience 'the first fruits of the Spirit', and in the hope they engender we find courage for our historical task.

9

Religion and the Labour of God

Israel saw God as labouring in creation and the events of their history. After creation God 'rested from all his work', according to the priestly source (Gen 2:2–3), whilst the Psalmist could speak of the events of the exodus likewise as God's labour (Ps. 106:13). In an oracle of the Second Isaiah God complains that, whilst he has not made Israel serve (*abad*) with cultic offerings, they have made him serve with their sins (Isa. 43:23–4). A later prophet in the same school speaks of God as one 'who works for those who wait on him' (Isa. 64:4). Jesus came calling labourers to God's harvest (Matt. 9:37) and offended religious sensibilities by 'working' on the sabbath (Mark 2:23—3:6). Reflecting both on this and on the Old Testament tradition, John records Jesus as saying, 'My Father is labouring still, and I am labouring' (John 5:17). (The word here is *ergazomai*, used for 'labour' also in, for instance, Matthew 21:28 and 1 Corinthians 4:12.) Paul speaks of members of the ecclesia as 'fellow workers' with God (1 Cor. 3:9; 2 Cor. 6:1) or alternatively as 'fellow workers for the kingdom of God' (Col. 4:11). God labours in human history – a pedagogical labour as distinct from his labour in creation – evoking a response in men and women, making them his fellow workers. The language used to describe the divine labour is that of the Spirit and of grace. The language used to describe the human response to this labour is often enough that of – religion. Where God's labour is recognised and responded to, the thesis runs, there is religion. But is religion really the category correlative to the labour of God? Whether it is possible to affirm this in the light of the biblical witness, at any rate undialectically, is very much a question.

THE MEANING OF 'RELIGION'

Before the Reformation 'religion' was used by Christian theologians only to refer to the sum of the rites and duties attendant on specifically Christian piety. Jerome Cardan was accused of atheism in 1552 for daring to compare Christianity with Judaism, Islam and paganism, and thus for putting all these, as religions, on the same footing.[1] In Herbert of Cherbury's essay *De Veritate*, published in 1624, 'religion' is treated as a meta-category under which to subsume both Christianity and all other religions. Herbert proposed that all religions were based on five 'Common Notions': belief in a supreme God; that this God should be worshipped; that the connection of virtue and piety was the most important part of religious practice; that repentance is necessary to expiate sin; and that there is reward or punishment after this life. Belief, worship, ethical practice, the need for confession, divine sanctions regarding human behaviour (it would hardly be possible to speak of an 'eschatology') – these are what constituted 'religion' for Herbert.

Herbert's ideas were taken up by the Deists of the end of the seventeenth century and the first half of the eighteenth. They rejected the idea of special revelation and the category of the supernatural and advocated a Christianity which was 'reasonable' (Locke) and 'not mysterious' (Toland). In a book which was translated into German and influenced Reimarus, Matthew Tindal argued that there was a religion of nature which was the basis of all the positive (i.e. historically determined) religions, and that the purpose of the gospel was but to free human beings from superstition for this original and authentic worship. These ideas were given enormous currency by Voltaire, who encountered them during his three-year stay in London, and by Rousseau, who advocated a civil religion based on 'natural religion' which was at the same time identical with the 'pure and simple religion of the gospel'.

What is being said by these writers is in the first instance polemical: religion is not a matter of creed and dogma. It is not magic and superstition. It is the articulation of what is perceived to be 'natural' human goodness and gratitude when this is not overlaid by ideology and so spoiled. As such it is the cement of human relations and has a role in fostering civic and international harmony.

Later in the eighteenth century Lessing explored the relationship between natural and positive religion in his play *Nathan the Wise*, as well as in *The Education of the Human Race*. In the play, which takes the form of a dialogue between a Christian, a Muslim and a Jew, Lessing told the fable of the three rings: a father possesses a miraculous ring which makes its wearer beloved of God and man. He has three sons whom he loves equally, and to avoid disappointing two of them he has two perfect imitations made – even he cannot tell the difference. After his death the three sons quarrel about who has received the true ring, and the judge who dispensed the rings counsels that each should strive to reveal the jewel's virtue 'by gentleness, a heartfelt tolerance, good works and deep submission to God's will'. They should return to the judgement seat after the lapse of a thousand thousand years during which time the power of the true ring will have come to light in the proof of 'spirit and of power', which is to say in what promotes tolerance, understanding and real human community. For Lessing the religion of the 'third age' which humankind is entering is reason, understood in this sense, the internalising of the moral law. On similar lines Kant described religion as 'the recognition of all our duties as divine commands', which he considered a religion 'solely within the bounds of reason'.

Reacting to this excessively ethical definition of religion ('piety is not an instinct craving for a mess of metaphysical and ethical crumbs') Schleiermacher, in his early period, preferred to describe religion in phrases like 'surrender to the universe', 'the sense and taste of the infinite', 'the sum of all relations of man to God, apprehended in all the possible ways in which any man can be immediately conscious in his life'.[2] What Edward Caird called 'the haze on the page' in Schleiermacher is particularly evident here. What is clear at this stage is on the one hand the rejection of religion as either a set of dogmas or a set of ethical beliefs, and on the other hand its identification with a more or less monist intuition, the 'sense' of the oneness of all reality. Further, Schleiermacher addressed his first book to the *cultured* despisers of religion, and he sought to show this audience that in the pursuit of philosophy, science and the arts the workings of the religious spirit might be discerned. 'See then,' he tells them, 'whether you wish it or not, the goal of your highest endeavours is just the resurrection of religion. By your endeavours this event must be brought to pass and I celebrate you as, however unintentionally, the rescuers and cherishers of religion.' 'Religion' then is a name for the human response to all 'promptings' for a more cultivated life, and in this way 'the sum of all the relations of man to God'. Naturally this means that there cannot be one religion which is 'true' at the expense of others, a position which Schleiermacher maintained even in his mature work. He tells his readers,

> You must abandon the vain and foolish wish that there should only be one religion, you must lay aside all repugnance to its multiplicity; as cordially as possible you must approach everything that has ever, in the changing shapes of humanity, been developed in its advancing career, from the bosom of the spiritual life.[3]

In his later work sense and taste for the infinite becomes the feeling of absolute dependence, something which is part of the 'absolutely general nature of man'. Every such essential element of human nature 'leads necessarily in its development to fellowship or communion', and in this way the positive religions develop. Beginning from the 'absolutely general', Schleiermacher naturally arrives at a position of degrees of truth. To the extent that all religions give expression to the feeling of absolute dependence all are equally true, but some have a more perfect and complete expression than others. By this stage Schleiermacher considers a 'predominating reference to the moral task' a mark of 'higher religion'. Although several religions belong to the same stage as Christianity 'it may yet be more perfect than any of them', an opinion ultimately defended in terms of his christology. 'Religion' is now therefore all expressions whatsoever of the feeling of absolute dependence, but also a graded reality in which it is important to speak of 'higher' and 'lower' according to a standard for which ethics provides the key. Schleiermacher assumes a developmental or, as it later came to be called, an evolutionary framework. Religion begins with fetishism, progresses through polytheism to monotheism, and amongst the monotheistic religions Christianity is the most perfect that has so far appeared.

Working with an evolutionary scheme, Lessing and the Deists, as well as the early Schleiermacher, all canvassed the possibility of Christianity being superseded. It was at this position that Troeltsch arrived at the end of his life. For him all the great religions (and therefore probably all the great world cultures) are a 'manifestation of the Divine Life itself', and all are based on 'a profound inner experience'. In the *Absoluteness of Christianity* he saw the Christian religion at the summit of the evolutionary spiral because it 'develops the personalistic religious idea and its liberating power to its maximum clarity and strength' and because 'its natural, spontaneous absoluteness is the purest and most inwardly oriented expression of the power of religion'.[4] Later on he renounced the possibility of objectively determining the relative value of the various religions, thus abandoning the developmental scheme.[5] Religion is for him human knowledge of and relation to God as this is articulated within different cultures, and each religion should 'strive to fulfil its own highest potentialities and allow itself to be influenced therein by the similar striving of the rest'.

RELIGION AS UNBELIEF

Karl Barth was brought up, not indeed in the school of Troeltsch, but still in a school where he heard that Schleiermacher's *Speeches* was the most important book written since the New Testament. Herrman, the author of this remark, along with Harnack, Gunkel, Bousset and nearly all the leading figures of pre-First World War theology worked with 'religion' as a central category. When this theological establishment collectively declared its support for the German war effort Barth was shocked into rethinking his theological foundations. In a fresh reading of the biblical texts he discovered that 'the polemics of the Bible, unlike that of the religions, is directed not against the godless world but against the *religious* world, whether it worships under the auspices of Baal or Jehovah'.[6] In his commentary on Romans, written whilst he was pastor of the small town of Safenwil, he elaborated a highly dialectical view of religion. On the one hand he saw it as the supreme human possibility, so that, 'There is for us no honourable alternative but to be religious men, repenting in dust and ashes, wrestling in fear and trembling, that we may be blessed; and since we must take up a position, adopting the attitude of adoration'.[7] Religion must be cultivated, nursed, stirred up, reformed, revolutionised. But 'the more zealously this labour is undertaken, the deeper we penetrate the valley of the shadow of death'.[8] For religion is 'the highest summit in the land of sin', the place where people most effectively screen themselves against God's demand. Therefore 'religion must die. In God we are rid of it'.[9] This dialectic Barth later took up in *Church Dogmatics*, using the ambiguous word favoured by Hegel, *Aufhebung*, meaning both the abolition but also the exaltation of religion. Here Barth understood religion more systematically as the attempt to forestall God's revelation, and also as the attempt at human self-justification. The religious man does not really believe, said Barth:

> If he did, he would listen; but in religion he talks. If he did, he would accept a gift; but in religion he takes something for himself. If he did, he would let God intercede for God: but in religion he ventures to grasp at God. Because it is a grasping, religion is the contradiction of revelation, the concentrated expression of human unbelief.[10]

In the same vein Barth spoke of the 'ultimate non necessity of religion'. The religious person is 'like a rich man, who in the need to grow richer (which cannot, of course, be an absolute need) puts part of his fortune into an undertaking that promises a profit'.[11] Whereas for Barth's antagonist, Schleiermacher, piety was a positive category, Barth singled it out for attack: 'It is the characteristically pious effort to reconcile Him to us which must be an abomination to God, whether idolatry is regarded as its presupposition or its result, or perhaps as both.'[12] As the document of a revelation which contradicts every religion of works, the New Testament contradicts all religion as such.

Barth is operating with at least two meanings of the word 'religion' in these passages. One is purely descriptive, phenomenological: 'religion' means the sum of beliefs and practices of any human system orientated towards humankind's transcendent goal. Thus Pure Land Buddhism, Indian Bhakti religion and Christianity are all indifferently 'religions' in this sense. But 'religion' is also a qualitative word for Barth: these systems are all without exception human attempts to do what God alone can do. This is not a negative value judgement based on religious science or philosophy – Barth too is not interested in evolutionary schemes. It follows from his understanding of God's historical revelation in Christ. If God is revealed in the human being Jesus, says Barth,

> It is not that some men are vindicated as opposed to others, or one part of humanity as opposed to other parts of the same humanity. It is that God Himself is vindicated as opposed to and on behalf of all men and all humanity. That it can receive and accept this is the advantage and pre-eminence of Christianity, and the light and glory in which its religion stands.[13]

The fact that revelation singles out the Church as the locus of true religion does not mean that the Christian religion is 'the true religion, fundamentally superior to all other religions'. All the same, because the Christian religion is 'the predicate to the subject of the name of Jesus Christ' we can speak of a religion – in the first sense used by Barth, of a system of belief and practice – which is created, elected, justified and sanctified by God, and therefore of a 'justified sinful religion' in the same way as we speak of a justified sinner. And this, maintain Barth's critics, despite all his efforts to insist that Christianity *qua* religion is more under judgement than other religions, his insistence on charity and caution in discussing other religions, his insistence on their human greatness, amounts to making a virtual exception of Christianity among all the world religions.

As a young pastor Bonhoeffer was excited by Barth's critique of religion and, writing from prison in 1944, he spoke of it as Barth's 'really great merit', though he felt that the critique ran out into a 'positivism of revelation'. As opposed to Barth he was less inclined to stress the 'human greatness' of religion and more critical of its dehumanising aspects. Barth opposed religion and revelation to one another, but Bonhoeffer drew a distinction between faith and religion. He felt that 'religion' was a partial reality which related especially to inwardness and conscience, whereas faith is 'something whole, involving the whole of one's life'. Identifying religion with piety, he thought that it concentrated on saving the soul, whereas in the Old Testament 'is not righteousness and the kingdom of God on earth the focus of everything?' Religion tends to look to the God who solves problems, the projection of human weakness, whereas 'the Bible directs man to God's powerlessness and suffering'. He saw the way in which religion was used to bolster the *status quo*, how it functioned as 'the strongest guarantor of the safety and continuation of the existing order, power structure and ways of thought', as his correspondent and later biographer Bethge puts it.[14] For these reasons he speculated on the possibility that religion was but a passing historical phase which humankind will grow out of, and seems to have envisaged a withering away of religion much as Marx envisaged the withering away of the State.

In the 1950s and 1960s Bonhoeffer's ideas were taken to be primarily concerned with a supposedly irreversible move towards secularism and decline in religious practice in the West. Barth's critique and the opposition of religion to faith was used in a very undialectical way to belabour other religions and establish the superiority of Christianity. Not surprisingly the new enthusiasm for religion which followed this very short-lived secularism has used this as an excuse for ignoring these critiques altogether, and much theology and 'science of religion' has sailed cheerfully back to the age of Troeltsch as if nothing had happened in between. But the question about how God works in history, and what he is redemptively up to, still remains, and with it the question of the role of religion in the redemptive pedagogy. Essential to the attempt to answer this question is an examination of Barth and Bonhoeffer's contention that an undialectical enthusiasm for religion runs counter to the biblical witness.

THE PLACE OF RELIGION IN THE BIBLICAL WITNESS

Reflecting on the theological implications of the book of Leviticus, B. S. Childs remarks that in that book:

> A witness is given that the institutions and rites which determine how Israel is properly to worship God derived from the divine revelation . . . The canonical shape provides a critical theological judgement against any reading of the tradition which isolates the priestly elements of the tradition from the so-called prophetic, or plays the one against the other.[15]

The prophets, it has been emphasised, were not opposed to the cult in principle but only to abuses in the cult. A prophet like Ezekiel was certainly interested in the restoration of the Temple cultus. The further thesis that the classical prophets of Israel emerged from the cult prophets common in ancient Near Eastern temples is probably overstated, but equally a simple opposition between the two groups cannot be granted. A great many if not all of the psalms seem to have come from Temple sources and the Wisdom literature may have originated in groups of scribes gathered round court and Temple. It is the 'priestly' writer or school who offers us the final redaction of many of the Old Testament traditions. 'Religion', in the sense of the structures of corporate piety, obviously plays a vital role both in the life of Israel and in the transmission of the biblical writings. Similarly, in the New Testament Jesus does not appear as a cult reformer: he frequents both synagogue and Temple, and he teaches his disciples to pray together. The early Church found it natural to gather round 'sacramental' practices such as baptism and eucharist, and believed this to be according to Christ's wish.

At the same time it is undeniable that religion itself is not the theme of the biblical witness. Even a book like Leviticus, where cultic prescriptions play a large role, moves from these to a description of the Jubilee Year, a radical political proposal for a more just society (Lev. 25). The theme of the Pentateuch taken as a whole is not the cultus but Israel in its historical societal existence, an existence in which religion (cult and ethical practice) plays a vital part but which cannot be reduced to religion alone. Likewise in the historical books the Ark, the Temple, the necessity to sacrifice, the contest with Canaanite modes of worship, all play their part, but religious practice can hardly be said to occupy the centre of the stage. The central concern of the prophets is not cult but the doing of God's will in establishing justice and righteousness, and the movement of the nations as instruments of God's judgement. The ethical practice involved here could only be called 'religion' in the very broadest Kantian sense of the word. At the same time the prophets develop a radical critique of the cult, a critique which no priestly redactor either dared or wished to eliminate. A prophet whose call seems to have come in the Temple could still protest:

Bring no more vain offerings;
  incense is an abomination to me.
New moon and sabbath and the calling of assemblies –
  I cannot endure iniquity and solemn assembly . . .
cease to do evil,
  learn to do good;
seek justice,
  correct oppression;
defend the fatherless,
  plead for the widow. (Isa. 1:13, 17)

A later prophet in the same tradition challenged the meaning of fasting when it was accompanied by oppression of workers:

Is this not the fast that I choose;
  to loose the bonds of wickedness,
  to undo the thongs of the yoke,
to let the oppressed go free,
  and to break every yoke? (Isa. 58:6)

The same note is echoed by most of the great prophets and indeed finds its way into the psalms (Ps. 51:16) and into the Wisdom literature (Ecclus. 34), and is later taken up by the author of James in his famous definition of 'true religion': 'to visit orphans and widows in their affliction and to keep oneself unstained from the world' (Jas. 1:27). The prophetic critique of the cult is directed at it as being the sign of an idolatrous and oppressive practice. What they demand in its place however is first of all right practice, described in the most 'secular' manner possible. Right cult by contrast usually figures as an eschatological reality.

Jesus stands squarely in this tradition. He does not come to reform religion or found a new religion, but he comes preaching God's kingdom, the need to 'do' Torah in a radical sense. As one who stands close to Pharisee belief and practice he illustrates in one encounter after another, and in many parables, the way in which religion can dehumanise people. When the institution of the sabbath is given a perverted sense for 'death' and not for life, Jesus is 'grieved' at the hardness of his opponents' hearts and freely sets the religious cultic obligations to one side in the interests of the restoration of human life (Mark 3:1–6). In conversation with a lawyer Jesus tells how religious obligations to offer service in the Jerusalem temple can destroy a person's humanity, making them blind to the true temple of God lying wounded by the roadside (Luke 10:25–37). Similarly, at the root of Paul's experience, as he speaks of it in Galatians, is the perception that an extreme religious zeal only led to destruction (Gal. 1:13–14). To make religious practice the central thing is to submit to a 'yoke of slavery', and in relation to this Christ offers a sovereign freedom, the freedom which follows from the fact that the Sabbath (and all religious observance) is made for man and not man for religious observance.

The account of religion in the biblical tradition is, therefore, highly dialectical. Cult, worship, temple, eucharist, even theology (as this is represented by scribal teaching) – all these may be regarded as 'God-given', but they are not the *raison d'être* of human life. As William Temple put it in an authentically biblical perception, 'It is a great mistake to suppose that God is only, or even chiefly, concerned with religion.' Religion is an essential part of the history of Israel, but the history of Israel is not the history of a religion. Israel is an *am*, a people, with a religion like all other peoples, but its history, from the exodus, through the settlement, the monarchy, the exile and return, is the history of that people's struggle for freedom and not of its religion. The disciples of Jesus, and the group which gather round them after the resurrection are not an *am* in the same way, but neither are they the devotees of a mystery cult or a gnostic religion. They are people caught up in the movement towards God's kingdom, a movement which involves corporate prayer and worship but is not identical with that worship. Thus religion is accepted, but it is strictly relativised at the same time as against the 'weightier matters of the law': obedience to God's will (1 Sam. 15:22); justice and righteousness (Amos 5:24); conduct informed by faithfulness (Hos. 6:6), love of the neighbour (Luke 10:37; 1 John 4:20). It is this will taking shape in a particular society, shaping the world in a particular way, which is the heart of the biblical witness. This will is certainly not apprehended without and apart from religion, from the whole tradition surrounding the cult, but it is not identical with any particular set of religious practices or indeed with religion as cultus at all. Here we should note the extreme secularity of, for instance, the court history (2

Sam. 12:20) or the story of Joseph, in which God's will is seen to be done in the course of 'secular' events which have scarcely any reference to cultus. In the same way Jesus lives what his more pious contemporaries regarded as a profane life (Mark 2:18, 7:5ff.) and certainly died a profane death. This death at once declares nothing to be outside the sacred (*pro fanum*) but at the same time points to a life offered up for others as the true shrine, the true sacrifice, the true religion (the theme of the letter to the Hebrews).

THE LABOUR OF GOD AND HUMAN WISDOM

God is labouring in human history, and according to the New Testament the meaning of that labour is revealed in Christ: its meaning is humanisation, the kingdom of God, the situation where all may be fully human because all are fully human.

In *The Unknown Christ of Hinduism* Raymond Pannikar proposed that God had provided the means of salvation for all human beings, and that these means were the great religions of humankind and their sacraments.[16] In other words, the principal fruits of God's labour are the religions. Two difficulties attach to this suggestion. One is the fact, which all the criticisms which Barth and Bonhoeffer bring against religion serve to illustrate, that religion may get in the way of the process of humanisation, as well as forward it, and that it may indeed be the most severe obstacle to God's purpose, alongside which mere atheism is a triviality. When Athanasius, in *Contra Gentes*, attacks pagan religion as the invention of demons, this may not be the product of a myopic Christian fanaticism but a product of the same perception as that of Barth and Bonhoeffer, that in their religious systems human beings have built for themselves towers by which every kind of oppressive structure is defended and sanctified. By the same token it needs to be remembered that Barth's attack on religion and natural theology appeared first during the First World War (when Barth's paper, 'Biblical Questions, Insights and Vistas', was written), in which the conflict was sanctified by the churches of both sides, and then during the period of National Socialism, when it was decisively influenced by his opposition to quasi-religious elements in that movement.

Secondly, if God is said to be revealed in a unique way in Christ, this raises the question of the relation of Christianity to the other religions. If it is correct, as Schleiermacher said, that it does not stand in the relation of the true to the false, then how are we to conceive the relation? This question was raised the moment Israel came into real contact with Greek culture, and the suggestion of 'the Wise', both in Proverbs and Ben Sirach, has provided a model which is followed to the present day. Ben Sirach suggested that whereas Wisdom was fully domiciled in Israel, God had left a certain portion to the nations 'according to his gift' (Ecclus, 1:10). Following up this suggestion Justin proposed that God's Logos was indeed to be discerned in all human strivings after truth and goodness but that it had been *fully* manifested only in Christ:

> Our religion is clearly more sublime than any teaching of man for this reason that the Christ who has appeared for us men represents the Logos principle in its totality (*to logikon to holon*), that is both body and Logos and soul. For all that the philosophers and legislators at any time declared or discovered aright they accomplished by the investigation and perception in accordance with that portion of the Logos which fell to their lot. But because they did not know the whole of the Logos, who is Christ, they often contradicted each other. (2nd *Apol.* 10.1)

This solution to the difficulty commended itself to many nineteenth-century missionaries, and was given classic expression by Farquhar who described Christianity as 'the Crown of Hinduism'. It is essentially this solution which Pannikar adopts, suggesting as he does that Hinduism is a preparation for the gospel. The problem in most of its expressions, and both Justin and Pannikar are good examples of this, is that it tends to suggest a highly intellectualist account of religion, concentrating on the noblest elements of Greek philosophy in the one, and on Advaita in the other. The religion of the Roman empire however was the worship of *lares* and *penates*, the Orphic and Mithras cults, and the worship of Caesar before it was Stoicism or Platonism. In the same way Hinduism is far more a religion of the wayside, of the village square, and of the home, than it is of the great philosophical systems. Where is the scale which measures the progress from 'religion' to 'quasi-religion', as all religions preserve large elements of superstition within them, much of which is far from harmless? And is there not a close relationship between all kinds of fundamentalistic chauvinism, such as is highly characteristic of all parts of the contemporary religious scene, and the quasi-religion of National Socialism, for example, with all its superstitious and idolatrous elements? It does not do to define 'religion' in too intellectual a manner.

Following the suggestion of Ben Sirach and Justin we will attempt to respond to these two different questions, though diverging from their answer at one important point. Pannikar points to religion as the main focus for the work of God, but if we begin with Paul's vision of Christ as the Wisdom of God a different focus is suggested. Using the tradition of Wisdom (already deeply implicit in the source of gospel tradition we call 'Q') Paul sees Christ as the heart of the meaning of creation (Col. 1:16). This image takes us, therefore, to the 5,000 million years in which 'there is no speech nor language', during which span of time this earth, and *homo sapiens*, slowly evolved from the raw unshaped energy God unleashed in the moment of creation. This energy takes on shape and form during this unimaginable length of time through what the priestly writers spoke of, in a moment of extremely profound insight, as the brooding of the Spirit (Gen. 1:2). This labour of God is not appropriately described in the same way as God's labour in history. That is a pedagogical labour which proceeds through dialogue, story-telling and sign-giving. This is a much more deeply veiled and hidden labour: the length of time, the seeming randomness, the wastage of evolution all bear witness to the fact that God does not work by producing things ready made, nor even by 'engineering', and it is perhaps in the patience that this immense process implies that God is most truly revealed. It is true that as a result of this labour the psalmist can say that 'the heavens declare the glory of God' (Ps. 19:1), but we can perhaps designate this labour of God's providence, as opposed to the story-telling which begins with Abraham or Moses, God's 'silent labour'.

With the emergence of *homo sapiens* there is an immense qualitative leap in evolution, so that there is now for the first time the possibility of an I and a Thou between God and the creature, and the question is, how is this I and Thou realised? The answer of Pannikar, and many Asian theologians, is that this I and Thou is reflected in all human religious traditions, but the difficulty with this position is the immense diversity of the human response, which contains mutually contradictory intuitions about the nature of ultimate reality. If there were really an I and a Thou, would we not expect some more fundamental agreement about this intuition? If we could imagine that representatives from a hundred different cultures all went to meet some great *starets* or guru who lived in seclusion in a remote spot, and if we further suppose that adequate time was given for meeting, and language difficulties were overcome, it is certain that the one hundred resulting accounts would differ, but they would differ so as to complement one another rather than to contradict each other. A further difficulty is this: an I and a Thou is always something very specific and very particular, occurring in this situation at this time and place between these people. 'I and Thou' means history, and history means the particular. The suggestion of this essay, echoing many distinctions familiar from the tradition, is as follows: what we have called God's silent or hidden work is his wooing of creation to the point where human beings evolve. It is a wooing of creation which wishes to elicit a 'Thou'. It is wholly the work of God. This work of God's Wisdom, 'fashioning all things', continues to give shape to creation even when creation becomes history, and the results of this work may be seen in the whole variety of human cultural traditions. If the goal of God's labour is 'hominisation', becoming like Christ, then the fruits of this labour may be seen in every cultural value which makes for human fullness. Thus the author of Proverbs ascribed the law and order which the Gentiles enjoyed to the Wisdom of God (Prov. 8:15). The fruits of this labour are the emergence of ever more human relationships, of more just social structures, of art and music, of philosophy and – as part of this whole complex – religion. Here 'religion' is understood as that combination of cultus, reflection and practice which relates directly to humankind's transcendent goal. As a human phenomenon religion in this sense is no more and no less a response to the silent wooing of God's wisdom than any other cultural phenomenon. No less: with Barth and Kraemer, and every missionary who has spent any length of time in close contact with the non-Christian religions, we can only express astonishment at the human greatness to be found in religion and in the cultural products the religions give rise to. But at the same time, no more! As Tillich especially has emphasised, a deep ambiguity runs through every human achievement and religion shares in this ambiguity. Every human tradition, including religious traditions (and including, of course, Christianity), contains much which is still chaos, the product of nothingness, the refusal of order, grace and the Spirit, and which may therefore serve de-humanisation rather than serving life. And we should not be misled, by the fact that religions speak explicitly about the transcendent, into thinking that for that reason it is to them we should turn if we wish to learn about God. There are many gods and many lords. Justin agreed with his accusers that Christians were atheists 'of such supposed gods as those of the heathen' (*Apol.* 1.6). Jesus and the early Christians were atheists of both Caesar and Mammon! Religion is not necessarily nearer God in its talk of what is divine but may rather represent the deepest human darkness. Here we should perhaps qualify the even-handed 'no more and no less'. When he came to the exegesis of Romans 13, Barth started from the insight that the God of whom Paul was speaking was truly revolutionary because his aim was the creation of the radically new. Therefore, said Barth, the revolutionary is far closer to the purposes of God than the conservative, but for that very reason stands in a far greater danger of perverting the gospel, by confusing his revolutionary programme with the divine initiative. Analogously the religious person, in the search for the transcendent which is God, is likewise in the place of greatest danger, and precisely in his or her religious speech and activity may be confronting God with the keenest opposition and the deepest obscuring of his revelation.

Alongside this 'silent work', not better than it, or as more truly the work of God, but exercising a different function within the one divine economy, arises the sign-giving and story-telling and the calling of Israel and Church. In both parts of the divine economy there is a response to God, but there is here an invitation to the particularity of I and Thou, a very particular direction to the divine human engagement. This distinction between the two aspects of God's work suggests the classical distinction between general and special providence or the later distinction between secular and salvation history. The problem with these distinctions is that they are not adequately rooted in christology. If we begin where Paul begins, with Christ as the Wisdom of God, then we have to say that there is only one form of God's providence, at work in the whole universe and in the whole of human history, the work of God's Wisdom or Logos, and that within the scope of that one providence God's Wisdom becomes flesh as the decisive means to accomplish the divine purpose that human beings should become fully human, that life should triumph over death. It is not, as Ben Sirach and Justin suggest, that God's Wisdom works in most places partially but in Israel and Church fully (for what would be a 'partial' working of God?), but that the Spirit works fully in the whole history of creation and, within history, is the 'agent' of the taking flesh of God himself. Again, there is only one history, which is salvation history. This does not mean that all human history is as such the history of salvation (God forbid!), but that the Word takes flesh within the whole of human history. This means that there are two responses to the question, 'What was God doing in my (Asian, African, North European, etc.) history before we received the gospel?' On the one hand the life-affirming aspects of that culture and religion are a response to God's 'silent labour', truly and completely the work of God in all human traditions. At the same time we can say that God was working in my history by working in Israel and Church, because it is part of the divine economy that the nations should tell one another their stories, that their stories should intermingle and flow into one another, and that the story of the crucified God should season all other stories by revealing what is idolatrous and what is not idolatrous in all other traditions. There is then one world history with many different parts; in every single part the Wisdom of God was and is silently at work; but for every single part that Wisdom took flesh. It is a matter of the economy of God's work, the two aspects of which are equal but different, and also of a fundamental *human solidarity*, 'in Adam' and 'in Christ' which transcends, even though it is articulated within, the different world cultures and races and in the name of which we must oppose all the chauvinisms which are such an ugly part of the contemporary scene.

From this point we can return to the question of the particular role of religion within the divine economy. At the Parliament of Religions held in Chicago in 1893 Vivekananda proposed that all the religions should unite in the face of the threat of growing secularism. But if Christ as the Wisdom of God is at the heart of reality, then secularism as such is not a threat. In the biblical witness people are not called to be religious first and foremost, and Jesus offers no new techniques or ideas for religious experience. Jesus calls people rather into an historical movement, a progress towards human freedom and fullness, towards life, in which 'religion' – prayer and corporate worship for example – plays its small but indispensable part in the process of humanisation. Human freedom and fullness are not there without religion, but religion without the concern for peace and justice is, according to both Jesus and the prophets, an empty charade, a way of death and not of life. The forces of death which are a threat to God's redeeming education are not identical with secularism and may, by contrast, be hallowed by religion, as for instance in the murder of tens of thousands of people in Latin America in the last thirty years in the name of the defence of 'Christian values and civilisation', or in the justification of apartheid or patriarchy from the Scriptures. From the biblical perspective, an atheist philosophy which opposed these forces of death would be closer to the kingdom of heaven than a religion which supported them. It is not religion as such which is the means of human salvation, but human salvation is attained through the pursuit of all those things which make for life *informed* by religion, by the practice of prayer and worship. If it would be an exaggeration to say that this applied to 'all religions', yet it may apply to many religious practices in many religions. At the same time the question of the relation of Christianity to the other religions cannot be avoided.

Revelation, said Barth, involves human beings being told what they cannot tell themselves, which means that revelation always runs counter to human expectation. From this perspective the specifically 'revelatory' aspect of what happens in Christ is that opposed to all human conceptions of the consolations of religion, of God the Father-figure who meets every need, God is revealed on the cross, his power is seen in powerlessness and his wisdom in folly. Revelation is thus not esoteric knowledge which may be guarded and manipulated by priests and theologians, but the disclosure of God's bias in history, of his presence alongside the oppressed. What is revealed therefore is the meaning and direction of world history and not a religious truth or system.

It follows from this that the objection, that to recognise a distinct revelation in Christ amounts to making virtual exception of Christianity amongst the religions, is not entirely accurate. God's act in Christ discloses the meaning of history and of world process. This does not make Christianity a better or more authentic religion than other religions, because we are not dealing with the revelation of religion as a means of salvation. Like all religions, and like all human cultures, Christianity responds to the mystery which is Christ, but unlike other religions it responds to the mystery become flesh and crucified. This is how we would restate Justin's Logos theology – not as partial on the one hand and complete on the other, but as hidden, pre-existent, working through the Spirit on the one hand and crucified on the other.

To argue thus is to reverse the procedure of Schleiermacher, who defined culture in terms of religion. Rather, we should seek to understand religion as one part of culture. Nevertheless it is also to accept his insight that what humanises may be taken as a response to God. When the nations come offering their treasures to God (Isa. 60:3ff.; Rev. 21:26), they are offering the fruit of what the Spirit has wrought in them. These fruits include, but go far beyond, religion (this applies even for countries such as India where religion and culture are closely, but not – as is often carelessly said – inextricably combined). If this humanist, because Christ-centred, tradition is accepted, it calls for a fresh perspective on inter-faith dialogue.

THE SCOPE AND NATURE OF INTER-FAITH DIALOGUE

Vivekananda liked to tell the parable of the blind men and the elephant: a number of blind men touch an elephant – one its soft and moist trunk, another the nails on its feet, another its tail, another its tusks, and so on. Just as the blind men's description of the one animal vary, so all the religions witness to the one God in different ways. In a variation of this parable, replacing the elephant by a seer, we have suggested that contradictory intuitions call the fundamental equality of the descriptions into question. Vivekananda's parable suggests that dialogue between religions is a matter of sharing different approaches to God, and indeed insofar as all religions represent a response to the mystery at the heart of reality there is some truth in this. But if we start from the incarnation (and our parable deliberately replaces the elephant with a human figure), this would indicate that to begin by talking about God is to begin at the wrong end. The crucial question in revelation is not first about God but about what is truly human, about what humanises, and then and in that context about God. Dialogue, says Freire speaking of the process of education, is 'the encounter between men, mediated by the world, in order to name the world', and this applies equally to the encounter between the religions.[17] This encounter must be conducted, as Lessing said, with 'heart felt tolerance', but what is meant by 'tolerance' is widely misunderstood, and Barth's warning on this score deserves quoting at length. Urging tolerance in the discussion between religions he went on,

> Now this tolerance must not be confused with the moderation of those who actually have their own religion or religiosity, and are secretly zealous for it, but who can exercise self-control, because they have told themselves or been told by others that theirs is not the only faith, that fanaticism is a bad thing, that love must always have the first and last word. It must not be confused with the clever aloofness of the rationalistic Know-all – the typical Hegelian belongs in the same category – who thinks he can deal comfortably and in the end successfully with all religions in the light of a concept of a perfect religion which is gradually evolving in human history. But it must also not be confused with the relativism and impartiality of an historical scepticism, which does not ask about truth and untruth in the field of religious phenomena, because it thinks that truth can be known only in the form of its own doubt about the truth. That the so-called 'tolerance' of this kind is unattainable is revealed by the fact that the object, religion and the religions, and therefore man, are not taken seriously, but at bottom patronised. Tolerance in the sense of moderation, or superior knowledge, or scepticism is actually the worst form of intolerance.[18]

On these grounds he could later say in the same volume, of the meeting of Catholics and Protestants, that such a meeting must be conducted with 'genuine dogmatic intolerance' – as between people who take each other seriously and do not patronise each other.

A 'tolerant' dialogue between human beings 'in order to name the world' consists then in attending on the revelation of the truly human as this is known and experienced and reflected upon in all human traditions. The presupposition of such a dialogue is *conversion*, which is not in the first instance a matter of changing religious traditions, nor even the psychological and moral experience of those William James called the 'twice born', but that new reading of history which is part and parcel of Paul's conversion. Paul's about-turn came when he encountered Christ in those he persecuted. This led him to a quite new understanding of God and his action in history: seeing God in the cross led him to see the strength of God in weakness and the wisdom of God in what to worldly eyes was folly. The radical judgement that this meant for him, the shaking of his foundations and the consequent need for re-creation – this is the deeper meaning of conversion which the Jewish-Christian Scriptures insist on for all people and all cultures. However, this conversion has echoes and analogues in all human traditions. It led Paul to read history henceforth from below upwards, as the history of the power of weakness, rather than from above down, as imperial history, in which he now saw the weakness of power. This kind of conversion, to the poor, to the weak, and to those of no account, is not restricted to Christianity, and has analogues in many traditions – in Hinduism in the Puranic literature for instance, which preserves stories critical of the theology which validated the great Hindu dynasties and legitimises caste. On the basis of this shared conversion to a new reading of history 'from below' a real dialogue becomes possible in 'tolerant intolerance' concerning genuine differences. In this dialogue concerning what humanises two criteria suggested by Bonhoeffer, worldliness and powerlessness, are important.

If dialogue is concerned with what fosters humanness, then it cannot begin by dividing the world into two realms, the secular and the sacred, and then advocating the union of all religions in the face of growing secularism. There is only one *saeculum*, of which religion is a part, and 'inter-faith dialogue' takes place within the one *saeculum* as part of the process of naming this world, seeing that all become the subjects of history and that creation's own rights are respected. Inter-faith dialogue becomes sterile if it is isolated and carried on in a 'purely religious' framework. Dialogue between the faiths has to begin concretely from local issues of unfreedom, with the question of womens' rights or caste oppression or race, for example. The question of God only becomes meaningful in this context, as such discussions throw up the question on which side God is on: for example, whether he is the dominating, White, Father figure, or whether he is on the side of the oppressed. In naming the world God is also named at a level beyond pious generalities, and real meeting becomes possible.

Similarly, if dialogue is concerned with what humanises, then it must reject conceptions of God, of whatever provenance, which alienate human beings and justify oppressive structures. The high God of all religious traditions, absolute and unquestionable solo power, has always been used to provide religious sanction for tyranny and non-representative power. The powerless God on the other hand subverts all such systems, as the lordship of Christ subverted the lordship of Caesar. In the same way Bonhoeffer draws our attention to the way in which the 'God' who is but the projection of infantile fantasies of omnipotence leads to escape from reality and to religion as opiate, whereas the suffering God points to the power of weakness. Thus what Moltmann calls 'the crucified God'

> brings liberation from the divinized father figures by which men seek to sustain their childhood. It brings liberation from fear in the ideas of political omnipotence with which powers on earth legitimate their rule and give inferiority complexes to the impotent, and with which the impotent compensate their impotence in dreams. It brings liberation from the determination and direction from outside which anxious souls love and at the same time hate.[19]

Dialogue between the religions therefore begins from the worldliness and powerlessness of God; it begins from 'the power of the poor in history' as Gutierrez calls it. It is an extension of that practice of attention whereby we wait for silence to approach and 'linger a moment over its transparent face', for the still pool in which God's reflection is found is not primarily my own consciousness but those Jesus spoke of as hungry, naked and imprisoned, and in whom he promised to meet us. It is only dialogue which begins here which can and does establish that community of equals, that meeting of human beings in freedom, respect and love, which Jesus announced as the kingdom, and it is in such dialogue that we recognise the divine education.

10

The Church in Human History

Beginning from Jesus' preaching of the kingdom of God, we have attempted to understand what God is redemptively up to in human history. Following the suggestion of Origen and other early theologians we have tried to grasp at least some aspects of this work through the image of a divine education. The strength of the image, compared with other images such as redemption and sacrifice which emphasise the 'once for allness' of what happened in Christ, is that it highlights God's patience and the nature of salvation as dialogue and continuing process. According to the so-called 'Farewell Discourses' of John's gospel (John 14–17) salvation is a history. Its root and ground is in the life, death and resurrection of Jesus, but the work of salvation goes on until the kingdom is 'delivered to God the Father', as Paul puts it (1 Cor. 15:24). Or as Bishop Westcott is supposed to have replied to the query 'Brother are you saved?', 'It depends whether you mean *esothen, sozomai* or *sothesomai*' (I was saved, on Calvary; I am in the process of being saved, through the work of the Spirit; I hope to be saved, in the consummation of all things). 'Salvation' does not just have a past tense but a present and a future, and each tense speaks equally of the work of the one God, the undivided Trinity. A problem, with Cullman's otherwise helpful distinction between 'D day' and 'V day' is that it suggests that what comes after Calvary simply consists in 'mopping-up operations'. As we have sought to conceive it, the incarnation is the crucial moment in redemption but not at all its sum. To claim this is to fail to grasp God's 'project' in the whole of human history which is realised both through incarnation and the work of the Spirit.

To speak of God as being at work in 'the whole of human history' raises the problem which we have stumbled across again and again in the preceding chapters. In the first place, human history is not only the record of response to the Spirit's wooing but also a history of flight, of refusal. Salvation is not only a history but the redemption of history. Secondly, 'history' is not a universal, but a record of particulars. God can only commit himself to history, work within history and redeem history by committing himself to the particular. To speak of God in this way is to discern his action in particular persons, places and times. Not all the plants of human culture are straining equally towards the light: monism and theism are mutually contradictory intuitions about the ultimate nature of reality; Gautama, Jesus and Mohammed cannot be equally the final word of salvation to human history. To understand God as the Lord of history, along with Amos, Isaiah and Paul, means to accept the 'scandal of particularity', the claim that the Spirit's working in the whole of human history is to be discerned especially in Israel, in the Jew Jesus, in the Church, and in the Jewish Christian Scriptures. Something of what it means to speak of this work of God has been seen in the account of the divine sign-giving and story-telling, but God not only gives signs and tells stories but calls into being a community, Israel and Church, and in these two we claim to find God's work of redemption forwarded. When it comes to making this claim for the Church, the scandal is compounded in a twofold way. Firstly, the Church of which we speak is the church of the crusades, the Inquisition, the wars of religion, the pogroms, the Concordat, a church which even today in places justifies apartheid and in places preserves a bitter hatred between Protestant and Catholic. Can God's redeeming education be discerned in *this* community? There is more to this scandal than particularity, and it cannot be brushed aside with clichés about ordinary people making extraordinary claims.

Secondly, the compromise formula which marked the end of the European wars of religion – *cuius regio, eius religio* (following the religion of the country you are in) – no longer applies anywhere in the globe, though various fundamentalisms seek to make it apply. In countries where there are large groups of people of different faiths, communities very easily fall prey to the evils of communalism – that situation where community solidarity is turned against other communities – Protestant against Catholic, Christian against Jew, Hindu against Sikh, Muslim against Hindu. In such a situation the

Church, which Jesus intended as the germ of a new universal humanity overcoming all distinctions, may be just one more group feeding the evil of communal strife. How then should we understand the Church's role in human history, what has traditionally been called its 'mission'? In attempting an answer we shall first outline the nature and role of the community as we discern it in the teaching of Jesus, and then turn to the relation of the Church to the body politic. The reflections of Bonhoeffer, especially in the prison letters, will be of great significance in that section. The answer given there makes it natural to ask the question of the role of baptism within the divine economy. Finally, a somewhat broader sketch of the Church's role in human history is attempted, which measures itself against various contemporary understandings of mission and evangelism.

THE COMMUNITY IN THE TEACHING OF JESUS

The Church derives not only from the life and teaching of Jesus but more fundamentally from the resurrection and from Pentecost. All the same, it is Jesus' life, death and teaching which are the crucial interpreters of these events. Thus, for instance, the charting out of the newly discovered territory 'ecclesia', which we find in John and Paul, has to be measured against the teaching of Jesus regarding the community. The question whether Jesus intended to 'found' the church is wrongly put, since the Church is founded on the events of Easter and Pentecost, but without doubt Jesus attracted disciples, chose twelve as the representatives of the 'new' Israel of Jews and Gentiles and addressed to this group a great deal of teaching about the 'lifestyle' of a group which lived by the messianic promises. From this teaching we can single out four related themes.

In the first place the community which Jesus calls and sends is a community of those who have burned their boats, who are on the road, who face the possibility of hostility, persecution and suffering. The community is constituted by the command to 'follow' (Mark 1:17) on a hard and narrow 'way' (Matt. 7:14) which involves the denial of security: 'And a scribe came up and said to him, "Teacher, I will follow you wherever you go." And Jesus said to him, "Foxes have holes, and birds of the air have nests; but the Son of Man has nowhere to lay his head" (Matt. 8:20) It is not so much a 'disciplined' community which Jesus calls into being but an 'action group' of the radically committed. Nothing is promised this group except Jesus' cup and baptism (Mark 10:38). The demand is made not only to the disciples but to the whole crowd: 'If any man would come after me, let him deny himself and take up his cross and follow me' (Mark 8:34). The 'cross' in this demand, whether this saying goes back to Jesus or to the early community, is not a symbol of 'suffering' in general. There is no reference here to either inner or otherworldly asceticism, in which Jesus was not interested. The cross is the punishment for those who get across the paths of the powers that be, in Jesus' time the power of imperial Rome, in the present time of all those governments of every political and religious persuasion which continue to demand homage to Caesar. The martyrdom of Bonhoeffer, Romero and Steve Biko, as well as of countless thousands of Christians less well known, mostly in 'Christian' countries such as Argentina, El Salvador, the Philippines, all resulted from refusing this fundamental homage. Jesus does not create a community which would glorify suffering for its own sake, but a community whose commitment makes them aliens, with no fixed address, in territory under the control of the powers.[1]

This uncompromising refusal to dally with the powers is the reverse side of the establishment by Jesus of a community committed to the values of the kingdom (Mark 10:13ff.; Luke 12:32ff.). The Beatitudes, and the teaching in the 'sermon' which Matthew and Luke gather round them, are not a starry-eyed picture of an ideal community but Jesus' outline of God's work of subversion. Jesus calls a community who will live by the mercy and compassion of God, which will give priority to the poor, the broken, and those without voice, who will be poor in the Spirit which rests on and empowers God's Messiah, who will work for God's *shalom*, and who will *therefore* be persecuted and reviled (Matt. 5:1–12). The community is that group in which God's transvaluation of values is apprehended and cherished as the clue to his redemptive purpose.

The transvaluation of values is at the heart of a third and very fundamental determination of the community. Although the debate about whether Jesus understood himself in terms of Isaiah 53 has reached no consensus, there can be no doubt that Jesus used the word 'slave', or servant, in a very fundamental way to describe the way he saw the vocation both of himself and his disciples. The saying recorded independently in Mark 10:45ff. and Luke 22:25ff. is central to this description. Which version of the saying is more authentic is difficult to determine, but it is unlikely that the Church which worshipped the exalted Lord would have freely created the story *ab ovo*.[2] In both gospels the context is a discussion with the disciples about future rule in the messianic kingdom. In both versions Jesus at once draws a contrast with Gentile rulers who glory in the exercise of power. Mark then follows: 'But it shall not be so among you; but whoever would be first among you must be your servant (*diakonos*), and whoever would be first among you must be the slave (*doulos*) of all.' Jesus explains the necessity of this in terms of his own self-understanding: 'The Son of Man came not to be served but to serve.' In Luke Jesus takes an illustration from their familiar table fellowship, 'I am among you as one who serves,' and thus the leader amongst the disciples is also to be 'as one who serves'. It is presumably some such piece of teaching that John takes up in his account of the 'last supper', where Jesus concludes: 'A servant is not greater than his master; nor is he who sent greater than he who sent him.' (John 13:16). Washing feet, as Jesus did on that occasion according to John, was the task of slaves. In addition to this there are a great many occasions where Jesus takes slaves as an illustration in parables which apply to the community. In another echo of the Johannine story Luke records that Jesus says, 'Blessed are those servants whom the master finds awake when he comes; truly I say to you, he will gird himself and have them sit at table, and he will come and serve them' (Luke 12:37). The disciples are to say of themselves, 'We are only unworthy servants' (Luke 17:10). Those who use their 'talents' are compared to 'faithful and wise servants' (Matt. 25:21). Thus if we ask who are the community according to Jesus we have to reply that they are *douloi*, slaves. It is this emphasis Paul takes up in Philippians where he speaks of Christ 'taking the form of a slave' and urges the community to 'have *this* mind amongst yourselves' (Phil. 2:5ff.).

Related to this is the fact that Jesus' call is addressed to the poor, those who are persecuted (Matt. 5:10), the 'little ones' (Mark 9:42, Matt. 10:42, 18:10), the 'least' (Matt. 25:40, 45) or 'simple ones' (Matt. 11:25 par.), people who are 'uneducated, backward and at the same time irreligious'.[3] Jesus called 'those who had been proscribed by the "remnant" groups. His command to his disciples to invite the poor, the crippled, the lame and the blind to their table (Luke 14:13) . . . amounts to a direct declaration of war on the Essene "remnant" groups'.[4] Jesus' attention to children, and his comparison of the community to children, also falls for consideration here: 'deaf and dumb, weak-minded, under age' was a repeated description in religious law. It is as those who have no voice that Jesus says to the disciples, 'to such belongs the kingdom of God . . . whoever does not receive the kingdom like a child shall not enter it' (Mark 10:14–5).[5] Here we are reminded of Paul's description of the Corinthian community in his first letter: 'not many wise . . . not many powerful, not many of noble birth; but God chose what is foolish in the world to shame the wise, God chose what is weak in the world to shame the strong, God chose what is low and despised in the world, even things that are not, to bring to nothing things that are' (1 Cor. 1:26–8).

The same applies to the conditions of discipleship. Jesus sends out the twelve with 'nothing' – except a staff (Mark 6:8). They are defenceless and unprotected like sheep among wolves (Matt. 10:16 par.). They will be refused hospitality and slandered. They will receive the blow on the right cheek which expresses 'the greatest possible contempt and extreme abuse'.[6] When the disciples discuss the power they are to have in the kingdom, Jesus promises them only his baptism and his cup (Mark 10:38). Again we are led to think of Paul's correspondence with Corinth, where Paul records that the 'answer' he received to the petition to be freed from his thorn in the flesh was 'my power is made perfect in weakness' (2 Cor. 12:9).

We can also point to images of hiddenness and patience in Jesus' teaching. The point of comparison in the parables of the leaven may not simply be the 'compelling certainty' of the coming of the kingdom, but may well include, as the image suggests, a silent and hidden growth. Similarly, the point of the salt parable in Matt. 5:13 is its flavouring, but salt only flavours by being lost in the stew. Jesus' word on the practice of God's providence, 'he makes the sun to shine on the evil and the good', likewise assumes a purpose hidden within given regularities (Matt. 5:45). This too is implied in the presence of Christ in the hungry, the strangers, the naked, the prisoners, which has not been discerned by those who actually helped them (Matt. 25:38). Paul too has a word on necessary patience amidst the groaning of the whole of creation (Rom. 8:25).

The community gathered round the promise of the kingdom has then a servant status, according to both Jesus and Paul; its strength is in weakness, and accordingly its 'progress' is hidden and often invisible to eyes which are not perceptive. It is in terms of this perspective that we must understand the great images used for the Church in the New Testament, the 'body of Christ', the 'people of God', the 'new creation', the 'bride of Christ', images which have so often suggested an undialectical understanding of power and glory.

Finally, and also part of the transvaluation of values, Moltmann has drawn attention to the importance of the category of friendship to describe the community. The community is to reject the pattern of hierarchical rule (Mark 10:42–5). In its place is the community of friends (Luke 12:4; Matt. 11:19; John 15:13–4) where people relate to each other in a brotherly way, as amongst equals.

> Friendship is an open relationship which spreads friendliness, because it combines affection with respect. The *congregatio sanctorum*, the community of brethren, is really the fellowship of friends who live in the friendship of Jesus and spread friendliness in the fellowship, by meeting the forsaken with affection and the despised with respect . . . Compared with the concept of the friend, the concept 'brother' implies the inescapable destiny to brotherhood – even in conflicts . . . Compared with the concept of brother, the concept 'friend' stresses freedom.[7]

These four elements of the community as found in the teaching of Jesus – the community of radical commitment, the community oriented to the kingdom, the servant community, and the community of friends and comrades – remain decisive for the community which derives from the resurrection and from Pentecost. Through such a community Jesus sees God's will for his world being accomplished. But already by the time John's gospel was written 'world' was a category to set over against the community: 'They are not of the world, even as I am not of the world,' says Jesus in that gospel (John 17:16). How then are Church and world related? The next three sections seek to answer this question in different ways: the first in terms of the relationship of the Church to the political order, the second in terms of what it means to be 'called out' in baptism, and the final section in terms of the wider sphere of human religions and cultures.

THE CHURCH AND THE POLITICAL ORDER

In Jesus word and act are one: he announces the kingdom and heals the lame, blind and deaf. He pronounces forgiveness of sins and, in an acted parable, tells the forgiven man to get up and run off home. He talks about the need for service and washes the disciples' feet. He preaches good news to the poor and feeds them with bread and fish. He teaches the disciples about the new covenant and at the same time breaks bread and shares wine. He abolishes the *lex talionis* and teaches love for the enemy, and he dies on the cross. The final astonishing instance of the unity of Christ's word and deed: he speaks of the need of repentance, new birth and new life; he is raised from the dead. Word and deed constitute a hermeneutic circle for the understanding of Jesus: the word is necessary to interpret the deed, but it is the deed which authentically interprets the word.

From the beginning the community understood itself in this unity of word and act. It could not be simply a preaching community with a 'purely religious' function; its preaching at once spilled over into action, according to Paul in the collection for the 'saints' in Jerusalem, and according to Luke in a new sharing community and in works of service. In the first three centuries the unity of word and act in the Church remained a question of the poor helping the poor, but after the establishment of Christianity as the religion of the state the act of the Church became, like its word, the act of a powerful, financially consequential organisation. It was not the act of a slave community on behalf of slaves but of a mighty community with a servant ideology. 'Servant' could now designate extremely powerful ministers of the crown as well as popes and bishops who could on occasion humble kings. The unity of word and act now involved the Church in an overt political role, and this proved profoundly ambiguous. On the one hand it reflected the correct perception that the Church's gospel has something to say about how people's lives are ordered and therefore that it has a political relevance. On the other hand it gave rise to the false identification of the Church with the Kingdom, the idea that salvation was guaranteed only within the Church, and consequent persecutions under the pretext of seeking salvation for those outside the Church.

This ambiguity of Christendom is not easily resolved, for it appeals to essential aspects of the gospel witness which cannot be surrendered. Above all, when we say 'church' we mean not a collection of individuals but a body, a community, and therefore an institution. The romantic dream of a non-institutional church is a piece of ecclesiastical docetism, a failure to take historical existence seriously. Thus the unity of word and act involves both community and institution, and the various Christendoms which developed from the fifth century onwards, as well as the Puritan theocracies of the sixteenth and seventeenth centuries were all ways of understanding the Church's political responsibility in a corporate sense. It seemed natural that if word should be accompanied by deed Christian states must be the result, and the same logic presumably underlies the 'Christian' Democratic parties and trade unions found today in Europe and Latin America. Compared with this, the Lutheran attempt to put religion on one side and politics on the other, or the Enlightenment attempt to make religion the affair of the individual and only politics the affair of the body corporate, must be recognised as a mistake. On the other hand, the experience of religio-political theocracy always resulted in the Church abandoning its servant status. This experience leads Hans Küng, from a Roman Catholic standpoint, to restrict the Church's role to 'spiritual *diakonia*'. 'How could the church ally itself with the powers of this world,' he asks, 'or identify itself with any secular unit, political party, cultural organisation, economic or social pressure group, or give uncritical and unqualified support to a particular economic, social, cultural, political, philosophical or ideological system?'[8] But if it fails to do this, how does it expect to have any effect? Parties, unions, organisations and pressure groups are the warp and weft of history, and if the Church chooses to ignore them she condemns herself to irrelevance. If we wish to change the world and not simply interpret it we have to involve with such groups. Meanwhile we see the group which wishes to restrict the Church's role to spiritual *diakonia* giving 'uncritical and unqualified support' to a political system which identifies the gospel with its opposite, the pursuit of Mammon. How then should the Church as body and institution exist in the unity of word and act?

Bonhoeffer came to reflect very profoundly on these questions in the last year of his life in prison in Tegel. His starting point is always the Lordship of Christ. The problem for him is not: how can a desperate and dwindling church respond to the 'challenge' of secularism. The problem is, given Christ's lordship, what does it mean to take that lordship seriously? It means, said Bonhoeffer, that Christ is already 'in' the world – the Church does not take him to the world but discovers his presence there. The starting point is positive, in the risen and therefore present Christ (the starting point of Bonhoeffer's lectures on christology). But the present Lord is also the crucified, and this has two consequences. In the first place it means that God's action and rule must be understood in terms of *powerlessness*. As Bonhoeffer put it in a now famous passage,

> The God who is with us is the God who forsakes us (Mark 15:34). The God who lets us live in the world without the working hypothesis of God is the God before whom we stand continually. Before God and with God we live without God. God lets himself be pushed out of the world on to the cross. He is weak and powerless in the world, and that is precisely the way, the only way, in which he is with us and helps us.[9]

The statement 'only the suffering God can help' should not be understood as a reduction of the gospel to *theologia crucis*, nor primarily as an answer to the question of theodicy, but as a description of *the mode of Christ's lordship*.

Secondly, Christ's lordship also involves *worldliness*, not in the profane sense but, as Bonhoeffer said, in the sense of being for the world. If Christ is really Lord of the world then discipleship consists not in church-related activities but in worldly activities: 'The Church must share in the secular problems of ordinary life, not dominating, but helping and sharing.' Christ liberates men 'to find their own responsible answer to life through his own powerlessness'.[10]

These ideas led Bonhoeffer to think of Christian life elliptically in terms of an arcanum, a 'secret discipline' of worship on the one hand, and complete involvement in worldly affairs on the part of Christians on the other. 'Christ is no longer an object of religion, but something quite different, really the Lord of the world,' he said. 'But what does this mean?' He was not given time to work his ideas out further, but it is these ideas which exercise a church deeply threatened by the evils of communalism, where everything that the Church does may be read simply as a form of boosting the Christian community over against other communities, Hindu or Muslim communities for example. Bonhoeffer seems to suggest that, whereas the Church 'gathers' (as institution) for worship, it acts, as it were anonymously, in and through its members. Just as the whole Church is involved in each congregation, be it never so small, because the whole Church is not the sum of its parts but is whole in each of its parts so, it might be argued, the whole congregation acts in each of its members, but these members act *in their secular role*.

The point of this elliptical view was twofold. On the one hand Bonhoeffer felt it protected the Christian faith from profanation – important in Nazi Germany, as today in those countries which ostentatiously espouse 'Christian' values and seek to enlist the Church to give justification for all sorts of chauvinist ventures. The arcanum makes the point that Christianity is not the religion of any country, race or party, and that there are demands which attach to Christian worship which may be incompatible with those of these other communities. Bethge goes on to point out that the 'arcane discipline' might also serve to protect the world from violation by religion, from the tasteless invasions of privacy common to the method of so many 'evangelical crusades' for instance.[11] This confusion of mission with crusade – the attempt to evangelise through non-evangelical means – leads on to the second point. In prison Bonhoeffer found himself irritated by some of his pious fellow prisoners, and drawn to those who professed no faith. He was not interested in 'evangelising' those prisoners, but he found it easy to speak about religion to them:

> While I often shrink with religious people from speaking of God by name – because that Name somehow seems to me here not to ring true, and I strike myself as rather dishonest (it is especially

bad when others start talking in religious jargon: then I dry up almost completely and feel somehow oppressed and ill at ease) – with people who have no religion I am able on occasion to speak of God quite openly and as it were naturally.[12]

Both in his letters and in the *Ethics* Bonhoeffer often notes the need for reserve, a kind of arcanum in human relationships, and this becomes the base for a non-aggressive, non-crusading Christian 'presence' which enables the gospel to be preached at a level much deeper than the pious clichés of crusades permit. Whilst Bonhoeffer was developing these thoughts from prison Simone Weil and Henri Perrin were also reflecting on Christian presence, in a way which led the latter on to the shop-floor as a 'worker priest', where his clerical identity was set aside and he 'witnessed' from his position of complete solidarity with the workers. After the war, spurred on by the reflections of Charles de Foucauld and the Little Brothers, the understanding of mission as presence became widespread. 'Presence' does not simply 'let the world set the agenda', but through the twofold practice of worship and solidarity it makes space for the integrity of the other. With regard to the question of the relation of Church and world it suggests that there is no specifically 'Christian' involvement but only complete solidarity in 'secular' affairs by Christians. This calls in question the 'Christian' label of so many projects and action groups in the Third World which only too often inadvertently contribute to communal tensions. If Bonhoeffer's perceptions are correct, for Christians to choose to work under 'secular' auspices rather than to plant a cross conspicuously wherever they go is not a cowardly retreat from mission, but the enabling of mission in the deepest sense.

Suggestive as this elliptical model is, it has its problems. Does the idea of the Church acting in each of its members really do justice to the corporate nature of the Church? Does it not leave the Church too exposed to the whims of eccentric and even downright mischievous individuals? And the idea of the arcane discipline, which refers to the practice of the early Church in barring the non-baptised from attendance at the eucharist, suggests a closed and ungracious practice, whereas the eucharist is the open, gracious messianic invitation to all peoples. Rather than this elliptical view of the Christian life, therefore, we could try to grasp the unity of the Church's word and act in terms of the differentiation of the so-called 'three offices of Christ' highlighted by Calvin who spoke of Christ as prophet, priest and king. Beginning from the axiom that every statement about Christ is at the same time a statement about the Church, Moltmann has elaborated the ecclesiological significance of the threefold office with great power and beauty.[13] The concern here is not to repeat what he has said but simply to understand how an ecclesiological reading of the threefold office might help illuminate the relation of Church and world. It can perhaps be set out as follows:

In its priestly ministry the Church continues the open table fellowship of Jesus, inviting especially the marginalised and oppressed (Luke 14:15–24), and it tells there the liberating story of God's act in Jesus. In the context of this fellowship the Church as institution gives thanks for and prays for the world. It gathers round the word of Scripture in the expectation that it will hear there 'a word which urgently concerns the very marrow of our civilization' (Barth), and in this way learns the direction of the action expected of it.

In its prophetic ministry the Church speaks, on the basis of its reading of Holy Scripture and in obedience to that, to the situation of the world in which it finds itself. The prophetic ministry is to 'cry out for the Jews' – the oppressed in every situation – and only that justifies the priestly ministry, 'singing Gregorian chant'. The prophetic ministry may be the concern of a few exceptional individuals within the community – Amos, for example, indignantly repudiated membership of any prophetic guild (Amos 7:14), and in the Second World War the 'preacher of Buchenwald' 'refused to worship idols' though not a member of the formal church opposition to Hitler. Equally it may be the concern of the Church-in-council, as at Barmen or Medellin, where the Church formally takes a stand against political positions incompatible with the gospel. What is precluded by this prophetic ministry is any kind of Concordat, a repetition of the war theology produced by theologians of all countries during the First World War.

In its kingly ministry the Church is the follower of the king who was a servant. She is not thereby limited to diaconal or charitable activity, filling in where the state fails to provide, a sort of 'church of the gaps', but is called to solidarity with the slaves, with the oppressed and this is the form of its rule. What was wrong with the Christian theocracies was not simply that the Church surrendered its critical role and lost sight of the 'eschatological proviso', but that it lost sight of its servant status. The Church is certainly involved in the power game, but from a particular direction, from below. It is certainly called to a royal office, but this does not mean arrogating the power of 'the lords of the Gentiles'. Its 'rule' is rather exercised through acts of solidarity, service and suffering with the victims of history. Only in this way, as Bonhoeffer saw, can the Church be faithful to the Lord who rules 'from the tree', and to the kingdom which comes in him. The Church therefore, even as an institution, is not called to forswear politics, to avoid all political alignments, for the idea that such a stance is possible is illusory. To preach the separation of religion and politics is simply to opt for the *status quo*. The question is not the avoidance of politics but which and what manner of politics, and the answer to this question is not in doubt. The good news to the poor which is the substance of Jesus' proclamation can call for only one kind of practice, a being alongside the 'oppressed'. Bonhoeffer saw this quite clearly, and for this reason in his sketch for 'a church of the future' he anticipated that the Church would have to dispense with all its inherited wealth.[14] To exercise its kingly rule, to live in the unity of word and act of Christ himself, the Church has to perceive the weakness of power and opt for the power of weakness.

In the form of these three ministries the Church is 'for' the world. This is the positive worldliness of which Bonhoeffer spoke which takes effect in specific words and actions in specific situations, in the interests of life where life is threatened or diminished, be this in the community or the environment. This worldliness involves the affirmation of a 'secular' state which cherishes the freedom of minorities and dissident groups, and opposes the attempt to impose by force any religious or political ideology.

BAPTISM AND THE ARCANUM

It is only at this point in the discussion that baptism can be considered. The traditional understanding of baptism was symbolised by the design of the medieval European church: this was a substantial building, often with a crenellated tower, which symbolised its garrison character. Near the door was the font, and baptism in the font was necessary for admission to the garrison and permission to go and eat there. Baptism was at once a moral and mystical reality: it incorporated the believer into the body of Christ, made them 'one' with Christ, and in so doing cleansed the believer from sin. It was 'the acknowledged rite of entry' into the Church, and in it 'everything needful for salvation' was given.[15] This view appealed to the New Testament in the light of a Cyprianic doctrine of the Church and of Augustine's understanding of sin and its remedy. Baptism was the indispensable prelude to the arcane mysteries of the eucharist – but perhaps it is baptism which belongs to the arcanum.

When John starts baptising in the river Jordan he is appealing to ancient traditions of covenant and cleansing, but his purpose is to prepare people for the coming of Messiah. Baptism is a kind of prophetic sign enacted with the people, a corporate acknowledgement that 'the kingdom of heaven is at hand' and that all must prepare for its coming. Jesus' baptism by John is one of the most secure parts of the gospel tradition, and this is recorded as a decisive step in Jesus' acceptance of a messianic vocation. Later, when he is challenged as to his authority, he replies, as Jeremias puts it: 'It rests on what happened when I was baptised by John'.[16]

The New Testament has four related ways of speaking of the significance of baptism. From the accounts of Jesus' own baptism derives the connection between baptism and the Spirit, a connection which was fundamental also for the experience of the early Church. This Spirit is of course not a spirit of religious enthusiasm but the Spirit of God's new age dawning in and through Jesus, the Spirit which enables the proclamation of justice to the nations and the taking up of the messianic task. 'Baptism in the Spirit' is the gift of discerning this purpose of God in the man Jesus, and so of discerning both God's openness to history and the openness of history to God.

In virtue of the connection with the Spirit baptism is also the sacrament of unity. Paul does not emphasise 'one baptism' because he thinks communal harmony is a nice thing but because the unity of Jews and Gentiles which has begun to be realised is an eschatological reality. Baptism is then an 'ecumenical' sign, a sign for the whole inhabited earth of the overcoming of all divisions – not only of Jew and Greek, but of slave and free and even of male and female. Baptism is thus for Paul the sign of a new humanity, and it is as such that it replaces circumcision, which still incorporated the convert into an '*am*', a specific people. The church for Paul was not another people but a *tertium genus*, that community called into being to signalise the end of all humankind's divisions.

The connection between baptism and death is not some more or less fortuitous reflection on the symbolism of the baptismal rite but expresses Jesus' own perception of what it costs to usher in God's kingdom. Luke records a saying in which Jesus thinks of his forthcoming death in terms of baptism: 'I have a baptism to be baptised with; and how am I constrained until it be accomplished!' (Luke 12:50). In Mark Jesus refers the disciples scarcely less clearly to 'the baptism with which I am baptised' (Mark 10:38). In these passages baptism refers to the struggle and suffering involved in commitment to the messianic promises of justice and upholding the downtrodden. When the disciples ask Jesus for seats on the right and left hand, he asks in turn whether they can undergo his baptism and they reply, 'Yes'. 'If Yes is your answer', says Jesus, 'you can forget about seats on the right and the left.' For baptism is an invitation to take up the same ministry and the same struggle as Jesus, and the consequences are likely to be the same.

All this goes to explain the significance of 'baptism into the name', for this was baptism into a name which was anathema to the Synagogue and dangerous in the Roman world. Christianity conquered the Roman world, it has been said, through the affirmation: 'Caesar is not Lord; Jesus is Lord'; but the cost of this affirmation can be found in the martyrologies of both the ancient and the contemporary Church.

In his discussion with the Christians in Rome Paul says that baptism is a sign that we are no longer 'slaves to sin' (Rom. 6:6), and he tells the Corinthians that an immoral Christian belies his own baptism (1 Cor. 6:11). From passages like these the Church derived a largely moralistic understanding of baptism, or came to see it as washing away inherited sin and as bestowing the first instalment of grace. But 'original sin', the power under which human beings are bound, as Paul puts it, is not something which we step outside of at any stage of our life. It is the sum of all those closed options and negative elements which demean and dehumanise and destroy people. In baptism we take an option against those powers, we choose between life and death. We stand in line with Jesus as he stood in line with his people going for baptism. We pledge ourselves in the cup in which he pledged himself, we undergo his baptism as a sign of commitment 'to a possibly painful struggle even unto death on behalf of the liberation of the oppressed and on behalf of a society which is more just and more human than it is now'.[17] Baptism then is not the making of a non-child of God into a child of God, for the witness of the Scriptures of both Old and New Testament is that every human being is made in God's image, that every human being is the object of his redemptive love and therefore that we may speak of all human beings as God's children (which is no more than what Gandhi insisted in calling outcastes 'harijans'), that therefore the Holy Spirit hovers over each birth, and each person may be regarded as the temple of the Spirit. Nor is it in the first instance a 'cleansing' from sin, for the emphasis of the New Testament is not negative but positive. Baptism is the sign of the new age of freedom and mutuality, of the new creature who gives his or her life for this reality, and this involves the unmasking and disintegration of the structures of 'sin'. Baptism is then, as Moltmann has finely said, 'a public confessional sign of resistance and hope', or as Barth prefers to describe it, a form of petition for the coming of God's kingdom. None of this is to make baptism a 'work of man', for – as Barth points out – 'Spirit baptism', which is the calling of God, the quickening of heart and mind and imagination which enables a person to see God at work in the crucified Jew and to want to commit their life for the kingdom he announced, necessarily precedes 'water baptism'.

For centuries infant baptism has been justified on the grounds that it is a sign of God's prevenient grace; but, if the eucharist derives from Jesus' table fellowship rather than exclusively from the 'last' supper, then it is this which is the sign of God's prevenient grace going to meet sinners. Baptism comes out of the eucharist rather than preceding it as its necessary condition. Encountered by this grace and surprised by this joy, baptism is the sober but at the same time glad and joyful response to the faithfulness of God, an acceptance of solidarity with Jesus and his fate just as Jesus' baptism was an acceptance of solidarity with sinful Israel. Just as it was for Jesus, who came to baptism at 'about thirty years of age' according to Luke, it is a moment for decision and commitment, for recognition of our calling. In baptism all is certainly not finished, for there we are 'sealed in the Spirit for the day of redemption' (Eph. 4:30). As it was for Jesus and for the disciples after Pentecost it is the sign of a new start, a recognition of and identification with God's purposes. It is a sign of grace: of God's self giving in Christ, appropriated in faith and tied into my story. When I am baptised 'into' Christ I am baptised into the movement he started, into the power of God's solidarity and into the hope of the resurrection in history, and in this sense into the Church. For this reason baptism belongs to the arcanum, for whereas Jesus calls all to sit at table with him, commitment to the coming kingdom, to justice, freedom and fellowship – and therefore for the oppressed and marginated and to the cost of such commitment – is something which must be freely chosen. As such baptism cannot be administered on the unknowing or half-unwilling, but is a mark of understanding and acceptance of God's story as this is rehearsed at the supper of the Lord.

THE TASK OF THE CHURCH IN THE DIVINE ECONOMY

'Politics' we could understand, without cynicism, as the attempt by human beings to frame a rational social order which enables people to live in peace and freedom. So far, in trying to understand the Church's role in human history, we have tried to give an account of its relation to the political order, which is where the vital themes of the prophets and of Deuteronomy, justice, righteousness and mercy, are given flesh. The Church is not called to play the role of the state, but neither is it indifferent to what goes on in the state, as if the kingdom were not of this world (for when John said this, of course, he had in mind the 'standards of this world', cynical power-mongering). Beginning from Jesus' account of the community, we have attempted to conceive this relationship in terms of the threefold office as the telling of the liberating story, protest, and solidarity. To the priestly work should of course be added prayer.

We now turn to the wider scene, taking up issues raised in chapters 8 and 9 about the relation of the Church to other cultures, religions and traditions. God is at work in all human traditions and yet in a special way through the Church. What does it mean to affirm this? What is the role of a sinful and divided church in the divine economy?

In the course of his ministry Jesus sent out the twelve to cast out demons, to heal, and to announce that the kingdom was at hand (Matt. 10:5f.). Matthew concludes his gospel with the so-called 'great commission' to make disciples of all nations, teach them the new law, and baptise them into the messianic movement (Matt. 28:19–20). Luke sums up all these things in the word 'witness': 'You shall be my witnesses in Jerusalem and in all Judaea and Samaria and to the ends of the earth' (Acts 1:8). The Church exists then as herald, teacher and witness; 'evangelism' or 'preaching the gospel' (Rom. 15:20) is the essence of its task. But both the charge to the twelve as well as the 'great commission' ought to alert us to the complexity of this task, and warn us against gross over-simplications.

For Paul salvation is a matter of being caught up in the new age which begins with the crucified and risen Lord, and redemption is from all the powers which destroy human beings and to that situation where there is no slave or free, male or female, but where all are one in Christ. The dimensions of salvation are cosmic, and so Paul speaks of both a new Adam, because redemption is something which applies to the whole of human history, and of a new creation, because redemption is not limited only to the human. 'Nobody understood Paul until Augustine except Marcion', said Harnack in a famous epigram, 'and Marcion misunderstood him.' But the truth is that even Augustine often failed to grasp the depth and universality of the New Testament message of salvation. Whilst Irenaeus in the second century still clearly perceived these universal dimensions they were more and more lost sight of until 'salvation' meant individual rescue from sin conceived moralistically. Imperceptibly the Church itself became the subject of the saving announcement, because it was the Church which mediated the grace without which there was no salvation. Since God willed the salvation of all, the task of the Church was to make the world Church, and this task was fulfilled at best through the work of 'mission' and 'evangelism' and at worst through the crusade. Although Christian action was recognised as a form of evangelism, the emphasis was on proclamation, and on drawing people into the Church as into the ark of salvation. This framework of thought, both terms of which are highly problematical, remains fundamental for large sections of the contemporary Church. We shall examine in turn each of the terms, the meaning of proclamation and the idea of the Church as the ark of salvation.

The American evangelist Peter Wagner speaks for this so-called 'evangelical' section of the Church in distinguishing between three types of evangelism, which he labels 'presence', 'proclamation' and 'persuasion'. By 'presence' evangelism he means such things as 'redeeming social structures', 'arousing the oppressed to take up arms against the oppressors', 'restoring manhood as reflected in Jesus'. His opinion of this kind of evangelism is conveyed in a comparison with 'proclamation' evangelism: 'a wide river of difference' separates these two. 'They represent two different philosophies, with two different starting points. Christian presence asks the world to set the agenda; proclamation sees it in sin . . . presence attempts to arouse a social conscience; proclamation attempts to arouse spiritual conviction'.[18] Condemnation could scarcely be less equivocal. In proclamation evangelism the Word is told 'orally and intelligently', whilst persuasion goes one better in making people committed church members.

There is a point in criticism of what Wagner calls 'presence' evangelism, though it is not a point he makes. Harvey Cox represents this point of view rather naively when he maintains that 'any distinction between evangelism and social action is mistaken', but as Karl Barth said long ago, 'Were Church social work as such meant to be proclamation it could only become propaganda, and not very good propaganda at that. Genuine Christian love with its all-too-human action would be shocked at the thought of giving itself out as the proclamation of the love of Christ'.[19] Although this is far from Cox's intention, Barth puts his finger on the point that the only motive for genuinely evangelical action is love, and love has no axe to grind – it does not act so that the other may do this or that but simply because the other is other. Action or service with one eye on conversion would, as Barth says, be propaganda, which is the attempt to win another to my position regardless of the truth, the equivalent in the sphere of dialogue of the doctrine that ends justify means.

Wagner's view of the true meaning of evangelism, on the other hand, represents that radical disjunction of word and act, gospel and world, religion and society, social conscience and spiritual conviction which we have already seen to be impossible with Jesus and which represents a truly staggering failure to understand the incarnation. Edwin Muir attacked just this failure in his poem 'The Incarnate One':

> How could our race betray
> The Image, and the Incarnate One unmake
> Who chose this form and fashion for our sake?
>
> The Word made flesh is here made Word again,
> A word made word in flourish and arrogant crook.
> See there King Calvin with his iron pen,
> And God three angry letters in a book,
> And there the logical hook
> On which the Mystery is impaled and bent
> Into an ideological instrument.

In the incarnation it is writ large that the spiritual is known and manifested in and through the material and that the attempt to understand sin apart from 'the problems of mankind in society', spritual conviction apart from social conscience, the Word apart from the world is a betrayal of God's purpose in creation and redemption. It is certainly no accident that such a *solum Verbum* gospel subscribes to the kind of political ideology which makes this convenient, permitting the affirmation that, as Escobar puts it, politics is worldly whilst business is not, membership of a union is worldly whilst membership of a group of real estate owners is not, giving alms to the poor is godly, organising them to fight the causes of poverty is not.[20] Such a combination of flight from and acceptance of different aspects of social reality is always characteristic of the docetism of this kind of theology, and the bondage of the Word to the ideology of the *status quo* is all the more secure for being unnoticed.

It is certainly the case that proclamation or, better, witness is required of the Church, but we see from the charge to the twelve and the 'great commission' what this involves: casting out the demons, which means every power which can rob persons of their humanity as Legion was robbed of his; healing, which includes what Jesus did to Zacchaeus as well as to the lame and blind, that restoration of humanity at which Wagner allows himself a sneer; the call to the costly commitment of baptism; proclamation of the kingdom which 'comes' in the doing of God's will. Much of what has come to be understood as 'evangelism' in the present century seems to be a very clear, even if subconscious, attempt to tailor the gospel to a world order of manifest injustice, and to make sure that the gospel does not disturb this order.[21]

We can turn now to the view that the task of the Church in the divine economy is to make the world Church, a view which seems so self-evident to a great many Christians that even to question it is taken to be a sign of lack of faith and genuine Christian commitment. We start from the point conceded by all, that the witness of the Church is not to the Church but to Christ. We must therefore ask: when we witness to Christ, to whom and to what are we witnessing? We must also insist that whatever Christian witness is it must be consistent with Christ, consistent with what we see him doing and saying in the gospel records. In answer to the question 'To whom?' we must say that the Jesus who is the heart of the gospel of the kingdom is, according to the testimony of the Church, the Word made flesh, which means the decisive clue to the mystery of the universe and ourselves. The Church has always taught that Jesus was 'sinless', which was never meant to be understood negatively (all sorts of things we do were absent from him) but positively: he is the mirror of true human being, the 'proper man' as Luther calls him. In Jesus God has revealed what human being is and therefore may become, what David Jenkins calls 'the glory of man'. This is not to put human beings rather than God at the centre of the gospel, but to put God's love for humankind at the heart of the gospel, to be amazed, like Paul and John, at the implications of Christ for ourselves. 'God so loved . . .' The dots extend across the page and lead to the breathtaking insight of Athanasius that God became human so that human beings might 'become divine', be drawn into the fellowship of God. It was on these grounds that the Logos theology of the second century taught that Christ might be found in all that makes for human dignity and fullness and freedom in all human traditions. But if this is the answer to the question 'To whom?', then this has tremendous implications for the question 'To what?'. What we are witnessing to is God's great movement of redemption, grounded once for all in Christ, continued in the work of the Spirit, which we spoke of in the first chapter as humanisation.

Because it is a distortion of being more fully human, says Freire, 'sooner or later being less human leads the oppressed to struggle against those who made them so. In order for this struggle to have meaning the oppressed must not, in seeking to regain their humanity (which is a way to create it) become in turn oppressors of the oppressors, but rather restorers of the humanity of both'.[22] But this is just the problem, for as Paul Lehmann has said, echoing Hannah Arendt, we know of no revolutions which have not ended by devouring their own children. It is this situation to which Christ comes and to which the Church addresses its gospel. Therefore, as Moltmann puts it, 'If Che Guevara is right that "the vocation of every lover is to bring about revolution", the Christian is he who has discerned that the vocation of every revolution is to bring about love.'[23] Humankind emerges from evolution after a labour of many thousands of millions of years, and in this emergence evolution becomes history and history acquires a subject. The 'project' of creation as this is perceived from the standpoint of Christ is that the hominid species may become fully human. It is this purpose which, according to the New Testament, is decisively forwarded and made ultimately possible through the life, death and resurrection of Jesus. The whole bevy of metaphors which the New Testament writers use – redemption, reconciliation, sacrifice, justification – all witness to this fact. They say that human beings on their own, what Paul calls *sarx*, are caught up in a 'totality' in which every human project is undermined and corrupted.[24] A 'totality' here means a self-enclosed and self-destructive system, that which leads revolutions to devour their own children. Precisely because it is a totality there is no way out within its own terms, through change, or growth or evolution: every option is already determined by the totality. Therefore Paul says: 'I have already charged that all men, both Jews and Greeks, are under the power of sin, as it is written: None is righteous, no not one . . .' (Rom. 3:9–10). However, the gospel is that the suspicion that this totality is final and self-enclosed is mistaken and that beyond this universe there is a God who is *sui generis*, not a member of any totality, and therefore not liable to be trapped by self-destructive systems. The New Testament writers do not say that this God is encountered only in Jesus, for he is encountered after all in Moses and the prophets, but they say that God is encountered in a totally strange and indeed unique way in Jesus – on the cross – and that through this encounter and through the Spirit of the crucified, God brings the human project to fruition through solidarity, through love, and in the power of weakness. They speak of God's entry into this created totality, which means also the totality of human history, and they speak of this as light in darkness, as breaking open the vicious circles of this totality, as rendering it permanently open to the humanity of God, to a love which cannot be overcome. This is the good news of the possibility of becoming human, of the possibility of a revolution which does not devour its children, where the oppressed do not become oppressors, which is committed to the Church and to which it is the Church's task to witness.

In his ministry Jesus rejected the Zealot and Essene options partly because, we may surmise, he did not want to create yet another small group of 'saved': such a purpose would be far too small a thing for the God Jesus called 'Father'. The dispute between Jesus and the Pharisees is not just about which people are to be invited into the Ark. As both Paul and John express it, Jesus came to bring salvation to 'the world'. Jesus does not come to make people 'Christians' but to make them human, to perfect God's image into the likeness, as Irenaeus puts it. If this is the case then the task of the Church cannot be primarily conceived as making the world into 'church', to rescue a few from the dangerous waters, to call into being a group of Christian Essenes. The Church's first task is to grasp the intention of God, as revealed in Jesus, with sufficient generosity and depth, and then to witness to that intention. This of course involves the retelling of Jesus' story (which includes the Jewish stories), which in turn certainly involves an invitation to join the messianic movement we call Church and, further still, an invitation to the recognition that it is in the adoration of the Trinity which includes the crucified Lord that human beings finally experience liberation. This story-telling and this gracious invitation is what is meant by 'witness' and 'proclamation', which should indeed be, as Wagner puts it, 'oral and intelligent'(!)

The story-telling and worship of the community, in which the world is invited to join, is the Church's part in the pedagogy of the Spirit which, as education, is a process. In this process God the Spirit continues that battle with the 'powers' which the Son waged in the days of his flesh, but these powers are not equivalent to other religions and cultures. Those religions and cultures are not 'conquered' but redeemed, and this means to be conformed to Christ. Does this necessarily imply becoming 'committed Christians'? There are at least two reasons for doubting this, and we can begin by earthing the discussion in contemporary India, where Christians form just over 2 per cent of the population. Failure to increase this percentage is often taken as a sign of failure of commitment amongst Christians, and church conferences frequently voice calls for the Church to 'redouble its efforts'. This frenetic, and therefore very un-christlike, concern with numbers seems to represent a failure to see the ways in which the gospel works as salt and leaven outside the Church. In the earlier part of the century the impact of the gospel, and at the same time the failure to come to 'faith in Christ' on the part of men like Gandhi or Tagore, was frequently commented on. But can we not see the 'salt' of Christ's gospel in the fact that, for instance, the Arya Samaj leader Swami Agnivesh has been led to a radical reinterpretation of the Vedas in terms of solidarity with the poor, a reinterpretation in which he cheerfully acknowledges Christian influence, or that the agenda of an all-India meeting of Hindu leaders consists of measures for 'restoring the humanity' of the oppressed?[25] The importance of this is not of course that it represents some unacknowledged 'victory' for Christianity, but simply that it happens. In its very happening there is some measure of conforming to Christ. And when we speak in those terms we have to recognise, as we pointed out at the beginning of the chapter, the 'contradiction of Christianity' in both the history and the present state of the Church. Like Israel of old the Church is a 'stiffnecked and disobedient people'. From the outside, joining the Church looks more like joining in a free-for-all than taking a step to be conformed to Christ. Here again lies the necessity of Barth's critique of religion, for God indeed works through the Church, because he is commited to human history, but he does so not through a model community self-evidently better than all others, but by refusing to let go of a community, in every respect as compromised as any other, by continually breaking and humbling it. The importance of the community lies not in its moral or spiritual practice (in which case we could do nothing but despair) but in the fact that it is the bearer of the liberating story, a story which continually renews it from within. From this point we can turn again to the question of the Church's task.

Indisputably the telling of the Christian story must include the invitation, 'Come let us adore him'. And yet just because it begins with Jesus, the Lord who is a servant, the man for God and the man for others, the vocation of the Christian is also to cup hands round the small flame of human dignity and creativity and freedom wherever it is found, in whatever cultural or religious context. As lantern-bearers the task of Christians is to guard the light, not to blow it out with the claim that our light is far bigger and superior. Recognising that the Father of Jesus Christ is the God of the immense patience of the evolutionary process, and also of the pedagogical patience of his dealings with Israel and Church, we have above all to respect that patience and have confidence in the salting and leavening power of the witness to Christ. We have every reason to believe that God is patient also with 'the nations'. He works through the Church but he is not its prisoner, and the time of redemption is in his hands and not in ours. The Church must 'witness' in season and out of season but: 'When you have done all that is commanded of you, say, "We are unworthy servants; we have only done our duty" ' (Luke 17:10). What then is this 'duty' and 'witness'? It is a matter of the story-telling, the invitation to the messianic table of peace and justice, of prayer for all sorts and conditions in the human race, and of the invitation to adore the crucified. At the same time it is, as Lehmann has taught us, to unmask the weakness of power and to live in solidarity with the power of weakness. As the bearing of good news it is the infection of others with the strength of God's solidarity and the hope of resurrection. In the midst of the great welter of traditions and stories and religions and cultures which constitutes world history, which represents not only the product of sin but also the human response to God's Spirit, the Church exists to maintain hope against hope in the name of the God of hope, to witness to the humanity of God and his messianic solidarity, and to the promise of resurrection for those who died 'not having received what was promised'. It is a witness to a light which cannot be overcome, a sacrament of a truly human future.

Conclusion

In different periods of Christian history different images of the atonement have assumed fundamental importance. Aulén drew attention to the significance for the patristic period of the image of Christ as victor over the powers of evil. Dissatisfied with crude versions of that account Anselm preferred to understand the cross as an act of 'satisfaction', whereby the shattered honour of the universe was restored. Many of the Reformers gave a prominent place to the image of sacrifice, understanding atonement principally as the expiation of sin. Liberal theology turned to Abelard and found in him a 'subjective' view of the atonement in which sin was overcome through Christ's example. In the light of Auschwitz and Hiroshima the decisive image since the Second World War has been the image of 'the crucified God', which in its own way is a version of the *Christus Victor* motif, stressing the dialectical nature of the victory.

In this essay the practice of liberation in small and undramatic ways in a Third World country has suggested the possibility of reworking the theme of Justin and Origen, of atonement through education. In chapter 1 we noted that 'education' might function differently to images like 'sacrifice' or 'satisfaction', in that it does not fix on ignorance as the basic human problem but explores the much broader concern of the bringing of humankind to fullness. Like the 'conflict' view of the atonement it thinks of a battle with the powers, overcome through their exposure. Like the 'satisfaction' view it thinks of the healing of the broken order of the universe, a healing which includes both the end of human divisions and also a restoration of peace to nature, as the prophets of Israel long ago envisaged (Isa. 11:6; Hos. 2:18). Like the sacrificial view the heart of this understanding of God's redemptive work is what happened 'once only, once, and once for all' in the life-offering of the Son of God which is the centre of the Christian story. Like the so-called 'subjective' view, importance is also given to the 'example' of Jesus, the fact that he too undergoes education, and to his teaching on the kingdom and its values. Compared with all these views, in a way anticipated by the great essay of Moberly mentioned in chapter 1, the image of education emphasises that redemption is the work of both Christ and the Spirit, one work but with two moments – grounded in the history of Christ, made history in the Spirit.

The life, death and resurrection of Christ are often spoken of as 'the great drama of redemption', but this is a very questionable description for neither creation nor history are God's 'theatre', and the agony of human history is not his 'play'. We have argued that history should be described in terms of both process and progress, but it is also a record of unimaginable waste and futility, deaths in skirmishes, battles, concentration camps; deaths due to natural disasters like droughts, earthquakes, volcanic eruptions; the nightly death of children from malnutrition and disease on the streets of Madras, Bombay and Calcutta, and every Third World city. This unthinkable waste is no drama but rather a desperate cry for redemption. The darkness of the cross and the new day of the resurrection together constitute a promise that it is not only the good and noble and beautiful but also this apparent meaninglessness that God redeemed and is redeeming and will redeem. To believe this and to act on it is to take to heart that dream which is 'dreamed in the heart, which only the heart can hold', a dream which is known in sign and story and in a broken but renewed community. 'Since the wise men have not spoken,' wrote Padraic Pearse, 'I speak that am only a fool':

A fool that hath loved his folly,
Yea, more than the wise men their books or their counting
    houses, or their quiet homes,
Or their fame in men's mouths;
A fool that in all his days hath done never a prudent thing,
Never hath counted the cost nor recked if another reaped
The fruit of his mighty sowing, content to scatter the seed;
A fool that is unrepentant, and that soon at the end of all

Shall laugh in his lonely heart as the ripe ears fall to the reaping
hooks
And the poor are filled that were empty
Tho' he go hungry.

I have squandered the splendid years that the Lord God gave
to my youth
In attempting impossible things, deeming them alone worth the
toil.
Was it folly or grace? Not men shall judge me, but God.
I have squandered the splendid years:
Lord, if I had the years I would squander them over again,
Aye, fling them from me!
For this I have heard in my heart, that a man shall scatter, not
hoard,
Shall do the deed of today, nor take thought of tomorrow's teen,
Shall not bargain nor huxter with God; or was it a jest of
Christ's
And is this my sin before men, to have taken him at his word?[1]

In the stories Christians tell there are many fools well known to us – Paul, Irenaeus, Athanasius, Francis, Luther, Fox, Bonhoeffer, Biko – all followers of incarnate 'Folly'. In the midst of human history this courage, this refusal to give up the dream (which we already encounter with a like passion in Romans 8 or Hebrews 11), this determination to see that the poor that were empty are filled, all of which is 'taking Christ at his word', all this is where we encounter and know the pedagogy of the Spirit and to this folly all are called. It is the present tense of redemption.

Notes

PREFACE

1. D. Barreto, *Analysis of Indian Society* (2), Bangalore 1977. The figures he gave for that year were 247 million in both sectors, but the population has increased considerably since then.
2. R. S. Thomas, 'The Small Window', in *Selected Poems 1946–68*, London 1973.
3. The translation of Romans 8:19ff. is C. K. Barrett's, in *A Commentary on Romans*, London 1962, p. 161.

CHAPTER 1. THE DIVINE PEDAGOGY

1. All quotations are from *Lessing's Theological Writings*, translated and edited by Henry Chadwick, London 1956.
2. The introductory statement of Kant's *Was ist Aufklarung*? (1784). Quoted in E. Bethge, *Dietrich Bonhoeffer*, London 1970, p. 770. Henceforward cited as 'Bethge'.
3. A. Grillmeier, *Christ in Christian Tradition*, 2nd edn, London 1975, p. 139.
4. Quotations from *De Principiis* are from the translation of G. Butterworth, *On First Principles*, London 1936. Patristic citations are generally from the *Ante Nicene Fathers*, and *Nicene and Post Nicene Fathers*, Edinburgh 1885, but the translation of Bettenson, *Early Christian Fathers*, London 1956, and *The Later Christian Fathers*, Oxford 1970, is sometimes preferred.
5. H. Kraemer, *The Christian Message in a Non-Christian World*, London 1938, p. 117.
6. Paulo Freire, *Pedagogy of the Oppressed*, London 1972, p. 56–7.
7. This is to adapt a phrase from Paul Lehmann, *The Transfiguration of Politics*, London 1975, which has influenced the direction of the whole essay.

8. M. Buber, *I and Thou*, tr. W. Kaufmann, Edinburgh 1970, p. 67.
9. J. M. Robinson, *The Problem of History in Mark*, London 1957, p. 6.
10. cf. S. Terrien, *The Elusive Presence*, New York 1978, whose ideas were suggestive for the present discussion.
11. Buber, op. cit., p. 162.
12. R. S. Thomas, *Between Here and Now*, London 1981.
13. Quoted in F. R. Barry, *Secular and Supernatural*, London 1969, p. 11.
14. Freire, op. cit., p. 80.
15. cf. B. Wielenga, *It's a Long Road to Freedom*, Madurai 1981, p. 27.
16. The real defect of the doctrine of the enhypostasia is that it fails to make this point. Otherwise it is unexceptionable.
17. K. Barth, *Church Dogmatics*, I, 1, (1st edn), tr. Thomson, p. 188.
18. Freire, op. cit., p. 63.
19. J. Moltmann, *Theology of Hope*, tr. Leitch, London 1967, p. 30.
20. Freire, op. cit., p. 61.
21. The formula is Terrien's, though I have changed it (Terrien, op. cit., p. 476).
22. R. C. Moberly, *Atonement and Personality*, London 1909, p. 149, 151.
23. Ton Veerkamp, 'In Lehrhaus, von der Einheit der heiligen Schrift', *Texte und Contexte* 22, July 1984. Bas Wielenga drew my attention to this article.

CHAPTER 2. THE KINGDOM OF GOD AND HISTORICAL PROCESS

1. R. Niebuhr, *The Nature and Destiny of Man*, vol. 2, London 1943, p. 254.
2. K. Löwith, *The Meaning of History*, Chicago 1949, p. 197.
3. ibid., p. 191.
4. E. Norman, *Christianity and the World Order*, Oxford 1979, p. 78–9.
5. A. Schweitzer, *The Quest for the Historical Jesus*, tr. W. Montgomery, London 1936, p. 369.
6. ibid., p. 397.
7. A. Harnack, *What is Christianity?* tr. Saunders, London 1958, p. 49.
8. N. Perrin, *The Kingdom of God in the Teaching of Jesus*, London 1963, p. 186. In a later work, *Jesus and the Language of the Kingdom*, 1976, Perrin tacitly recognised the inadequacy of his earlier interpretation and sought to understand 'kingdom' through the categories of myth and symbol. But he concludes that work, 'in the last resort my option may not produce a result significantly different from "a Bultmannian understanding of the eschatology of Jesus" '! It is doubtful whether the

category of myth can take us beyond this, though symbolic language possibly can: the two should not be confused.

9. Perrin, *The Kingdom of God*, p. 41.
10. C. H. Dodd, *The Parables of the Kingdom*, London 1961, p. 152.
11. H. Conzelmann, *An Outline of the Theology of the New Testament*, London 1969, p. 113.
12. Perrin, op. cit., p. 193. Perrin follows Jeremias in assuming that the Lucan text, which omits 'Thy will be done', is original. This assumption rests on no stronger grounds than that liturgical expansion of texts is commonly attested. We could argue equally that the parallelism of the Matthean version is a semitism strongly in favour of its originality.
13. Cf. Matt. 5:19, 5:44, 6:1, 7:12, 7:24, 8:9, 23:3, 23:23, 24:46, 25:40.
14. Löwith, op. cit., p. 196.
15. G. von Rad, *Old Testament Theology*, vol. 1, tr. Stalker, London 1962, p. 229.
16. In B. J. Kidd, *Documents Illustrative of Church History*, vol. 3, London 1941, p. 73.
17. O. Cullmann, *Christ and Time*, tr. Filson, London 1962, p. 149.
18. J. Jeremias, *Jesus' Promise to the Nations*, tr. Hooke, London 1958.
19. ibid., p. 46.
20. N. Dahl, 'The Parables of Growth', *Studia Theologica*, 5 (1951), pp. 132–66.
21. W. Kasper, *Jesus the Christ*, tr. Green, London 1976, p. 78.
22. J. Jeremias, *New Testament Theology*, tr. Bowden, London 1971, p. 113.
23. Freire, op. cit., p. 24.
24. Schweitzer, op. cit., p. 396.

CHAPTER 3. SOLIDARITY AND REDEMPTION

1. There is an extremely profound discussion of solidarity as a redemptive category in Kasper, op. cit., p. 216ff., which takes its start mainly from Anselm.
2. Freire, op. cit., p. 66.
3. Dodd, op. cit., p. 155.
4. Löwith, op. cit., p. 170.
5. ibid., p. 184–5 (my italics).
6. Whether this is really the view of Ecclesiastes is a moot point. It is interesting that Barth used Ecclesiastes as the text for his Tambach lecture on 'The Christian's Place in Society'. Eccles. 3:1–11 can certainly be read as an exhortation to revolutionary patience.
7. K. Barth, *Dogmatics in Outline*, tr. Thomson, London 1960, p. 123.

8. D. Jenkins, *The Contradiction of Christianity*, London 1976, p. 143. The phrase 'concrete utopia' is H. Gollwitzer's.
9. E. Brunner, *Christianity and Civilization*, in McIntyre (ed.), *God, History and Historians*, Oxford 1977, p. 82ff.
10. ibid., p. 94.
11. Moltmann, op. cit., p. 119.
12. T. de Chardin, *Activation of Energy*, quoted in J. Cowburn, *Shadows and the Dark*, London 1979.
13. Cf. J. N. D. Kelly, *Early Christian Doctrines*, London 1965, p. 172, 378.
14. I am here drawing on material published in *Expository Times*, vol. 95, no. 1, under the title 'Title and Metaphor in Christology'.
15. R. Girard, *Des Choses cachées depuis la fondation du monde*, Paris 1978, p. 275ff.
16. L. Fischer, *Mahatma Gandhi*, London 1951, p. 93.
17. B. Wielenga, *Biblical Perspectives on Labour*, Madurai 1982, p. 83.
18. It was the function of Irenaeus' theory of recapitulation to make this point. It emphasises that in order for the human situation to be changed an 'underivably new start' is necessary in human history. Schleiermacher also spoke of Christ, for this reason, as having his origin in an 'absolutely miraculous fact'. By contrast Barth emphasised that the *sarx* which Christ took was sinful flesh. The problem with the underivably new start is that it easily lapses into docetism, and it more or less did so with Schleiermacher. The 'new creation' in Christ is to be found in the direction of messianic politics rather than in any theory concerning Christ's nature, though of course, as this chapter has emphasised, the incarnation was necessary for those politics to begin.

CHAPTER 4. THE SPIRIT AND THE KINGDOM – I

1. N. Gottwald, *The Tribes of Yahweh*, London 1979.
2. ibid., p. 705.
3. ibid., p. 708.
4. G. Nathan, in Chappell (ed.), *Hume*, London 1968, p. 422.
5. As for instance in J. Fison, *Fire on the Earth*, Edinburgh 1958, ch. 1.
6. I owe this exegesis of Numbers 11 to Gabrielle Dietrich, *Would that All the Lord's People were Prophets*, WSCF 1979.
7. B. S. Childs, *Introduction to the Old Testament as Scripture*, London 1979, p. 554.
8. For this period, cf. J. Jeremias, *New Testament Theology*, London 1971, pp. 76ff.; E. Schweizer, *The Holy Spirit*, tr. Fuller, London 1981, pp. 29ff.
9. Freire, op. cit., p. 36.

CHAPTER 5. THE SPIRIT AND THE KINGDOM – II

1. S. Smalley in *Novum Testamentum*, 15 (Jan. 1973), pp. 59–71.
2. W. Hollenweger, in I. Fraser, *Reinventing Theology as the People's Work*, London, undated.
3. P. Lehmann, op. cit., p. 39.
4. Klaus Wengst, *Bedrängte Gemeinde und Verherrlichter Christus*, Neukirchener Verlag 1981.
5. Schweizer, op. cit., p. 46.

CHAPTER 6. THE HISTORY OF GRACE

1. T. F. Torrance, *Grace in the Apostolic Fathers*, Edinburgh 1948, p. 140.
2. C. K. Barrett, *Commentary on 2 Corinthians*, London 1973, p. 316.
3. Simone Weil, *Waiting on God*, Fontana 1959, p. 71.
4. *De Correptione et Gratia* 14.45.
5. *Enchiridion* 98.
6. *De Ciritas Dei* 21.17ff.
7. For example, 'On Grace and Free Will' 45.
8. *Sermon* 99.6, my italics.
9. *De Correptione et Gratia* 12.38.
10. N. P. Williams, *The Grace of God*, London 1930, p. 26 (my italics). My account of Augustine's thought on grace in indebted to Williams' account.
11. For instance in *De Bapt.* 4: The Spirit comes down upon the baptismal waters after the invocation 'sanctifying them by his own power; and being thus sanctified they are imbued at the same time with the power of sanctifying'.
12. II *Sent.* 26.1.1 quoted in Aquinas, *Summa Theologiae*, New Blackfrairs edn, London 1967, vol. 7, p. 95.
13. *Summa Theologiae* la 2ae 108.1.
14. ibid., 110.1.
15. ibid., 110.2.
16. ibid., 109.1.
17. ibid., 109.3.
18. *S.T.* 3a 62.1
19. *S.T.* 1.23.5.
20. 'Confession Concerning Christ's Supper', 1528, *Luther's Works*, vol. 37, Philadelphia 1961, p. 368.
21. 'Exposition of the Lord's Prayer', 1519, ibid., vol. 42, p. 41.
22. 'Treatise on the New Testament', 1520, ibid., vol. 35, p. 84.

23. Preface to Romans, 1522, in *Martin Luther*, ed. Rupp and Drewery, London 1970, p. 95.
24. Calvin, *Institutes* II.3.6.
25. Schleiermacher, *The Christian Faith*, tr. Mackintosh, Edinburgh 1928, 100.1–2, p. 426.
26. ibid., 100.3, p. 429 (my italics).
27. ibid., 108.5, p. 491.
28. ibid., 100.1–2, p. 426.
29. ibid., 124.1, p. 575.
30. Schweitzer, op. cit., p. 62.
31. N. Lash, *A Matter of Hope*, London 1981, p. 189.
32. Padraic Pearse, 'The Fool', in *Plays. Stories. Poems*, Dublin 1980. Cf. Paul Lehmann: 'Realpolitik is politics with the accent upon the primacy of power over truth. Political realism is politics with the accent upon the primacy of truth over power.' op. cit., p. 56.
33. J. Moltmann, *Theology of Hope*, p. 25.
34. I owe the reference to John Tinsley in a sermon preached in the University Church, Oxford, in May 1978.
35. A. Ecclestone, *Yes to God*, London 1975, p. 12.
36. M. Chagall in *Chagall*, ed. Sorlier, London 1979, p.8.

CHAPTER 7. SIGNS OF HOPE

1. Augustine, *Sermon* 272.
2. *Treatise on John* 26.11
3. *Epistle* 98.9.
4. P. Tillich, *Systematic Theology*, London 1968, vol. 3, pp. 130–1.
5. G. von Rad, op. cit., vol. 2, p. 342.
6. C. K. Barrett, *Commentary on John*, London 1958, p. 64.
7. T. A. Lacey, in *Hasting's Dictionary of Religion and Ethics*, vol. 10, Edinburgh 1918, p. 904.
8. *Procatechesis* 12.
9. *Catechesis* 23.22.
10. *Epistle* 138.7.
11. *Civ. Dei.* 10.5/6.
12. *De Vera Religione* 33; *Epistle* 54.1.
13. 'On the Babylonian Captivity of the Church', *Luther's Works*, vol. 36, p. 124.
14. *S.T.* 3a 65.1.
15. John Oman, *Grace and Personality*, Fontana 1960, p. 151.
16. ibid.

17. K. Barth, *Church Dogmatics*, IV, 1, tr. Bromiley, Edinburgh 1956, p. 296.
18. K. Barth, *Church Dogmatics*, IV, 2, tr. Bromiley, Edinburgh 1958, p. 40.
19. K. Rahner, *Theological Investigations*, vol. 14, tr. Bourke, London 1976, pp. 161ff.
20. H. Zwingli, *Exposition of the Christian Faith*, in Library of Christian Classics, vol. 24, Philadelphia 1953, p. 247–8.
21. Oman, op. cit., p. 189.
22. *Large Catechism*, Augsburg, Minnesota, 1967.
23. T. Balasuriyea, *The Eucharist and Human Liberation*, London 1979, p. 21.
24. *Ad Simplicianus* 2.2.
25. *Institutes* IV 14.17.

CHAPTER 8. A MEAL AND A STORY

1. Thinking of the relation of baptism and eucharist in this way is at least in some areas a matter of missionary practice also. Over the past ten years the eucharist has been celebrated regularly in Madurai jail. The vast majority of those who attend the service are non-Christians. Many of these present themselves for 'communion', and it would be deeply ungracious to refuse them. From this 'open table' a steady stream of requests for baptism have come.
2. J. Jeremias, *The Eucharistic Words of Jesus*, tr. Perrin, London 1966, pp. 186ff.
3. op. cit., p. 218.
4. op. cit., p. 255.
5. Drawing on a paper by Samuel Rayan at Tamil Nadu Theological Seminary in September 1982, to which the whole exposition is indebted.
6. Sermon 272.
7. *Didache* 9 and 10.
8. J. Jungmann, *The Early Liturgy*, tr. Brunner, London 1959, p. 37.
9. In *The Fathers of the Church*, vol. 10, New York 1950, p. 389.
10. Letter 62 in *Ante Nicene Fathers*, vol. 5 (letter 63 in the Oxford edition).
11. W. H. Frend, *The Donatist Church*, Oxford 1952, pp. 76ff.
12. Cited in Jungmann, op. cit., p. 197.
13. The Quartodeciman controversy concerned the following of Jewish practice in the celebration of Easter on the same day as Passover, Nisan 14. It had some prominent supporters, like Polycarp and Melito of Sardis, and the sect formed from the controversy survived to the fifth century.
14. M. Buber, *Tales of the Hasidim*, vol. 2, New York 1948, p. 93.
15. Freire, op. cit., p. 61.

16. *Pesahim* 10.4.
17. R. de Vaux, *Ancient Israel*, London 1961, p. 429.
18. C. Westermann, *Isaiah 40–66*, tr. Stalker, London 1966.
19. Sermon 227.
20. *Luther's Works*, vol. 35, p. 99.
21. E. Dussel, 'The Bread of the Eucharistic Celebration as a Sign of Justice in the Community' Concilium, 152 (1982), which this section follows closely. Succeeding quotations are from this article.
22. Samuel Rayan in the unpublished paper referred to in note 5.

CHAPTER 9. RELIGION AND THE LABOUR OF GOD

1. I take this from Chadwick, *Lessing's Theological Writings*, p. 9.
2. F. D. E. Schleiermacher, *On Religion, Speeches to its Cultured Despisers*, tr. Oman, New York 1958, pp. 39ff., Second Speech.
3. ibid., p. 214.
4. E. Troeltsch, *The Absoluteness of Christianity*, tr. Reid, London 1971, p. 145.
5. E. Troeltsch, *Christian Thought*, tr. von Hügel, London 1923.
6. K. Barth, *The Word of God and the Word of Man*, tr. Horton, London 1935, p. 70.
7. K. Barth, *The Epistle to the Romans*, tr. Hoskyns, London 1933, p. 252.
8. ibid., p. 255.
9. ibid., p. 238.
10. Barth, *Church Dogmatics*, I, 2, p. 285.
11. ibid., p. 315.
12. ibid., p. 310.
13. ibid., p. 356–7.
14. Bethge, op. cit., p. 780.
15. B. S. Childs, op. cit., p. 187.
16. R. Pannikar, *The Unknown Christ of Hinduism* (1st edn), London 1964, pp. 50ff.
17. Freire, op. cit., p. 61.
18. Barth, *Church Dogmatics*, I, 2, p. 299.
19. J. Moltmann, *The Crucified God*, tr. Wilson and Bowden, London 1974, p. 216.

CHAPTER 10. THE CHURCH IN HUMAN HISTORY

1. Cf. the famous remark of the second-century Epistle to Diognetus: Christians 'live in countries of their own, but as sojourners. They share all things as citizens; they suffer all things as foreigners. Every foreign land is their native place, every native place is foreign.'
2. See J. Jeremias, *New Testament Theology*, tr. Bowden, London 1971, p. 293.
3. ibid., p. 111.
4. ibid., p. 177.
5. ibid., p. 227.
6. ibid., p. 239.
7. J. Moltmann, *The Church in the Power of the Spirit*, tr. Kohl, London 1977, p. 316.
8. H. Küng, *The Church*, tr. Ockenden, London 1967, p. 99.
9. D. Bonhoeffer, *Letters and Papers from Prison*, Fontana 1959, p. 122.
10. ibid., p. 166.
11. Bethge, op. cit., p. 786.
12. Bonhoeffer, op. cit., p. 92–3.
13. Moltmann, *The Church*, p. 76ff.
14. Bonhoeffer, op. cit., p. 166.
15. So Flemington, *The New Testament Doctrine of Baptism*, London 1948, pp. 62, 144.
16. Jeremias, *Theology*, p. 56.
17. Samuel Rayan in the lecture mentioned in the notes to ch. 8; the previous two paragraphs are also indebted to this presentation.
18. P. Wagner, in *Christ the Liberator*, ed. Stott, London 1972, pp. 97–8. Part of this section was published under the title 'Evangelism and Incarnation' in *Indian Journal of Theology* 30 (1981).
19. Barth, *Church Dogmatics*, I, 1, p. 55.
20. In Stott, op. cit., p. 105.
21. Cf. the cynical use of both fundamentalist and charismatic preachers in Costa Rica and the Philippines.
22. Freire, op. cit., p. 21.
23. Cited in Lehmann, *Transfiguration*, p. 70.
24. The category of 'totality' used here is taken from the Jewish philosopher B. Levinas, and I owe the introduction to it to E. Dussel.
25. Cf. *Indian Express*, Madurai, 2 Nov. 1985 under the heading 'Hindus Urged to Fight Social Evils': 'The Dharma Samsad today called on Hindus to collectively launch a strong mass campaign against the evils of dowry, corruption and untouchability . . . people should be persuaded not to perpetrate cruelty on the backward and down-

trodden.' Swami Agnivesh has been disowned by certain sections of the Arya Samaj because of his involvement in justice concerns.

CONCLUSION

1. Padraic Pearse, 'The Fool', op. cit.

Index